"ZIMBABWE WILL NEVER BE A COLONY AGAIN!"
Sanctions and Anti-Imperialist Struggles in Zimbabwe

Munoda Mararike

Langaa Research & Publishing CIG
Mankon, Bamenda

Publisher
Langaa RPCIG
Langaa Research & Publishing Common Initiative Group
P.O. Box 902 Mankon
Bamenda
North West Region
Cameroon
Langaagrp@gmail.com
www.langaa-rpcig.net

Distributed in and outside N. America by African Books Collective
orders@africanbookscollective.com
www.africanbookscollective.com

ISBN-10: 9956-550-22-1

ISBN-13: 978-9956-550-22-7

© **Munoda Mararike** 2019

Dedication & Homage

To my father 'Think Quickly and Act' – Mr Ishmael Mujere Mararike: An educationist and philanthropist "The Headmaster". After pioneering at Goromonzi High School in 1946, he established Mukondomi School in 1952 in Buhera, Manicaland.

I also dedicate this book to the suffering children of the State of Palestine: they bore the ugliest brunt of fighting against imperialism and occupation with only one weapon at their disposal: 'rekeni' or David's biblical sling!

About the Author

Munoda Mararike is an *Alma Mater Studiorum* of the University of Zimbabwe (UZ) where he was student leader in the Student Representative Council (SRC) in 1986, graduates with a Bachelor of Arts and a BSc Special Honours degree in Sociology. Munoda was involved in students' politics through the *Society of African Studies* and *The Focus*, and *Students' Eye,* magazines. Munoda, a holder of a Diploma in Personnel Management and various certificates in Training and Human Capital Development gained post-graduate qualifications at the University of Central England in Birmingham - PG Diploma in Management Studies (DMS) & Master's in Business Administration (MBA). Munoda also holds post-graduate qualifications in Teaching in Higher Education from University of Northampton, UK and a Diploma in Higher Education from University of London at St Georges. He read for his Doctorate in the Department of Law and Politics at London Middlesex University. He remains a stoic fighter against imperialism, neo-colonialism and economic sanctions. Munoda is a Fellow of the UK Higher Education Academy. *Areas of focus:* Political Sociology, Liberation Struggle politics, labour migration and diasporic transitions; decolonialism critical theory.

Table of Contents

Acknowledgements

This book would not have taken off the ground had it not been for my academic heroes – research assistants who helped me carry out essential fieldwork research. I salute team *'Restore Order'* in the UK who helped me research, sift through massive data, interview transcriptions and process interview data. In Harare, I am deeply indebted to a leading light at Zano Remba Housing Cooperative, Willard Njagu, and other progressive forces, including Mr Bote and the team at the Central Statistics Office at Mukwati Building. I thank Professor Oliver Mutapuri at University of Kwa Zulu Natal for his forensic read and many eyes – *"zvinoda maziso akawanda"*. I thank my son Gamuchirayi Mujere for his techno-savviness, and for originating the front cover. Last, although I hold very strong atheist views, I thank my God for this life and guidance.

Munoda Mararike
Mill Hill, Barnet - London, UK, April 2018

Preface to the First Edition

Munoda Mararike's *"Zimbabwe will Never be a Colony Again!" Sanctions and Anti-Imperialist Struggles in Zimbabwe* is a thought-provoking original book. It is structured in Africa's contemporary post-colonial liberation politics of development economics. This exciting publication uses Zimbabwe as a synthesis of microcosmic study that provide accessible in-depth analysis of key aspects of sanctions as a weapon of control wielded by the so-called 'powerful' governments.

We see power differently. You can be powerful because of your humanity and human-ness – and that is what we believe to be supreme. Nations can equally be powerful by showing compassion and solitude to the poor and disadvantaged and not ruthlessness. Powerful nations should not fight the poor citizens of other countries with fire because it is, ironically, those poor citizens whose wealth has provided them with fire in the first place. Sanctions, even when called targeted, are non-discriminatory as they affect ordinary citizens with the same ferocity and savagery as against intended target, albeit often missing the target. Sanctions are lethal in that they are discriminatory often contrasting the rich and poor, the rulers and those who are ruled. Sanctions are a graveyard for the poor, weak and vulnerable.

The book features a wealth of empirical case studies of how Zimbabwe experienced illegal economic sanctions. Humanly constructed obstructions – from external remittances/finance flows into the country - to finance embargos or total financial blockages are deliberately created by the so-called powerful governments to deal with an 'errand' country. The infamous Zimbabwe Democracy Economic Recovery Act of 2001 (ZDERA) is part of a raft of punitive measures and discourses that the USA, UK and Europe used to make the economy, in the words of US's Chester Crooker "scream". It is the same 'powerful' countries who allow their Multinational Corporations to loot while they impose sanctions against African governments and their peoples to make them scream.

Sanctions induced both corruption and suffering with equal measure. We see no humanity in this panoply of debauchery. The reason why Zimbabwe has endured a total of thirty-one (31) years of colonial and post-2001 land reform economic sanctions is to do with its 'curse' of rich natural mineral ore resources that the west is exploiting and stealing in broad daylight.

This well-researched work provides scholarly platforms to understand historical evolution of imperialism in Africa. It also conceptualizes the genesis of neo-colonialism. *"Zimbabwe will never be a Colony Again!" Sanctions and Anti-Imperialist Struggles in Zimbabwe* interrogates nuanced successes and failures of Zimbabwe economic sanctions as that account explores depredations and trails of destruction they caused particularly in rural poor communities. The situation in Zimbabwe is emblematic of far wider problems, including failed foreign policy engagements where diplomacy and direct engagement were available as humane alternatives to those sanctified with humanity.

Themes of this account draw upon powerful waves of rhetoric and demagogic stance taken by both Blair and Mugabe – repeatedly played to unfairly undermine precarious democratic institutions under Blair's well-bolstered threats of regime change. This book is, therefore, a blistering expose of western hypocrisies and the destructive nature of sanctions policies. Is Robert Mugabe a liberator or a dictator as he dropped bombs on bridges that link imperialism to the African renaissance and self-determination? Is he some apoplectic and irate suicide bomber who detonated landmines that liberated his own people from economic slavery through reclamation and empowerment? History will be the supreme judge.

Yet again, neo-colonial links constitutes the gravest affront to African independence and Zimbabwean sovereignty to be precise. Was Mugabeism a catalyst or change agent considering current demands for fast-track land reforms by desperate Black South Africans? A controversial expose? What are deep implications of the rise and "fall" of Mugabe? Did the 'brutal dictator' called Mugabe fall? If he did, why has his spirit reincarnated in Namibia and South Africa in form of an invocation for urgent land tenure reforms?

This remarkable and shocking book captivates repertoires of anger and pain; anguish and vituperation in its factual preponderance. There is a reason: Colonial discourse is about expressions of intense emotions – usually involving hostility, rancorousness and indignation. It is about potent emotions invoking provocation, hurt and threat. Author Munoda Mararike is good at handling that language in his deployment of decolonial critical theory. In Chapter 4 *Rodinising Economic Sanctions: How Sanctions Destroyed Zimbabwe* Namibia suffers the ordeal of colonial sexual orgies perpetuated by its three serial colonizers, leaving the country in profanity of multi colonial rape cases. That debauchery leaves the debased and violated colony reeling in agony of a lethal colonial gonorrhoea disease which was only to be cured through the protracted SWAPO liberation armed struggle! Colonialism is criminal and canal.

But it is not only Namibia but most of southern and central Africa wobbling in colonial misogynism. Kenya, Tanzania, Uganda, Zambia, Botswana, Malawi, Angola, Mozambique and South Africa are examples connected with the same umbilical code of economic enslavement by the United States of America, the United Kingdom and the European Union.

Last, but certainly not the least, the author provocatively and tantalisingly argues about the legitimacy of sanctions to Zimbabwe and calls capitalism a form of genocide against vulnerable poor citizens. According to Chinondidyachii Mararike, it is for that very reason that Zimbabwe should guard against devils and scarecrows masquerading as 'investors' - in its fight against destructive sanctions and imperialism!

Professor Oliver Mtapuri,
University of Kwa Zulu Natal, South Africa

List of Abbreviations

ANC	African National Congress
BSAP	British South African Police
CTC	Chitungwiza Town Council
DRC	Democratic Republic of Congo
EFP	Economic Freedom Party
EU	European Union
FCA	Financial Conduct Authority
GATS	General Agreement of Trade and Services
HMRC	Her Majesty Revenue and Customs
IDA	International development Agency
IMF	International Monetary Fund
MDC	Movement for Democratic Change
OFAC	Office of Foreign Assets Control
POSA	Public Order and Security Act
UDCORP	Urban Development Corporation
UDI	Unilateral Declaration of Independence
UN	United Nations
WB	World Bank
WTO	World Trade Organisation
ZANLA	Zimbabwe African National Liberation Army
ZANU PF	Zimbabwe African National Union Patriotic Front
ZAPU	Zimbabwe African People's Union
ZDERA	Zimbabwe Democracy and Economic Recovery Act
ZIPRA	Zimbabwe People's Revolutionary Army
ZNA	Zimbabwe National Army
ZINARA	Zimbabwe National Roads Administration
ZIMRA	Zimbabwe Revenue Authority
ZINWA	Zimbabwe National Water Authority
ZSE	Zimbabwe Stock Exchange
ZRHC	Zano Remba Housing Cooperative

Introduction

Aluta Continua!
Consciousness and reincarnation of the struggle against Imperialism and Neo-colonialism

The neo-colonial space in which Zimbabwean sanctions were imposed arbitrarily through the treacherous ZDERA in 2001 by Britain and America is all about hidden and open struggles of power and resistance. It is about imperial love and infectious Rhodesian sentiments by the British, upholding the Commonwealth values and the expression of their love of *'Little England'* in Zimbabwe's Eastern Highlands', *Nyanga – Manicaland* – which they preferred to sentimentally call *'Scenic Melsetta'.* That desire by genres in different generations for connectivity with glorious sentiments of the past has recreated the present conflict between Rhodesia and Zimbabwe. Caucasians holding on to what belonged to them in the past while Zimbabweans seek to hold on to their heritage by birth right. It is also a reincarnation and creation of some attachment that links with never let go syndrome of colonial reminiscence which is passed from generation to generation through historicism and histograms.

This account pigeonholes colonisers into a reprehensive state of denial, into ambivalent bitter-sweet situations. Yet conflict is a battle of situational and hardened willpower, which if unchecked, degenerates into fallout. The story imposition of sanctions on Zimbabwe can best be described as a conspiracy of power struggles between of the past and the present: By this I mean that Zimbabwe has a past colonial history which must be understood in the context of the present. At the same time, to understand the present is to understand the past that Zimbabwe went through as a colony. Zimbabwe being an emblem of present day symbol of true African independence – defining its moments of truth through resistance in its opposition of dominance. Economic sanctions are a form of protracted conflict in power struggles and politics. What I mean is that there are differences in terms of perceptions regarding governance and politics. Differences have created conflict resulting in imposition of sanctions. Their use -as last resort- is representative of failed mind battles and foreign policies of sender countries in which protagonists end up behaving like schoolmasters wielding the big stick of sanctions on innocent, poor and vulnerable victims in receiving countries. That is what colonial master Britain ended up doing under Tony Blair in as far as imposition of sanctions on Zimbabwe is concerned.

In this book, I look at reasons for imposition of abominable sanctions on Zimbabwe, their forms and structure including various processes that unfolded at international levels. I look at the 'axis of evil' protagonists George Bush (Jnr) and Tony Blair – in terms of the way they altered their countries' foreign policies on Zimbabwe in league with their international financiers and backers. I also trace roots of global sanctions and their implications not only in terms of their impact of on the Zimbabwean populace, but those countries affected by them. This is illustrated in Chapter 2 *America: Goliath walking on clay feet: Policing the world through Sanctions and Embargos.*

Chapter 3 *Sanctions: Functionalist Foundations of their Success and Destruction* lays foundations for consciousness and theoretical repertoire around the subject of colonial being and sanctions. We use these book chapters as a discursive intervention that enables us to understand the Zimbabwean condition of coloniality in terms of how it came into being and how it has been perpetuated by our colonisers to exploit our natural resources. We delve into the Chimurenga uprising to encapsulate the spirit of our struggle for our land which was stolen from us by settlers who came from faraway lands – some of whom were bandits, rascals, vandals, convicts and criminals running away from prosecution in their own countries. Three Chimurenga uprisings are all part of the subject of generational sequences of consciousness under the vocative spirits of our ancestors – who guided us to reclaim our land.

Chapter 4 *The Rodinisation of Economic Sanctions in Zimbabwe: GDP and Roots of Poverty in Africa* is a global interface of how Europe has, over the years undermined, Africa's potential through underdevelopment. Analysis of Rodney statistics on GDP at the time in the 60's and now in the new millennium confirms the global onslaught and agenda of neo-colonialism and exploitation of African states. It is eternal, unabated and unrelenting. It is important to highlight that imperialism works well and effectively in countries that have been ravaged by war and poverty – because at that stage, exploitation of resources is easy and unchallenged. Imperialism works well in countries with weaker government, warlords and banditry.

We posit that the economic strategies of creating desperation through poverty by the West – through deprivation, war and famine has been used successfully in countries like Ethiopia, Chad, Southern Sudan Somali, Eretria, Malawi and the Democratic Republic of Congo. Imperialism has also created irredentist states in form of Eretria and Somaliland and "recognised" their independence and war lords' leaders through divisions among the same people. The case of Saharawi Arab Republic remains one of the cornerstones of western double standards. Rodney's thesis is important because it illustrates that is easy to manipulate unstable governments in these countries for purposes of exploiting their wealth and resources. If a country is unproductive and dependent on foreign aid for the survival of its people, then it becomes easy to exploit. Malawi is a disturbing and tragic example – even pop stars are stealing innocent children in broad daylight with the support of the government of the day!

In Chapter 5, *Love and Infection: British coloniality and Imperialism – A Repository of Zimbabwe's illegal post-2000 Land Reform Sanctions* we state that strategies of political demonization, use of rhetoric escapades, deployment of downright threats and hostility pitches multiple actors, politicians or interests' groups on collusion course and curse in matrices of colonial subjugation. This is where strongmen like Robert Mugabe pitches battles against imperialism and neo-colonialism. Mugabe is probably the only post-colonial leader in Africa who was able to stand up to the Whiteman's double Dutch by telling them where exactly they belong. Even Europe at one stage did not know how best and practical to deal with Mugabe as they became mindful of his 'pollutant' ideas crossing over the Limpopo river border into their preserved prized possessions – South Africa. As in 2000 when land reform and black empowerment started in Zimbabwe, imperialism was not yet ready for South Africa to be contaminated by its boisterous neighbough. Even South African blacks in the powerful African National Congress (ANC) confound fears of gaining political and not economic independence at the time when Mandela was a public relations officer of international capital. The doctrine of Mugabeism and land reform programme hence 'strikes fear into the heart of the Whiteman'.

Under ZDERA of 2018, we witness a global web of capitalist strategies literally engulfing Zimbabwe as financial, trade and bilateral lines of credit are withdrawn abruptly deliberately causing irreparable damage to the populace that traditionally vote ZANU PF and its strong leadership to power. Themed with withdrawal of financial support is the wider strategy by the west of getting rid of liberation war political parties that are bedrocks of liberation political ideology and decolonial political narratives.

Under Zimbabwe economic sanctions, international financial organisations under the auspices of the World Bank and IMF are routinely audited for compliance with US Department of Treasury OFAC standing instructions. They are robustly monitored for prohibited transactions cited in the US Federal Register, through Executive Orders 11288, 13391 and 13469. Compliance with Executive Orders of November 2005 ensures that financial institutions are blocked from conducting financial transactions with individuals and organisations deemed to be undermining democratic processes in Zimbabwe. Using reinforced concrete evidence, my research gains credible insight into how various international statutory legislations have been applied to prevent the organisations from sending money and financial assistance to Zimbabwe. I look at theoretical repositories of Zimbabwean economic sanctions from a punitive juncture inflicted onto that country for implementation of fast-track land reforms from 2000.

Chapter 6 - *Counting the toll of Zimbabwe's Economic Sanctions: A Case Study of Zano Remba Housing Cooperative in Chitungwiza Township* is a summary of cumulative and adverse effects of economic sanctions especially in poor and vulnerable communities. We draw on palpable evidence of existence of high poverty levels that started to show in half a decade after the passage of ZDERA in 2001. The question of shortage of housing and homelessness are part of "insufficiency of basic needs" or being in a state of "insufficiency of earnings". In the same vein, costs of construction of pre-fabricated core houses, those without toilets and basic amenities, are part of poverty stratum especially in radicalised and deprived communities. When building material costs escalate to some levels beyond affordability; when residents invade other people's private core houses by force or through corrupt means – we then look at the economic baseline of residents who are involved in that war of attrition. We apply Runciman's relative deprivation theory to interpret what economic sanctions can do to a chosen population. Relative deprivation and the Gini coefficient are premised on the relative merits of the two satisfaction measures that are contrasted on comparative satisfaction and differentiation models to measure social injustice.

We also stress that this study is a microcosmic report of how post economic sanctions housing cooperatives worked in Zimbabwe: burdened by corruption and depravity, endemic poverty, conflict and other social evils including crime, prostitution, malnutrition, poor health facilities, underfunded local authorities, shortages of schools, absence of rule of law, violence and death. The picture of *Zano Remba Housing Scheme* and its tribulations as a troubled estate in the heart of Chitungwiza near Harare is a demonstration that, in implementing punitive sanctions, Western government do not care of outcomes and impact to ordinary citizens. It is amazing how communities in such catchment areas are oblivious to such destructive factors – largely because of poor levels of conceptualisation and lack of proper education.

Chapter 7 is entitled *Remarks on Imperialism and Plundering of African Resources by the West:* This is a posthumous collection of articles written by Chinondidyachii Godfrey Tichafara Mararike, who at the time of his death was a lawyer, writer, political analyst, and secretary-general of *Davira Mhere*, an activist Pan-African organisation. This chapter is not about iconizing Robert Mugabe, but it is about conceptualisation of his ideas of de-coloniality and neo-coloniality. Mararike exposes asymmetrical ideas that are being pursued by the western world to disseminate and dislodge the African race through western sponsored economic sabotage, including cutting off aid as punitive measures and excessive demands for good governance. Persuasive diagnosis calls for compelling solutions – Chino advocates for consciousness -that awareness by Zimbabweans that rekindles nationalism. Revolutions are fought and won by a people aware of their circumstances, aware of the forces operating around them.

The USA and Britain have used threats or military discourse to silence their oppressed opponents. They have used this option because they want to dominate world political events through power. According to Chinondidyachii Mararike the doctrine of Mugabeism is shaped by colonialists and is snowballing to define a new impetus in the struggle for self-determination and freedom of Zimbabweans and Africa as a whole. Chino writes with passion and a fierce sense of identity, originality, ownership and excitement. There is something that is not materialistic in his writings, but some form of a spiritual connectivity – something that one cannot buy.

Chapter 8 *The New Scramble for Africa: Re colonising the Continent* – There is a new form of imperialism which involves re-colonizing the continent using globalisation as a front. Using such strategies, Western Europe has chosen specific countries which they have turned into satellites of neo-colonialism. One such country is Rwanda – which because of Western imperialism – was involved in tribal genocide in 1994. The reason why Europe converged on this country is to clean up scars of their guilty conscience when United Nations failed to act on genocide. This Chapter looks at how European companies and western Europe are involved in land grab deals with corrupt governments like Sudan, leaving poor communities sunk in poverty and starvation.

Chapter 9 is a *Postscript: Zimbabwe Democracy and Economic Recovery Amendment Act 2018.* After gathering eclectic evidence from desktop sources of data in Chapter 5, it is necessary to integrate and analyse neo-colonialism themes in paradigms. We look at western attempts to preserve the status quo by colluding with opposition politics in Zimbabwe. This is what the British themselves call 'political meddling' should it happen in their country – and they would never allow any country on the face of earth to do that in Westminster! Their foresight is economic: their companies in Zimbabwe must thrive. They must share spoils and dividends. Imperialism works well without Mugabe or his 'venerated and loathed' ZANU PF party and ZANLA liberation movement whose intricate military structures, strategies and force were rated third behind those of Palestine's *Hamas* and Lebanon's *Hezbollah* during the liberation war struggle. Related to that, we also look at the role played by mostly British firms in exploiting rich mineral ores from Zimbabwe and this chapter impress upon the need for re-negotiation of balanced terms of trade in investment during post-Mugabe era. Calls for a trade-off for lifting of sanctions must remain measured, fair, balanced and mutually beneficial between countries who seek to invest in and trade with Zimbabwe in the new Mnangagwa era. Zimbabwe must be given space for its self-determination.

Reference

Runciman, W.G. (1966) Relative deprivation & social justice: study attitudes social inequality in 20th century England. Found at: http://www.citeulike.org/group/2546/article/1361362/Accessed 12 May 18

Chapter 1

The Socio-politico Construct of a Sovereignty State in Zimbabwe: Nationalism as a mass mobilising tool for post-independence Struggles

"...The subject of colonizing "natives" has never been qualified on refined qualities... there is nothing like better colonizers ... anyone who dominates a people through colonialism demeans a whole race and its generations. It is evil and despicable. That is modern cannibalism.... a new death sentence – whether it is from the USA or China! ..."

Munoda Mararike: The Big Debate. Zimbabwe Economists
WhatsApp Group 11/01/2019

Sovereignty and Nationalism

In conclusion, Agnew (2005) states that the concept of sovereignty has predominated modern political theory. Such theory relies on the idea of exclusive political authority exercised by a given state over a given territory. This concept emerges from Westphalia and was developed along with Enlightenment and Romantic ideas of popular patriotism. Governments and their leaders use the concept in describing their relations with the contemporary world. The sovereignty regime of Zimbabwe was a combination of centralised state authority that western countries perceived as dictatorial. The dictatorial leadership was guided by tenets of absolute territoriality which relied on 'internal sovereignty' to try and dismantle the impact of globalisation and capitalism to a former colony. Land reform was one such programme in which ZANU PF leadership countered globalist / imperialist influence and neo-colonial control.

In order to understand socio-political construct and context of sovereignty, this chapter looks at four inter-related aspects, namely the political background of liberation politics; nationalism and the Chimurenga liberation struggle; post-independence agenda, land reform programmes sanctions and nationalism. This chapter is important in introducing sovereignty as a concept of nation state – and forms the heart of the title of this book. The statement in the title of the book suggests that the question of sovereignty and nationalism are the core of anti-imperialist struggle personified by the resolution of land question in Zimbabwe. In this book, other individual chapters offer perspectives on eminent domains including human rights, governance and economic sanctions.

According to Agnew (2005) conventional political discourse of sovereignty is about central state authority: '… this is a relationship in which an agent of a state can makes commands that are voluntarily complied with by those over whom the state claims authority…' (439). The incorporeal realm of the state is part of a "body", an adult and a leader – whole function is to lead a sovereignty nation or a territory. The concept of sovereignty of any nation state relies on its power as its authority and political territoriality. We take it that power struggles between Zimbabwe's Robert Mugabe and England's Tony Blair (since his election as British Premier in 1997) were part of responses to inter and intra state conflict that were based on land and mineral resources. These were also in part issues that had not been resolved by the Lancaster House Constitution of 1979.

Post-independence Agenda and Sovereignty

In pushing the governance agenda of Zimbabwe forward, Robert Mugabe related to the concept of national independence at four broad strata: 1) state sovereignty; 2) parliamentary sovereignty; 3) territorial sovereignty and international relations sovereignty. I will explain why these aspects are the four cornerstones of Zimbabwe's sovereignty. International relations are encapsulated in Mugabe's anti-sanctions drive and rhetoric that he delivered especially at national events like Heroes Holiday, National Independence Day, Unity Day, Workers and May Day. He took the opportunity to deliver the sovereignty position of the country especially when he felt that the country was under threat of recolonization. He took apt opportunities to address the nation whenever a hero of the liberation struggle of Chimurenga was being buried at the national heroes' acre shrine. He linked international sovereignty with the defeat of imperialism. In terms of state sovereignty, Mugabe asserted his influence and beliefs by creating provincial heroes' acres in every province – where the doctrine of nationalism was imparted especially to communities who directly participated in the liberation struggle. The all-inclusive approach became his rally point against neo-colonialism for rural communities who participated in the liberation of Zimbabwe – thereby clearing sending anti colonial and anti-imperialism doctrine.

Parliamentary sovereignty in Zimbabwe is based on representation – "the people's voice". Election of members of Parliament is based on democratic principles of grassroots support of the masses – those masses that participated and supported the liberation struggles of Zimbabwe in the three phases of Chimurenga War of Liberation Struggles. Robert Mugabe continuously worked on building party structures from grassroots – from cells, branch, districts, provincial, to national structure levels because this forms the buttress of parliamentary democracy and representation in ZANU PF.

Territorial sovereignty looks at Zimbabwe's position in relation to other African states, positionality in terms of regional politics and integration. During the 1980s, Zimbabwe was part of the frontline Pan African States that became a buffer zone that fought against apartheid and white minority rule in South Africa. Together with Tanzania, Mozambique, Zambia, Angola, Botswana Lesotho, Swaziland, the Front Line States (FLS) were a loose coalition of African countries that formulated a uniform territorial sovereignty policy towards destruction of the pernicious apartheid system. Thus, such identity of nations for a common cause formulated territorial sovereignty in the war against imperialism. Such sense of purpose and pan African solidarity scares imperialism – Samora Machel had to pay a high price for it on 19 October 1986 at Mbuzini when he was assassinated by P.W Botha's racist apartheid regime.

The connectivity of the struggle for Zimbabwean independence was reincarnated in national politics as a weapon of liberating the minds of especially younger generations. Once he became the Prime Minister of Zimbabwe in 1980, he specifically renamed strategic roads towns and holidays after those who fought in the liberation struggle of three waves of Chimurenga War of Independence. Rhodes and Founders, for example, was a holiday which celebrated white supremacy on the 'founding' of the repressive colonial state of Rhodesia under the auspices of the infamous Pioneer Column of 12 September 1890. This holiday was abolished by Robert Mugabe in 1980. Overcrowding political spaces with liberation struggle beacons constituted nationalism. Political discourse was undoubtedly one of the strategies that he used in regenerative politics especially when articulating the doctrines of struggles against imperialism and colonialism. Thus, reinforcement and definition of sovereignty became enshrined in the concept of total liberation, emancipation and empowerment of his people – and this was detested by western imperialism.

In the structural construct of state sovereignty, the post-independence state of Zimbabwe is based on production and normative conception which linked (his) authority ("my Zimbabwe") as a territorial space and population. The possessive figure of speech ("my people are tired of these odious and evil sanctions"); the personification of the nation ("as Zimbabwe …we are saying this to you Blair…". The first republic of Zimbabwe used this instalment in accordance with the cardinal principles of nationalism.

According to Biersteker and Weber (1996) the range of state authority raises boundary issues of territorial integrity – which is one of the arms of state positioning. Sovereignty recognition is traditionally and normatively is dependent on state claims to hold a monopoly on the legitimate use of violence within its boundaries to protect its territory. This is the reason why Chimurenga 3 which brought about land redistribution to landless peasants in Zimbabwe was deemed to be a "war of liberation" (by President Mugabe) whose maxim was aimed at "overcoming" the struggle by defeating enemies of state including Tony Blair and his western allies. It is a struggle in which "individual members of the state of Zimbabwe claimed and exercised legitimate authority to mobilize the peasants in what the western governments termed "land grab". Mugabe thus underscored his understanding of relationships between components of the state sovereignty and change as part of the struggle to liberate the minds of Zimbabweans. Sovereignty is also in part, a component of state accessories aimed at improving material conditions of citizens through empowerment. This can also be located in the source of religious legitimacy even by some rogue states using "...in God we trust..." as a rallying point.

From another different perspective, Kratochwil (2012) in *Leaving Sovereignty Behind: An Inquiry into the Politics of Post Modernity,* has argued ferociously that sovereignty should be considered "... an institution analogous to private property, which changes scope in terms of application and the range of activities allowed within its domain... (p.127). It is valid to argue that the relational identities of state and sovereignty are not fixed meaning but co-exist in interpretation as they undergo structural changes in a revolution like in the case of Zimbabwe. Figuratively "my Zimbabwe" is possessive normative of sovereignty juxtaposed with "your England" as properties or entities defining geographical boundaries of a map.

In *Theorizing the State Geographically: Sovereignty, Subjectivity and Territoriality* political scientist Agnew (2005) makes a value addition instalment by submitting that the state is "...an autonomous subject which strengthens the territorial conception of power and conversely the conception of the sovereignty state as a territorial unit bolsters the assumption that the state is the singular subject of international politics..." Mugabe was embroiled in international politics because of property rights – rights that safeguard capitalism and accumulation.

According to Agnew (ibid) administration is a central theme in political geography as part of power, authority community and obligation. The importance is in conceptual premises of sovereignty and the role of politics in state control and authority. The interlinked concepts help to highlight national identity exercised through territorial integrity.

State, Sovereignty and articulation of Economic Sanctions

Zimbabwean struggles against economic sanctions are mainly for political identity in terms of space and time. Frames of reference in terms of time fall within the post land reform programme dating back to 2001 when the Zimbabwe Democratic and Recovery Act

(ZDERA) was enacted and passed into law by the USA Federal government. We witness the dollarization of cultures of nations as mainly the United Kingdom, the United States of America and the European Union cooperate and connive in implementing punitive measures against Harare. Western Europe and the EU adopted ZDERA as a common approach based on their identity and common causes as imperialists; with that sense of unitary connection in some shared enterprise of production, international trade and cooperation. Punishing Zimbabwe is based on universalising cultural conditions, rights and interests fostered in collective belief or purposes for exploiting mineral ores and land resources. This is so because western powers have economic interests in Zimbabwe based on emerging global financial culture and connections. This causes writers and theorists from sovereignty perspectives to view economic sanctions as part of imperialist global machinery emphasizing on variable autonomy of state officials led by those at the top. According to Max Weber's political sociology thesis, politicians, bureaucrats and military officers develop identities, interests and ideology to fight and defend the sovereignty state

Liberation Politics

When Zimbabweans were fighting all the Chimurenga wars, one theme running in all the epochs is the wider outlook on politics of liberation, yes – liberation of the mind. This is what makes the post-land reform politics complicated. Liberation struggle parties like ZANU-PF believe that the political stalemate between the ruling party and Movement for democratic Change cannot be solved by the ballot box per ser. They believe so on the premise that behind the so-called democratic change or under the US-backed regime change agenda lies imperialist interests. It is – therefore – an ideological conflict. The conflict has created polarized groups with distinctive identity features: The MDC as a sponsored party designed to dismantle ZANU PF out of politics; and on the other one hand, the ruling party ZANU PF fighting to crush the insurgency of imperialism behind MDC and its handlers and backers. The important objective which can easily be lost is that the sovereignty state of Zimbabwe and its people needs to find each other by first and foremost defining what Zimbabwe is through inclusivity. This is one of the fears of western powers particularly the United States and Britain. If Zimbabweans differ on policy and governance but agree on national values, then imperialism will suffer a devastating blow. It is on that basis that liberation struggle influence becomes a danger for western powers agenda in Zimbabwe. The post 2018 harmonised elections have generated a lot of debates on narrowing differences by political groups for the benefit of sovereignty. Questions like 'why are we now so different' and statements like 'Let's work for common goals' are potential obstacles in terms of slowing down imperialist designs.

Imperialism and Mineral resources in Zimbabwe

The subject if imperialism raises the following key issues in Zimbabwe. First, we trace the history of politics and constitutionalism to understand what really happened in the first ten years of Zimbabwean independence. The British had good experience in negotiating political and independence settlement in former colonies. Kenya for example, went through the same Lancaster House settlement as it was bludgeoned into accepting terms and conditions of their independence using intimidation and deception – way back on 12 December 1963 under Jomo Kenyatta. They used that experience under the Lancaster House Agreement to incorporate hostile terms and conditions that were designed to protect white colonial settlers.

For Zimbabwe, Prime Minister Mugabe found himself implementing a constitution that his government could not amend in any way – within the first ten years of independence. From 1980 to 1990, the Zimbabwean constitution was disproportionately in favour of white settlers by granting them 20% of the votes even if that group constituted only 3% of the voting population.

Under the 1979 Lancaster House Agreement, Zimbabwe was granted bi-lateral terms and conditions in which the USA and Britain would fund $75 million a year towards agrarian reforms over a period of ten years (1980 to 1990); and $1 billion for the same period from Britain. The question of a non-amendable constitution remained non-negotiable until Britain started to make overtures for Mugabe to go in 1990. Mugabe was under pressure from his own party and his electorate to address the land question. War veterans were aware that the Chimurenga War of Liberation was all about land. They wanted Mugabe to bring closure to this emotive subject.

Stepping back into colonial history, Rhodesian colonialism was about land and mineral resources. The Colonial administration was – from 1890 – determined to consolidate their gains for land expropriation: Under the heading "Crown Gets Matabeleland"- 'Decision of British Privy Council in Case Involving 48 000 000 Acres'

"LONDON, JULY 29, – By a decision of the Privy Council announced today the domination of some 48 000 000 acres of land in Southern Rhodesia remains in the Crown, but the British South African Company will continue to administer financial matters…With the decisions one of the biggest actions ever brought in the British Courts has finally been settled. Therefore, four claimants to the land, which is known as Matabeleland, and before 1888 was ruled by Lobengula, chief of the Matabeles. These claimants were The Crown – in other words the imperial Government, the Legislative Council, The British South Africa Company or as it is commonly called The Chartered Company and the natives. The company occupied the country after the overthrow of Lobengula and asserted that it was the owner of the unalienated land of Southern Rhodesia. The Crown submitted that by assuming a protectorate over the territories Queen Victoria assumed complete rights and powers over them. The natives contended that the country never was annexed by Great Britain, while the Legislative Council claimed the land on behalf of the inhabitants of Southern Rhodesia" From *The New York Times,* Published July 30, 1918.

The above judgement is evidence that imperialism was about expropriation of land. It was about depriving and disadvantaging the 'natives' through theft and deception. Where, in the name of justice, would a judgement for such a case be delivered in the absence of aggrieved party? Were 'natives' invited to London to hear their case? As if that was not enough, the British were jostling among themselves about ownership of their loot, having conquered and displaced natives who fought settlers using spears, bows and arrows!

It is correct to point out that expropriation of land was systematically in phases that used colonial statutes to consolidate imperialism. It is worthy pointing out that the decision by the Front-Line States (FLS) in 1990 also gave way to complex logistical and legal dimension of Zimbabwe's land question. In 1990, Julius Nyerere and Kenneth Kaunda argued that raising the land question in Zimbabwe at the expiry of the 10-year arbitrary constitutional stalemate would jeopardize South Africa's ANC and PAC war on liberation in that country. They argued for total liberation of South Africa first and notably the unconditional release of Nelson Mandela as a prerequisite. In that meantime, Britain and the United States of America took advantage of the Frontline States' strategic option to renege on funding for Zimbabwean land reform. Britain and the United States also put certain conditions, among many, for the removal of Robert Mugabe from power (before releasing further funding) because they perceived his land policy and ideology to be highly dangerous in the region. Western thinking at that stage was that – if Robert Mugabe's land reform was successful, then the contagion effect would spread not just to South Africa, but to Southern Africa as a whole. Mugabe had to be stopped.

This book interrogates a new awakening by asserting that Africa is not a dark continent. Any country that has mineral resources is not dark. Zimbabwe has gold reserves that are in excess of 20 billion tonnes – and that is not a dark country! Zimbabweans are increasingly becoming aware that the reasons why the west is dangerously interfering and meddling in Zimbabwean politics is because of mineral ore resources which the country is endowed with. The creation of unpopular leaders is also part of the agenda. Working on the premises that Mugabe was an evil leader, that contradiction rooted in post-independence Zimbabwean politics, is that he was – to a very large extent, created and nurtured by the west. The West managed to create conditions that were untenable for a one-party state in Zimbabwe because they controlled the means of production. Whites feared nationalisation of their assets as part of the grand socialist plan that ZANU PF government had mooted. Second, because of the clauses and legal trappings of the Lancaster House Constitution of 1979 – of necessity required western governments to work with Mugabe to preserve their status quo. The Reconciliation Plan that started in 1980 was part of a plan aimed at diluting the spirit of nationalism and the liberation struggle.

The British were aware of the Gukurahundi massacres (1983 - 1987) in Matebeland. At the time of the atrocities, Margaret Thatcher's government had 'transformed' and integrated the Zimbabwe National Army (ZNA) through aid and funding and it had also managed to retool the Zimbabwe Defence forces Industries. The short 'industrialisation' of the army was started General Peter Walls who was appointed – on the recommendations of the Zimbabwe British Governor – Lord Soames to head the army at independence. In essence what I confirm in this post-colonial era in Zimbabwe is that Britain was complicit to creating roots of post-colonial and toxic politics in Zimbabwe. At that time, from 1980 -1990 Mugabe was compelled to serve the interests of British imperialism; and British imperialism was also about the creation of bad leaders. As if that was an oversight, it was no coincidence that Mugabe was knighted at the Commander of the Order of the Bath in 1994 as an inducement for retirement! What the Zimbabwean population is aware of is that – when Britain calls Mugabe "an evil dictator" it resonates as part of their creation and sinister agenda all ingrained at their desperation to maintain their power in Zimbabwe. Post-Mugabe years are about maintaining their power and influence in Zimbabwe through creation and funding of opposition parties.

What followed was that instead of stepping down in 1990 as demanded by the British government, Mugabe went down the nationalist and sovereignty lane – agitating for empowerment and land redistribution to 'his people'. This did not only surprise the British but angered them into hostility. There are two theoretical perspectives. According to western interpretation, an 'unpopular leader' imposed himself and started to rig elections to stay in power in order to frustrate their democratic interests. Western interests are fronted by proxy opposition parties. This has created and reinforced mainly two political groupings. The first group comprise of those who see western governments as champions of democracy, human rights, good governance through enforced through economic sanctions and restrictive measures. This group is desperate for change at any cost irrespective of sovereignty consequences.

The second group is made up of those nationalist and liberation struggle elements who view the west as part of a new wave if imperialism. The group has accused western governments of using abstract political rhetoric including "champions of democracy", "new world order", "economic and restrictive measures" or economic sanctions to subjugate Zimbabwe through "economic and repressive measures". This group is cautious but conservative about western engineered change. It is that group that the west aims to clobber and arm twist into submission by accusing them of rigging elections and electoral fraud. The overall strategy is for the west to capitalize on such divisions to advance and realise their agenda. Zimbabweans are aware that the forces behind the opposition MDC is far too strong politically and financially in that they hold the key to ending two decades of economic sanctions.

Nation State and Political Settlement

In finding political settlement to the ongoing Zimbabwean chapter of economic sanctions, there is the need to acknowledge the liberation agenda in any political settlement. Previous political settlement through economic sanctions was used in the past to make ordinary Zimbabweans aware about the devastating effects of sanctions. It is important to underline the fact that the three waves of post settler liberation struggles and land issue are national values. They are founding principles of the nation state of Zimbabwe. On the same wavelength, there is the need to address governance issues and political issues. The compromise for any settlement and resolution must be dominated by those founding principles of the nation state. A situation in which conflict resolution in Zimbabwe is drawn on the norms and values of nationalist principles is likely to bring settlement, resolution and closure of this protracted political conflict. Settlement on Zimbabwe that seeks to remove ZANU PF from power on the basis of perceived threats to imperialist interests is likely to re-ignite another long drawn Chimurenga Four war of liberation.

References

Biersteker, T.J and Weber, C. (1996) State Sovereignty as Social Construct, Cambridge University Press, United Kingdom. https://books.google.co.uk/books?hl=en&lr=&id=qy97O2Eo n0gC&oi=fnd&pg=PR9&dq=biersteker+and+weber&ots=a1J XEy7Pyv&sig=tLQXbdZ7eRrf2MfvmtLAKthVFMc#v=onepa ge&q=biersteker%20and%20weber&f=false

Kratochwil (2012) in *Leaving Sovereignty Behind: An Inquiry into the Politics of Post Modernity,* in Legality and Legitimacy in Global Affairs, Falk, R., Juergensmeyer, M. and Popovski, V (Ed) Oxford University Press, USA. https://books.google.co.uk/books?id=5lpgicFU1hcC&pg=PA 29&dq=kratochwil,+nationalism.+sovereignty&hl=en&sa=X& ved=0ahUKEwjL3qX6uMbfAhUsxIUKHd_CAYwQ6AEIMT AB#v=onepage&q=kratochwil%2C%20nationalism.%20sovere ignty&f=fal.

Agnew J, (2005) 'Sovereignty Regimes: Territoriality and State Authority in Contemporary World Politics'

Annals of the Association of American Geographers, Vol. 95, No. 2 (Jun, 2005), pp. 437-461, Taylor & Francis, Ltd. Published on behalf of the Association of American Geographers Stable URL: http://www.jstor.org/stable/3694127. Accessed as https://is.cuni.cz/studium/predmety/index.php?do=download &did=85804&kod=JMMZ108

Chapter 2

America: Goliath walking on clay feet: Policing the world through Sanctions and Embargos

"With what moral authority can [the US] speak of human rights... the rulers of a nation in which the millionaire and beggar coexist; where the Indian is exterminated; the black man is discriminated against; the woman is prostituted; and the great masses of Chicanos, Puerto Ricans, and Latin Americans are scorned, exploited, and humiliated... Where the CIA organizes plans of global subversion and espionage, and the Pentagon creates neutron bombs capable of preserving material assets and wiping out human beings"

Fidel Castro

Historical anecdotes confirm that the United States of America has been called names for its acclaimed 'Policeman of the World' status in its acrid maintenance of power and domination. The 'imperialist powerhouse of the world' comes from accusations of interference in domestic and foreign policies of strategic countries that it deems weaker, inferior or fragile. On the preponderance of 'rugged American nationalism' the US has bludgeoned other nation states into towing its line of thinking, its mind-set and psych without due regards to political configurations of victim countries. It is countries like Russia, Cuba, China and Zimbabwe who have stood up to such threats, waging wars from trenches of international law or rhetoric demonization of "a goliath to our midst who threatens the extinction of other countries"[1]

It is well known from historical evidence that the USA government has a history of declaring specific countries to be a "national security threat." This is deemed on the basis that such victim countries pose significant threats in terms of frustrating or

---

[1] Mugabe addressing the 72nd United Nations session of the General Assembly http://www.dailymail.co.uk/wires/afp/article-4908326/Mugabe-UN-stands-Giant-Gold-Goliath-Trump.html/ Accessed May 4,19

obstructing US interests. Thus, the policy of declaring a country, no matter how small, a threat to the U.S. is perceived in terms of normative comparison and competing interests with the economically-and-militarily-largest country in the world. This dates back and is regulated by the US "Trading with the Enemy Act" of 1917. This act works in conjunction with the International Emergency Economic Powers Act (IEEPA) of 1977. We also note that the 2001 Patriot Act, which was passed in the aftermath of the 9/11 attack on the World Trade Centre and the Pentagon, further expanded the IEEPA to include "terrorist" organizations.

Sanctions programmes include against China (1949), North Korea (1950), Cuba (1960), Iran (1987 and 1996), Iraq (1990), Sudan (1997), Burma (1997), Western Balkan (2001), Zimbabwe (2001), Syria (2004) Belorussia (2004), Democratic Republic of Congo (2006) Lebanon (2007), North Korea (2008), Somalia (2010), Libya (2011), Ivory Coast (2011), Lebanon (2012), Yemen 2012, Russia (2012) South Sudan (2013), Ukraine/Russia (2014), Central African Republic (2015), Venezuela (2015), Burundi (2015) There are countries – once they buckle to US and European demands, have had sanctions lifted. There are also countries that – after forcibly being put into enduring and perpetual situations of imposed change – have also had sanctions lifter. For the later, this has been necessary largely to fulfil imperialist objectives in terms of politics, finance and trade.

For example, in Burma stringent sanctions were put in place including a ban on all inward investment in 1997 and were gradually relaxed in 2012 because USA was succeeding in planting their impostor Ms Aung San Sue Kyi within the conservative and reclusive Burmese political elite. President Obama proceeded to terminate sanctions. However, later developments in Burma about Kyi caught the USA government wrong footed as the impersonator Kyi was assimilated back into Burmese political structures of the ruling elite. This defeated the imperialist agenda of infiltration to undermine the Burmese government.

For Liberia, sanctions of the EU lifted in its entirety on June 20th, 2016, based on UNSCR 2288 (2016) with respect to the actions and policies of former Liberian President Charles Taylor. Sanctions were terminated November 12, 2015. This was after Charles Taylor was arraigned to serve his 50-year sentence for war crimes in a British prison following announcement of a final ruling by the United Nations-backed Special Court for Sierra Leone (SCSL) in The Hague. Britain generously volunteered to take Charles Taylor to HM Prison Frankland in County Durham. Since then, diamond trade with Sierra Leonne is thriving and both the UK and France are happy with the country's 'conducive' trade investment climate despite Africa being a disturbing "scar of the world".

U.S. SANCTIONS PROGRAMS

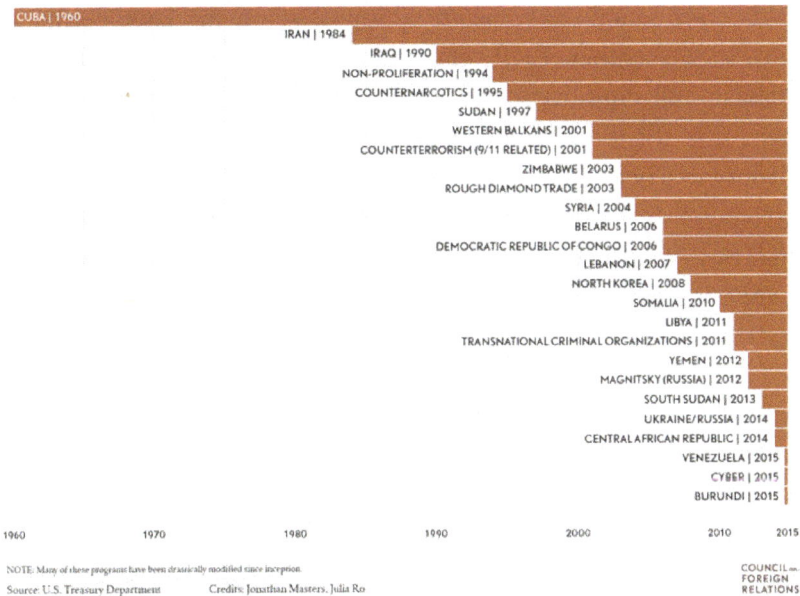

CUBA	1960					
	IRAN	1984				
	IRAQ	1990				
	NON-PROLIFERATION	1994				
	COUNTERNARCOTICS	1995				
	SUDAN	1997				
	WESTERN BALKANS	2001				
	COUNTERTERRORISM (9/11 RELATED)	2001				
	ZIMBABWE	2003				
	ROUGH DIAMOND TRADE	2003				
	SYRIA	2004				
	BELARUS	2006				
	DEMOCRATIC REPUBLIC OF CONGO	2006				
	LEBANON	2007				
	NORTH KOREA	2008				
	SOMALIA	2010				
	LIBYA	2011				
	TRANSNATIONAL CRIMINAL ORGANIZATIONS	2011				
	YEMEN	2012				
	MAGNITSKY (RUSSIA)	2012				
	SOUTH SUDAN	2013				
	UKRAINE/RUSSIA	2014				
	CENTRAL AFRICAN REPUBLIC	2014				
	VENEZUELA	2015				
	CYBER	2015				
	BURUNDI	2015				

1960   1970   1980   1990   2000   2010   2015

NOTE: Many of these programs have been drastically modified since inception.

Source: U.S. Treasury Department   Credits: Jonathan Masters, Julia Ro

COUNCIL on FOREIGN RELATIONS

From Council on Foreign Relations: 2018

Chinese Sanctions 1949-1970

The United States Trade embargo on China from 1949 to 1970 was designed to isolate China both politically and economically. At the same time, the United States wanted to inhibit China's military growth in the era of cold war politics. In response, China raised doubts on embargo's motive, effectiveness and rationale in consideration of historical relations of the two countries. However, at the time, the United States maintained legality of sanctions on international law and trade policy. Historical and economic links stretched as far back as Canton in 1785 under the British East India

Company trade protocols when the United States formalised the signing of the Treaty of Wanghia in 1844. The People's Republic of China's (PRC) Central Committee of the Chinese Communist Party proclaimed that the question of sanctions and acts of foreign disagreements were "completely contrary to the will of the Chinese people" and therefore vowed not to honour terms and conditions of the United States imposed sanctions[2]. Luke, T.L & McCobb (Jnr) (1971), Redick, C.F (1973) document this ugly historical interface.

The war between the United States and the People's Republic of China over sanctions subjectively imposed on the later continued until 15 December 1979 when the two countries agreed to re-establish full diplomatic relations[3]. What is important is that this paved way for the establishment of new institutional framework of relations. Thereafter, several trade-related bi-lateral relations agreements and commercial partnerships were signed by two countries, acknowledging not only their super power status but opened a new chapter of equality and mutual respect in their international relations.

Cuban Sanctions 1959-2016 [then from 2017 to date under President Donald Trump]

Kaplowitz (1988) describes sanctions against Cuba as 'an anatomy of a failed embargo'. As in all cases of political and international relations going sour, before 1959, United States was the Island's biggest trading partner. Things turned nasty at the onslaught and victory of the Sandinista Cuba Communist Revolution which was led by Fidel Castro and Che Guevara in 1959. Commentators like Haney & Vanderbrush (2005) notes that the Cuban the Cuban embargo was the 'domestic politics of an American foreign policy'. Cold war analysts such as Fontaine & Ratliff (2000) discredit the

---

[2] *See* Cohen , *Chinese Law and Sino-American Trade* , in *China Trade Prospects and U.S. Policy 128–30*, 141–43 (Eckstein A. ed. 1971)Google Scholar. *See generally*, Lee & McCobb , *United States Trade Embargo On China, 1949–1970: Legal Status and Future Prospects* , 4 N.Y.U.J. Int'l. L. & Pol. 1 (1971)

[3] See Joint Communique on the Establishment of Diplomatic Relations between the United States of America and the People's Republic of China. 18 International Leo. Mat. 274. (1979)

United States of America's failure of foreign policy on Cuba as a 'flip flop in the Caribbean' because it was at a loss in terms of how to deal with Cuba especially after Cuba managed to put very successful sanction bursting measures in rebuffing the United States' imperialist designs.

The timeline for Cuban Sanctions is a fearful representation of powerful nations designed to exterminate smaller nations, powerful nations set deface forms of civilisations from the face of this earth. It is a case in which 'smaller nations' are transformed in greater and larger nations because of the way they handle and absorb threats ushered by giants in clay feet. It has milestones of horrific and classic dreadful madness: for example, after President Obama paid a state visit to Cuba to reverse sanctions, restore diplomatic relations thereby ending cold war of the two powerful nations, Donald Trump reversed the deal at the stroke of a pen as soon as he entered the Oval Office in 2017!

Here is Cuba's timeline of economic sanctions:

7 February 1962 Full embargo of sanctions is announced

14-28 October 1962	The Cuban Missile Crisis
March 1982	US labels Cuba a 'Terrorist State and Sponsor'
20 May 1985	US launches a Propaganda Station for Cubans
23 October 1992	US tightens Cuban sanctions after the collapse of Soviet Union
12 March 1996	Helms Burton Act is signed into law
12 September 1998	Cuban five arrested sparking a major diplomatic row
21 November 1999	Elian Gonzales: Another Diplomatic War
30 October 2000	Aluta Continua: Partnership with Hugo Chavez

24 February 2008	Raul becomes President of Cuba: Aluta Continua
3rd December 2009	U.S. Aid Worker Arrested in Cuba for espionage
2011-2013	Cuba embarks on massive economic reforms having beaten counter effects of sanctions of US-engineered sanctions. Cuba recorded a GDP per capita growth of 6,760.15 USD (2013); with a life expectancy of 80 years.
28-29 January 2014	Cuba Hosts Regional Summit for the first time the Community of Latin American and Caribbean States (CELAC) summit, during which regional leaders discuss trade, peace, and human rights. The US is jolted by the union of CELAC – which is endorsed as an alternative to the U.S-dominated Organization of American States (OAS), from which Cuba was ousted in 1962.
17 December 2014	A move to restore diplomatic ties: Barack Obama and Raul Castro announce they will restore full diplomatic ties following the exchange of a jailed U.S. intelligence officer for the three remaining Cuban Five prisoners. U.S. subcontractor Alan Gross, imprisoned since 2009, is also released. The prisoner swap and release of Gross comes after nearly eighteen months of secret talks between U.S. and Cuban officials that were brokered, in part, by Pope Francis. Obama says the United States plans to reopen the embassy in Havana, while hard-line members of the Republican-controlled Congress condemn the move and vow to uphold the economic embargo.

29 May 2015	Cuba Removed from 'Terrorism List': The U.S. State Department removes Cuba from its list of state sponsors of terrorism. The designation, first imposed in 1982, had prevented Cuba from accessing international finance and was a sticking point in U.S.-Cuba talks on normalizing relations. Obama had called for Cuba's removal from the list in April of that year, after the State Department found that 'Cuba had not sponsored terrorism in recent years and vowed not to do so in the future.'
20 July 2015	U.S. and Cuba reopen embassies: The United States and Cuban embassies, which had been closed since 1961, reopen. The U.S. trade embargo, which cannot be lifted without congressional approval, remains in place, as Obama's term of office nears its end.
21 March 2016	U.S. President makes a historic visit to Cuba. Obama becomes the first sitting U.S. president in nearly ninety years to visit the Great island nation of Cuba to meet a Cuban sitting President, Dr Raul Castro.
21 November 2016	The Revolutionary leader of Cuba, Fidel Castro dies.
16 June 2017	Donald Trump reinstates travel, business restrictions: President Donald J. Trump announces that he will reinstate restrictions on Americans traveling to Cuba and U.S. business dealings with a military-run conglomerate but will not break diplomatic relations. The Obama administration's loosened restrictions stating that they "do not help the Cuban people—they only enrich the Cuban regime," Trump's argument is that U.S.

sanctions will not be lifted until Cuba frees all its
political prisoners, respects freedoms of
assembly and expression, legalizes opposition
parties, and schedules free and fair elections.
Trump is good at monitoring developments in
other countries when he cannot [even] control
gun crime in his own backyard.
[I think I have heard this language script being
repudiated by Robert Mugabe as he labels it
hypocritical, Janus-faced and evil!]

This chapter is significant in several ways. First it sets the scene
to the political environment in which the United States gains
notoriety as a policeman of the world. That situation has been
described to imply poking noses into affairs of other states. Others
have termed such acts of gross interference as part of the US foreign
policy which is buttressed by threats, intimidation and bullying.
American historians and politicians refer to this as some form of
power ingrained in the state of its nation as they assert their capability
and strength. It goes beyond assertiveness and aggression because
even the most powerful must also exercise restraint. What is the cut-
off point of aggressiveness and restraint and who sets out the
criterion? Is it possible for the most powerful nation on earth to put
in place mechanisms to check on its excessive power – and if so,
how? What is "excessive"? Thus, the success and failure of America's
self-control lies in its foreign policy and how it relations with other
individual nations or blocks of nation states.

Furthermore, let me explain a bit about how the US has worked
with other nation states. They weigh the power of others in
comparison with their power. They challenge and threaten as they
become boisterous. Their language of engagement especially when
dealing with nations who disagree with their foreign policy is that of
threats and aggression. When other nations disagree with American
foreign policy they feel challenged. The soul of every nation lies in its
power – the power to lead other nations and dominate over them.
Domination is a form of control in that it weakens those nations to

becoming victims. The United States of America relies on its power to influence world events through domination. When a state is referred to as powerful, then it goes without saying that it has the capacity to change and influence events through political and economic means.

Most sanctions and embargoes deployed to European or Eastern bloc countries by the USA are based on ideological differences especially during the time of the cold war. Middle Eastern countries have suffered the brunt and ravages of exploitation of their resources especially oil. Incapacitating oil rich countries like Iran through sanctions destroys all international trade lines because of trade restrictions. Another way of compelling victim nation to sell resources on terms and conditions dictated by sender countries is to impose restrictive measures and trade/financial embargoes.

All the countries blacklisted on the USA sanctions list are nations that have disagreed and challenged USA foreign policy. The common thread of victim states dealings with the USA are characterised refusal and non-conformity to the dictates of the USA or its allies. Victim countries including Zimbabwe have asserted their determination and resolve to fight against imperialism and domination. Other nations highlight repression involved in deploying sanctions or even wars where the US is often found wanting in terms of defining its position in the new world order of democracy.

Sanctions Risk Countries (See notes below)[4]

Iran (1984)
- Joint Comprehensive Plan of Action (JCPOA) was implemented on 16 January 2016 (see *JCPOA*).
- restrictions on admission of certain persons
- *JCPOA* freezing of funds and economic resources
- valid until 13.4.2019
- embargo on telecommunications monitoring and interception equipment
- embargo on equipment which might be used for internal repression

---

[4] Compiled from internet sources including Business and Sanctions Consulting Netherlands. See also http://www.bscn.nl/ Accessed 07 May18

- ban on provision of certain services
- embargo on arms and related materiel
- embargo on nearly all dual-use goods and technology
- embargo on certain goods and technology which could contribute to enrichment-related, reprocessing or heavy water-related activities, or to the development of nuclear weapon delivery systems or to the pursuit of activities related to other topics about which the IAEA has expressed concerns
- prohibition of procurement from Iran of arms and related material, nearly all dual-use goods and technology and certain other goods and technology
- (arms and other embargoes related) ban on provision of certain services
- (arms and other embargoes related) ban on certain investment
- controls on export of certain other sensitive goods and technology
- control on provision of certain services
- control on certain investment
- embargo on key equipment and technology for the oil and natural gas industries
- ban on provision of certain services (to the oil and natural gas industries)
- ban on certain investment (in the oil and natural gas industries)
- ban on certain Iranian investment (nuclear industry)
- ban on new commitments for grants, financial assistance and concessional loans to the Government of Iran
- *JCPOA* restrictions on transfers of funds to and from Iran
- restrictions on establishment of branches and subsidiaries of and cooperation with Iranian banks
- restrictions on provision of insurance and re-insurance
- restrictions on issuance of and trade in certain bonds
- vigilance over business with Iran
- inspection of and prior information requirement on cargoes to and from Iran
- restrictions on access to EU airports for certain cargo flights
- ban on provision of certain services to certain vessels and aircraft
- restrictions on admission of listed natural persons

- freezing of funds and economic resources of listed persons, entities and bodies
- measures to prevent certain specialised teaching or training
- prohibition to satisfy claims made by certain persons, entities or bodies
- import ban on crude oil and petroleum products- ban on provision of certain services, including transport (related to crude oil, and petroleum products from Iran)
- *JCPOA* import ban on petrochemical products
- *JCPOA* prohibition on transport of Iranian crude oil
- *JCPOA* ban on provision of certain services (related to Iranian crude oil)
- *JCPOA* ban on provision of certain services (related to prohibition on the provision of insurance and reinsurance and transport of Iranian crude oil)
- ban on provision of certain services (related to petroleum products)
- *JCPOA* ban on provision of certain services (related to petrochemical products)
- embargo on key equipment and technology for the petrochemical industry
- ban on provision of certain services (to the petrochemical industry)
- ban on certain investment (in the petrochemical industry)
- *JCPOA* ban on trade in gold and precious metals with the Government of Iran
- ban on trade in diamonds with the Government of Iran
- ban on provision of new Iranian banknotes and coins
- ban on provision of specialised financial messaging services to those subjected to the freezing of funds and economic resources
- import ban on natural gas
- ban on provision of certain related services (related to natural gas)
- embargo on graphite
- embargo on certain raw and semi-finished metals
- ban on provision of certain services (related to graphite and metals)
- embargo on key naval equipment and shipbuilding technology
- ban on provision of certain related services (related to key naval equipment and shipbuilding technology)
- prohibition of construction of new oil tankers for Iran

- embargo on certain software for integrating industrial processes
- ban on provision of certain related services
- ban on Member States' commitments for financial support for trade with Iran
- control of transactions of EU financial institutions with banks domiciled in Iran and their subsidiaries, branches and other financial entities outside Iran
- ban on provision of flagging and classification services to certain vessels
- *JCPOA* ban on 'supply' of certain vessels to Iran
- vigilance requirements for EU financial institutions in their activities with banks domiciled in Iran and their branches and subsidiaries
- ban on certain Iranian investment (nuclear industry)
- monitoring of activities of EU branches and subsidiaries of credit and financial institutions domiciled in Iran
- enhanced vigilance as regards transactions of EU financial institutions with credit and financial institutions domiciled in Iran and with the latter's branches and subsidiaries

Iraq 1990
- confirmation of embargo on arms and related materiel
- restrictions on trade in cultural goods
- freezing of funds and economic resources
- transfer of such funds and economic resources to Development Fund for Iraq
- *expired on 30 June 2011* immunities and restrictions concerning payment for petroleum and gas exported by Iraq
- prohibition to satisfy claims with regard to contracts and transactions whose performance is affected by the measures taken in accordance with UN Security Council Resolution 661(1990) and related resolutions

Yugoslavia 1992/1995
- withdrawn 29.10.2014
- prohibition to satisfy certain claims in accordance with UN Security Council Resolution No 757 (1992)

- prohibition to satisfy claims about contracts and transactions the performance of which was affected by UN Security Council Resolution No 757 (1992) and related resolutions

South Sudan (1997)
- embargo on arms and related materiel
- ban on provision of certain services (related to arms and related materiel)
- restrictions on admission
- freezing of funds and economic resources
- prohibition to satisfy certain claims of certain persons, entities and bodies
- restrictions on admission for certain persons
- embargo on certain goods which might be used for the manufacture and maintenance of products which could be used for internal repression
- ban on provision of certain related services

Burma (1997)
- No sanctions: entirely lifted in October 2017

Afghanistan (1999)
- measures against the Taliban:
- embargo on arms and related materiel
- ban on provision of certain services
- freezing of funds and economic resources
- restrictions on admission
- freezing of funds and economic resources
- ban on provision of certain services

Western Balkan (2001)
- see Bosnia and Herzegovina and/or Moldova and/or Serbia and Montenegro

Zimbabwe (2001)
- embargo on arms and related materiel
- ban on exports of equipment for internal repression
- ban on provision of certain services

- restrictions on admission (suspended for specific parties)
- freezing of funds and economic resources (suspended for specific parties)
- valid until 20.2.2019
Sanctions against Zimbabwe

Description of the sanctions
1. Arms embargo, etc.

The arms embargo covers the sale, export and supply of arms, ammunition, military vehicles and equipment to Zimbabwe, as well as any associated financial and technical assistance. Exemptions may be granted for equipment that is to be used for humanitarian or protective purposes by the UN or the EU. There is also a prohibition on the export of equipment that might be used for internal repression, as well as any associated financial and technical assistance.

2. Travel restrictions

The travel restrictions involve a prohibition on entry and transit for individuals involved in activities that seriously undermine democracy, respect for human rights and the rule of law in Zimbabwe. The persons covered by the travel restrictions are included on a list, which is updated continuously. The list mainly includes people linked to President Mugabe and ZANU-PF. Exemptions may be made on urgent humanitarian grounds or, in special exceptional circumstances, for participation in intergovernmental meetings in which dialogue directly promoting human rights and democracy is conducted. A special procedure applies to these exemptions. As stated in the section on the background to the sanctions, the EU has now removed a large number of people from the EU list of people covered by restrictive measures and has decided to suspend the restrictive measures against the majority of the remaining people and companies on the list.

3. Freezing of assets

The restrictions mean that assets and economic resources belonging to certain identified individuals in the regime in Zimbabwe or linked to it are to be frozen. The restrictions also apply to entities controlled by these individuals, such as companies. It is also prohibited for others to place assets and other resources at their disposal. Exemptions may be granted for funds necessary to cover basic living costs and for expenditure to cover legal costs. The persons covered by the freezing of assets are included on a list which has subsequently been amended. The group is described as members of Zimbabwe's government and persons and entities linked to it. The list includes the same natural persons as the list of those covered by the travel restrictions, with the addition of certain companies. As stated in the section above, the EU has now removed a large number of people and companies from the EU list of people and companies covered by restrictive measures and has decided to suspend the restrictive measures against the majority of the remaining people and companies on the list.

Syria (2004)

- embargo on certain goods which might be used for the manufacture and maintenance of products which could be used for internal repression
- ban on provision of certain related services
- embargo on certain goods which might be used for the manufacture and maintenance of products which could be used for internal repression
- ban on provision of certain related services
- control of export of certain other goods which might be used for the manufacture and maintenance of equipment which might be used for internal repression
- control of provision of certain related services
- import ban on arms and related materiel
- ban on provision of certain related services
- embargo on telecommunications monitoring and interception equipment
- ban on provision of certain services (related to such equipment)
- import ban on crude oil and petroleum products
- ban on provision of certain services (related to crude oil and petroleum products)
- embargo on key equipment and technology for the oil and natural gas industries
- ban on provision of certain services (to the oil and natural gas industries)
- ban on provision of new Syrian banknotes and coins

- ban on trade in gold, precious metals and diamonds with the Government of Syria

- embargo on luxury goods

- ban on certain investment (in the oil and natural gas industries, in construction of power plants for electricity production)

- prohibition to participate in the construction of new power plants for electricity production

- restraint on commitments for public and private financial support for trade with Syria and ban on new long-term commitments of Member States

- ban on new commitments for grants, financial assistance and concessional loans to the Government of Syria

- prohibition for the European Investment Bank to make certain payments

- restrictions on issuance of and trade in certain bonds

- restrictions on establishment of branches and subsidiaries of and cooperation with Syrian banks

- restrictions on provision of insurance and re-insurance

- restrictions on access to airports in the EU for certain flights

- inspection of certain cargoes to Syria and prior information requirement on cargoes to Syria

- restrictions on admission of certain persons

- freezing of funds and economic resources of certain persons, entities and bodies

- prohibition to satisfy claims made by certain persons, entities or bodies

- valid until 1.6.2018

- restrictions on trade in cultural goods (with list)

- embargo on jet fuel and certain additives

- ban on provision of certain services (related to jet fuel and certain additives)

- embargo on equipment used in the construction of new power plants for electricity production

- ban on provision of certain services (related to the construction of such power plants)

- specific exception for Central Bank of Syria (freezing of funds and economic resources)

- ban on exports of certain goods which might be used for the manufacture and maintenance of equipment which might be used for internal repression
- ban on provision of certain services
- ban on exports of luxury goods
- prior information requirement on cargoes to Syria
- information on competent authorities
- authorisation to apply an embargo on equipment which might be used for internal repression
- authorisation to ban the provision of certain services
- amendment of the exception to the ban on exports of certain goods which might be used for the manufacture and maintenance of equipment which might be used for internal repression
- amendment of the prohibition to satisfy claims made by certain persons, entities or bodies
- prohibition of circumvention of the restrictive measures
- restrictions on admission of persons suspected of involvement in the planning, sponsoring, organising or perpetrating of the murder of former Prime Minister of the Lebanon, Rafiq Hariri on 14 February 2005
- commitment to cooperate with international investigation into that murder

Belarus (2004)
- embargo on arms and related material
- ban on exports of equipment for internal repression
- ban on provision of certain services
- restrictions on admission
- freezing of funds and economic resources
- valid until 28.02.2019
- 15.02.2016 Council conclusions on Belarus

1. Arms embargo, etc.

It is prohibited to sell, supply, transfer or export to Belarus arms and similar equipment as well as equipment that might be used for internal repression. It is also prohibited to provide technical or financial assistance related to such products. There are certain exceptions with regard to, for example, equipment for EU and UN crisis management operations.

2. Individually targeted restrictive measures (travel restrictions and freezing of assets)

The group of persons, entities and bodies who may be subject to sanctions is described in detail in the legal acts, but can be briefly summarized as follows: Persons responsible for (1) four notable disappearance cases in 1999 and 2000; (2) electoral fraud, serious human rights abuses, repression against peaceful demonstrations in connection with the parliamentary elections and referendum in October 2004; (3) electoral fraud and repressive measures against the opposition and civil society in connection with the presidential election in March 2006; (4) electoral fraud and repressive measures against the opposition, civil society and the media in connection with the presidential election in December 2010; (5) serious human rights abuses, repression of civil society and political opposition in general; and (6) persons and companies benefiting from or supporting the Lukashenko regime, for example through financing.

Four persons are currently covered by individually targeted restrictive measures. These persons have been listed since they are considered to be responsible for four notable disappearance cases in the period 1999–2000 (category 1 according to the summary above).

Democratic Republic of Congo (2006)
- embargo on arms and related material
- ban on provision of certain services
- freezing of funds and economic resources
- restrictions on admission
- Article 3(2) shall apply until 12.12.2018

1. Arms embargo, etc.

It is prohibited to directly or indirectly supply, sell or transfer arms and related materiel, including ammunition, military vehicles and equipment, paramilitary equipment or related spare parts to all non-state entities and individuals in the territory of the DRC. It is also prohibited to offer technical and financial assistance in connection with the arms embargo. These sanctions do not apply to materiel intended solely for support to the UN stabilization mission in the DRC (MONUSCO). Also, non-lethal military equipment intended solely for humanitarian or protective use may be supplied. The UN Security Council has established a Sanctions Committee concerning the DRC to handle issues related to exemptions from the arms embargo. Exemptions must be reported to and approved by this Committee to be approved by the competent national authority.

2. Travel restrictions

The persons listed are prohibited from entry into, or transit through, the European Union. Persons who may be listed include those who violate the arms embargo, political and military leaders of both Congolese and foreign armed groups who impede disarmament, demobilization and reintegration, or those who recruit or use children in armed conflict as well as persons who commit serious crimes against children or women in situations of armed conflict. Additional persons may be listed. This applies to persons who commit acts in the DRC that constitute human rights violations or that constitute crimes or violations of international humanitarian law; prevent humanitarian access, illegally support armed groups in eastern DRC through the illicit trade of natural resources; act for or on behalf of a listed person; or participate in attacks against MONUSCO, UN staff and members of the UN Group of Experts on the Democratic Republic of the Congo. The list of the persons concerned is drawn up and amended by the UN Security Council Sanctions Committee concerning the DRC, which can also grant exemptions in some cases. The EU continuously implements the decisions of the Sanctions Committee.

3. Freezing of assets

All assets and economic resources belonging to listed persons or entities are to be frozen. It is also prohibited to place assets or economic resources at their disposal. The criteria for listing persons and, where appropriate, entities are the same as for travel restrictions. As mentioned about travel restrictions, the list is drawn up and amended by the Sanctions Committee. The EU continuously implements the decisions of the Sanctions Committee. Certain exemptions from the freezing of assets may be permitted for humanitarian purposes,

Lebanon (2006)

- embargo on arms and related material
- ban on provision of certain services
- restrictions on admission of persons suspected of involvement in the planning, sponsoring, organising or perpetrating of the murder of former Prime Minister of the Lebanon, Rafiq Hariri on 14 February 2005
- freezing of funds and economic resources of those persons
- commitment to cooperate with international investigation into that murder

Description of the sanctions

1. Arms embargo

The arms embargo means that the sale or supply, etc. of arms is prohibited to entities, natural and legal persons and others in Lebanon. The same applies to the provision of technical and financial assistance and other services associated with arms and related materiel. The prohibitions do not apply to the sale or supply of goods or services for use by the UN Interim Force in Lebanon (UNIFIL) or by the Lebanese armed forces, or if the transaction has been authorized by the Government of Lebanon or UNIFIL. Sales and supplies of this kind must always be approved by the competent national authority.

2. Travel restrictions

Individuals suspected of involvement in the planning, sponsoring, organizing or perpetrating of the attack on Rafiq Hariri and some twenty other persons are subject to a prohibition against entry into or transit through the EU. The EU list of those subject to travel restrictions is to reflect the list prepared and updated by the UN Security Council Sanctions Committee for Lebanon. To date, no individuals have been listed by the Sanction Committee.

3. Freezing of assets

Individuals suspected of involvement in the planning, sponsoring, organizing or perpetrating of the attack on Rafiq Hariri and some twenty other persons are subject to having their funds and economic resources frozen. The EU list of those subject to having their assets frozen is to reflect the list prepared and updated by the

UN Security Council Sanctions Committee for Lebanon. To date, no individuals have been listed by the Sanction Committee.

North Korea (2008)

- embargo on arms and related materiel
- ban on exports of certain goods and technology
- prohibition of procurement from DPRK of arms, related materiel and other goods and technology
- ban on provision of certain services
- ban on provision of new DPRK banknotes and coins
- ban on trade in gold, precious metals and diamonds with the Government of DPRK
- ban on exports of luxury goods
- ban on public provided financial support for trade where such support could contribute to DPRK's nuclear-related, ballistic missile-related or other weapons of mass destruction-related programmes
- ban on new commitments for grants, financial assistance and concessional loans to the DPRK
- enhanced monitoring of the activities of EU financial institutions with banks domiciled in DPRK and their subsidiaries, branches and other financial entities outside DPRK
- restrictions on establishment of branches and subsidiaries of and cooperation with DPRK banks
- restrictions on issuance of and trade in certain bonds
- inspection of and prior information requirement on cargoes to and from DPRK
- restrictions on access to EU airports for certain flights
- ban on provision of certain services to certain vessels and aircraft
- restrictions on admission for certain persons
- freezing of funds and economic resources
- measures to prevent certain specialised teaching or training
- enhanced vigilance over DPRK diplomatic personnel
- prohibition to satisfy certain claims made by certain persons, entities and bodies

- ban on import and purchase of goods and technology (which could contribute to North Korea's nuclear-related, other weapons of mass destruction-related or ballistic missile-related programmes)

- ban on provision of certain services (related to such goods and technology)

- ban on exports of luxury goods

- additional ban on exports and imports of certain goods and technology which could contribute to DPRK's nuclear-related, ballistic missile-related or other weapons of mass destruction-related programmes

- prior information requirement on cargoes to and from DPRK

- measures to be applied by EU credit and financial institutions to exercise vigilance over their activities with banks domiciled in DPRK and their subsidiaries, branches and other financial entities outside DPRK

- restrictions on access to EU ports for certain vessels

- ban on provision to certain DPRK vessels of bunkering and ship supply services

- restrictions on certain flights (EU airports, overflight)

Eretria (2009)

Description of the sanctions

1. Arms embargo

It is prohibited to sell or supply weapons and related materiel to Eritrea. Corresponding prohibitions apply to technical and financial assistance linked to such products. The arms embargo does not apply to protective clothing that is temporarily exported to Eritrea by UN personnel, representatives of the media, and humanitarian personnel and aid workers solely for their personal use. Nor does the arms embargo apply to non-lethal military equipment intended solely for humanitarian use or for providing protection following prior approval from the UN Security Council Sanctions Committee for Somalia and Eritrea.

Inspection regime

All Member States are called upon to inspect, in their territory – including seaports and airports – all cargoes to and from Eritrea if the state concerned has information that provides reasonable grounds to believe that the cargo contains items whose supply, transfer or export is prohibited. For this reason, special cargo declarations must be submitted for such transport.

2. Travel restrictions

A prohibition to enter or transit through the EU applies to individuals and entities listed by the UN Security Council Sanctions Committee for Somalia and Eritrea and that violate the arms embargo, provide support from Eritrea to armed opposition groups that aim to destabilize the region, etc. To date, no individuals or entities have been listed by the Committee or, consequently, by the EU.

3. Freezing of assets

All funds and economic resources that are owned or controlled, directly or indirectly, by individuals or entities listed by the UN Security Council Sanctions Committee for Somalia and Eritrea and that violate the arms embargo, provide support from Eritrea to armed opposition groups, etc., are to be frozen. Nor may funds or economic resources, directly or indirectly, be made available to, or used for the benefit of, such individuals or entities. To date, no individuals or entities have been listed by the Committee or, consequently, by the EU.

Somalia (2010)

- confirmation of embargo on arms and related materiel
- ban on provision of certain services
- inspection of and prior information requirement on certain cargoes to and from Somalia
- embargo on supplying arms and related material
- ban on provision of certain services
- freezing of funds and economic resources
- restrictions on admission for certain persons
- import ban on charcoal
- ban on provision of certain related services (related to charcoal)
- ban on supplying arms and related material meant for the Security Forces of the Federal Government of Somalia to any person or entity not in the service of such forces
- vigilance requirement for EU Member States about certain goods related to military activities and the provision of certain services

- inspection of certain vessels to stop illegal trade in charcoal, arms and related materiel
- prior information requirement on cargoes to and from Somalia

Libya (2011)
- embargo on arms and related materiel
- embargo on equipment which might be used for internal repression
- ban on provision of certain services
- prohibition of procurement from Libya of arms and related materiel and of equipment which might be used for internal repression
- commitment to inspect vessels and aircraft bound to or from Libya, if certain conditions are met
- commitment to deny permission to aircraft to land in, take off from or fly over a Member State's territory, if certain conditions are met
- inspection of and specific restrictions on certain vessels in order to stop illegal exports of crude oil from Libya
- restrictions on admission
- freezing of funds and economic resources
- confirmation of the freezing of certain funds and economic resources which were frozen as of 16.9.2011
- vigilance requirement when doing business with Libyan entities
- prohibition to grant certain claims to listed persons and entities and any other persons and entities in Libya, including the government of Libya
- prior information requirement on cargoes to and from Libya
- restrictive measures against three specific persons valid until 02-10-2018
- export restrictions on certain goods to Libya which may be used for smuggling migrants and trafficking in human beings

Ivory Coast (2011)
No, sanctions of the EU lifted in its entirety on June 9th, 2016, based on UNSCR 2283 (2016)

Tunisia (2011)
- freezing of funds and economic resources
- valid until 31.1.2019

All funds and economic resources belonging to natural and legal persons responsible for misappropriation of Tunisian state funds, and natural or legal persons, entities or bodies associated with them are to be frozen. Furthermore, no funds or economic resources are to be made available to them. In certain cases, however, exemptions can be granted, e.g. on humanitarian grounds. Frozen assets may also be released in certain cases for the enforcement of judgments etc., in order to facilitate their return to the Tunisian state.

Guinea Bissau (2012)
Description of the sanctions
1. Travel restrictions

A prohibition to enter or transit through the EU applies to all persons listed by the UN Security Council or the Security Council Sanctions Committee for the Republic of Guinea-Bissau, as well as persons designated by the EU who engage in or provide support for acts that threaten the peace, security or stability of the Republic of Guinea-Bissau and persons who are associated with them. Certain exemptions may be granted.

2. Freezing of assets

All funds and economic resources, owned by individuals or entities involved in or supporting actions that undermine the peace, security or stability of Guinea-Bissau and individuals or entities associated with them shall be frozen. It is also prohibited to directly or indirectly make funds or economic resources available to such individuals or entities. Exemptions may be granted in certain cases to satisfy basic needs

Yemen (2012)
- restrictions on admission of certain persons

- freezing of funds and economic resources

- embargo on supplying arms and related material to certain persons, entities and bodies

- ban on provision of certain services to these persons, entities and bodies

- commitment to inspect vessels and aircraft bound to or from Yemen, if certain conditions are met

- prohibition to satisfy certain claims

Sanctions against Yemen

Description of the sanctions

The sanctions involve an arms embargo, travel restrictions, the freezing of assets and a prohibition on providing access to assets for the persons designated by the United Nations Sanctions Committee for Yemen.

1. Arms embargo

The direct or indirect sale, supply or other provision of arms and arms-related equipment, including military vehicles and paramilitary equipment, is prohibited to persons and entities listed by the UN Sanctions Committee for Yemen. Corresponding prohibitions also include persons acting on behalf of, or under the direction of, these listed persons. It is also prohibited to provide technical or financial assistance to the same sphere of persons.

Within the framework of international law, Member States are to inspect cargo bound for Yemen within their own territory, including ports and airports, when reasonable grounds exist to assume the cargo contains prohibited goods as outlined above. Upon discovery, the goods are to be seized and removed.

2. Freezing of assets and travel restrictions

Persons who may be subject to the sanctions are those conducting or providing support to acts that threaten peace, security or stability in Yemen through acts that in various ways obstruct or undermine the successful completion of the political transition as outlined in the Gulf Cooperation Council (GCC) Initiative and Implementation Mechanism Agreement, or through planning, directing or committing acts that violate human rights or international humanitarian law in Yemen.

Persons who provide support to the acts outlined above may be subject to the freezing of assets. The freezing mechanism may also include persons and entities that are instructed to commit any of the above acts, and entities that are owned or controlled by a person who commits any of the above acts.

Exemptions from travel restrictions may be made by the Sanctions Committee on humanitarian grounds or where entry or transit would further the objectives of peace and national reconciliation in Yemen.

Exemptions from the rules concerning the freezing of assets may be made by EU Member States for basic needs and, in certain cases, to fulfil previously agreed obligations.

Russia Federation (2012)

- see also Ukraine
- embargo on arms and related material
- embargo on dual-use goods and technology, if intended for military use or for a military end-user
- ban on imports of arms and related material
- (arms and related materiel related) ban on provision of certain services
- (dual-use goods and technology related) ban on provision of certain services
- (deep water, Arctic and shale oil related) controls on export of certain equipment/items for the oil industry
- controls on provision of certain related services
- prohibition of procurement from Russia of arms and related material
- restrictions on issuance of and trade in certain 'bonds, equity or similar financial instruments' (i.e. securities and money-markets instruments)
- prohibition to satisfy certain claims made by certain persons, entities and bodies
- valid until 31.7.2018
- ban on the supply of dual-use goods and technology to certain persons, entities and bodies

Sanctions with respect to Russia and Ukraine

There are three systems of sanctions with respect to Russia and the developments in Ukraine, all introduced by the EU.

The first system consists of measures against persons in Ukraine identified as responsible for the misappropriation of Ukrainian public assets and persons responsible for human rights violations in the country. These sanctions involve the freezing of assets and have so far been imposed on former Ukrainian President Viktor Yanukovych and a number of other representatives of the former regime.

Sanctions due to the situation in Ukraine

The second system of sanctions consists of measures concerning actions that threaten or undermine the territorial integrity, sovereignty, independence, stability or security of Ukraine, or obstruct the work of international organizations in the country, and the transfer of ownership of companies in Crimea and Sevastopol in contravention of Ukrainian law. This system is, in turn, divided into two. One system involves individually targeted measures in the form of the freezing of assets and travel restrictions and has been imposed on several persons and some organizations and companies on a list that has gradually been extended. The second, established later, involves special sectoral sanctions that were introduced against Russia and later stepped up because of Russia's conduct that is destabilizing the situation in Ukraine.

Sanctions due to actions threatening Ukraine's sovereignty, etc.

The third system consists of restrictions on the import of goods from Crimea and the city of Sevastopol and has subsequently been extended to include measures against certain exports to, and a prohibition on investments in, these areas. Tourism-related services have also been prohibited. This is in response to Russia's illegal annexation of these areas.

Sanctions due to Russia's illegal annexation of Crimea and Sevastopol

Central African Republic (2015)
- embargo on arms and related materiel
- ban on provision of certain services
- restrictions on admission of certain natural persons
- freezing of funds and economic resources
- commitment to dispose of arms and related materiel that are in breach of the embargo
- ban on provision of certain services
- prohibition to satisfy claims

Description of the sanctions
1. Arms embargo

It is prohibited to directly or indirectly supply, sell or transfer arms and related materiel, including ammunition, military vehicles and equipment, paramilitary equipment or related spare parts to the Central African Republic. It is also prohibited to offer technical and financial assistance in connection with the arms embargo. The sale, delivery, transfer or export of arms and related materiel intended solely for use by various international forces and other peacekeeping missions in the country are exempt from the embargo. To deal with issues concerning the arms embargo and other matters, the UN has established a sanctions committee for the Central African Republic. Exemptions from the arms embargo must be approved in advance by the sanctions committee. Member States have a mandate to confiscate goods covered by the arms embargo.

2. Travel restrictions

It is prohibited for persons designated by the sanctions committee, and who on this basis have been listed by the EU, to enter or transit through the EU. Persons who may be subject to listing include those who participate in actions that undermine peace, security and stability in the Central African Republic, who violate the arms embargo, who support armed groups or criminal networks with weapons or in some other way, who in any way have participated in crimes against human rights or international humanitarian law, who recruit or use child soldiers or who obstruct the delivery of humanitarian assistance.

3. Freezing of assets

All assets and economic resources owned by persons or entities designated by the United Nations Sanctions Committee, and who on this basis have been listed by the EU, shall be frozen. It is also prohibited to place assets or economic resources at their disposal. The criteria for the listing of persons and, where appropriate, entities are the same as for travel restrictions. Certain exemptions from the freezing of assets may be permitted for humanitarian purposes,

Egypt (2015)
Description of the sanctions

All funds belonging to persons responsible for misappropriation of Egyptian public assets, and natural or legal persons, entities or bodies that are associated with them and that are placed on the EU's sanctions list shall be frozen. Furthermore, no funds or financial resources are to be made available to these persons. In certain cases, however, exemptions can be granted, e.g. on humanitarian grounds. Frozen assets may also be released in certain cases for the enforcement of judgments etc., to facilitate their return to the Egyptian state.

The persons who have had their assets frozen are listed in the annex of Council Regulation (EU) No 270/2011; see the section entitled 'Relevant documents'.

Venezuela (2015)
- Freezing of funds and economic resources
- embargo on arms and related materiel.
- (arms embargo related) ban on provision of certain services

Sanctions against Venezuela
Description of the sanctions
1. Arms embargo
The arms embargo means that the sale, delivery, transfer or export of arms and arms-related materiel of all types is prohibited. Furthermore, a specific prohibition also applies to technical assistance, brokering and other services linked to military activities.

2. Embargo on certain equipment
The embargo on certain equipment includes the sale, delivery, transfer and export of equipment that could be used for internal repression against the Venezuelan population. Examples of such equipment could be aids to conduct surveillance activities and the interception of telecommunications and internet among the civilian population. Providing funding and economic support for this type of equipment are prohibited.

3. Restrictions on entry
Persons responsible for serious violations, crimes against human rights or repression of civil society and the democratic opposition are prohibited from entry to and transit through EU Member States. A

list of persons covered by the restrictions will be prepared by EU Member States.

4. Freezing of assets

All assets and economic resources that are owned, held or controlled by natural and legal persons who are responsible for serious violations, crimes against human rights or repression of civil society and the democratic opposition are to be frozen.

Burundi (2015)

- restrictions on admission of certain natural persons
- freezing of funds and economic resources
- valid until 31.10.2018
- prohibition to satisfy certain claims

Travel restrictions

The travel restrictions involve a prohibition on entry into and transit through EU Member States for individuals involved in activities that seriously undermine democracy or obstruct the search for a political solution in Burundi, e.g. by acts of violence, repression or inciting violence. The persons subject to the travel restrictions are listed in the Annex to Council Decision (CFSP) 2015/1763; see under 'Relevant EU documents'. The entry ban does not oblige a Member State to refuse its own nationals entry as this would contravene the right to return to their own country of citizenship. Exemptions are also made for travel restrictions when they are contrary to obligations under international law, e.g. agreements on immunity. In addition, exemptions may be granted by the Council, e.g. on grounds of urgent humanitarian need or, in special exceptional circumstances, to attend intergovernmental meetings that directly promote the policy objectives of restrictive measures, including human rights and democracy in Burundi. A special procedure applies to these exemptions; see Article 1, points 2–8 of Council Decision (CFSP) 2015/1763.

Freezing of assets

These measures mean that all funds and economic resources belonging to, owned, held or controlled by individuals, entities or bodies listed shall be frozen. The list is contained in the Annex to Council Decision (CFSP) 2015/1763 and in Annex I of Council Regulation (EU) 2015/1755. No funds or economic resources may be made available, directly or indirectly, to or for the benefit of those included on the list. Exemptions may be granted for funds necessary to cover basic living costs and for expenditure to cover legal costs.

Sudan (North) – (2017)
- restrictions on admission
- freezing of funds and economic resources
- embargo on arms and related material
- ban on provision of certain services

Mali (2017)
Sanctions against Mali
Description of the sanctions
1. Travel restrictions
A prohibition to enter or transit through the EU applies to individuals and entities listed by the UN Security Council Sanctions Committee for Mali and that threaten peace, security and stability in Mali. To date, no individuals or entities have been listed by the Committee or by the EU.
2. Freezing of assets
All funds and economic resources that are owned or controlled, directly or indirectly, by individuals or entities listed by the UN Security Council Sanctions Committee for Mali and that threaten peace, security and stability in Mali are to be frozen. Nor may funds or economic resources, directly or indirectly, be made available to, or used for the benefit of, such individuals or entities or any other individuals or entities acting on their behalf. To date, no individuals or entities have been listed by the Committee or by the EU.

Ukraine (See Russia Federation above)
- ban on imports of goods from Crimea or Sevastopol
- ban on provision of certain services
- prohibition to satisfy certain claims made by certain persons, entities or bodies

- valid until 23.6.2018
- ban on investment in real estate in Crimea and Sevastopol
- ban on investment in entities in Crimea and Sevastopol
- embargo on certain goods and technology for use in certain sectors (transport, telecommunications, energy, oil, gas and mineral resources)
- ban on provision of certain services (related to such goods and technology)
- ban on provision of certain services related to infrastructure in certain sectors (transport, telecommunications, energy, oil, gas and mineral resources)
- ban on provision of certain services related to tourism
- prohibition for certain ships to enter ports in Crimea and Sevastopol
- restrictions on admission of (a) certain natural persons responsible for, actively supporting or implementing, actions or policies which undermine or threaten the territorial integrity, sovereignty and independence of Ukraine, or stability or security in Ukraine, or which obstruct the work of international organisations in Ukraine, and certain natural persons associated with them; (b) certain natural persons actively supporting, materially or financially, or benefitting from, Russian decision-makers responsible for the annexation of Crimea or the destabilisation of Eastern Ukraine; (c) certain natural persons conducting transactions with the separatist groups in the Donbass region of Ukraine
- freezing of funds and economic resources of (a) certain natural persons responsible for, actively supporting or implementing, actions or policies which undermine or threaten the territorial integrity, sovereignty and independence of Ukraine, or stability or security in Ukraine, or which obstruct the work of international organisations in Ukraine, and certain natural or legal persons, entities or bodies associated with them; (b) certain legal persons, entities or bodies supporting, materially or financially, actions which undermine or threaten the territorial integrity, sovereignty and independence of Ukraine; (c) certain legal persons, entities or bodies in Crimea or Sevastopol whose ownership has been transferred contrary to Ukrainian law, or certain legal persons, entities or bodies which have benefitted from such a transfer; (d) certain natural or legal persons, entities or bodies actively supporting, materially or financially, or benefitting from, Russian decision-makers responsible for the annexation of Crimea or the destabilisation of Eastern Ukraine; (e) certain natural or legal persons,

entities or bodies conducting transactions with the separatist groups in the Donbass region of Ukraine

- valid until 15.9.2018

- freezing of funds and economic resources of certain persons responsible for the misappropriation of Ukrainian State funds, of certain persons responsible for human rights violations in Ukraine and of natural or legal persons, entities or bodies associated with such persons

- valid until 6.3.2019

- prohibition to satisfy certain claims made by certain persons, entities or bodies

Guinea Bissau Conakry (2018)

Description of the sanctions

1. Travel restrictions

EU Member States shall take necessary measures to prevent entry to or transit through the EU for persons identified by the International Commission of Inquiry as responsible for the events in Guinea on 28 September 2009 and persons associated with them.

2. Freezing of assets

All funds and economic resources that belong to or are owned, etc. by persons identified by the International Commission of Inquiry as responsible for the events in Guinea on 28 September 2009, and all natural and legal persons, entities or bodies associated with them, shall be frozen.

Notes adopted and compiled from internet sources. Rationale and some comments provided by the author

Also refer to Government Offices of Sweden at: http://www.government.se/government-policy/foreign-and-security-policy/international-sanctions/Accessed 09 Mar 18

References

Haney, P.J & Vanderbrush, W (2005) *The Domestic Policy of an American Foreign Policy,* University of Pittsburgh Press, Pittsburgh, USA

Kaplowitz, D.R (1988), *Anatomy of a failed embargo: US sanctions against Cuba,* Lynne Rienner Publishers [Google Scholar]

Luke, T.L & McCobb (Jnr) (1971). 'United States Trade Embargo on China, 1949-1970: Legal Status and Future Prospects', N.Y.U. *Journal of International Law and Politics* 1 (4), Hein Online

Ratliff, W & Fontain (2000), *A Strategic Flip Flop in the Caribbean: Lift the Embargo on Cuba, Hoover Institute on War, Resolution and Peace,* Stanford University, USA

Redick, C.F (1973), 'The Jurisprudence of the Foreign Claims Settlement Commission: Chinese Claims', *American Society of International Law* 67 (4) 728-740,
http://doi.org/10.2307/2198570.

Chapter 3

Sociological Foundations of Sanctions:
their Success and Destruction

"I'm against everything
Against war and those against
War. Against whatever diminishes
the individual's blind impulse..."

Dambudzo Marechera

Sanction, as a noun is a form of threatened penalty for disobeying laws and standing protocols aimed at deterring abuse. As a verb it conveys approval of action, implying both to 'allow, encourage' [5]and to 'push to deter'. The word 'sanction' is derived from a Latin word *sanctio*, meaning 'a law or a decree that is sacred or inviolable under penalty of a curse'. The noun is related to the verb *sancere* which means 'to render sacred inviolable decree'. The Latin verb can be used in its extended meaning 'to forbid' – since something that is forbidden lies in the power of an inviolable decree. It is the historical reconstruction and evolution of this word that has brought a paradigm shift in terms of its contextual application.

However, there has been difficulties in quantifying the 'success' of sanctions especially in situations when a target country does not comply or accede to demands from sender countries. In the case of Zimbabwean sanctions, land reform programme on which sanctions were imposed upon as an indiscriminate punitive measure onto the entire population, land re-distribution was not reversed at the end of the Mugabe era in November 2017. If at all the incoming Mnangagwa

---

[5]Houghton Mifflin Harcourt, (2006) More Word Histories and Mysteries from Aardvark to Zombi. Visited at:
https://www.google.co.uk/search?q=more+word+histories+and+mysteries+fro
m+aardvark+to+zombie&rlz=1C1HLDY_enGB693GB698&oq=more+word+
histories&aqs=chrome.1.69i57j0.10950j0j8&sourceid=chrome&ie=UTF-8/
Accessed Mar 09, 18

government upheld and hailed the Mugabe era land reform as a successful story. By insisting on redistribution of land to Zimbabweans – to both peasants and petit bourgeoisie alike - was a plausible and revolutionary decision on the part of the ruling ZANU PF party. However, the incoming Mnangagwa government was inadvertently sending strident signals to the West. Wary of the fact that the new dispensation was going to uphold ideological values on which the Zimbabwean struggle's 3rd Chimurenga was waged, the West, especially 'Colonial Master' Britain adopted a wait and see attitude. Their inevitable diplomatic face saver was by putting demands and conditions for the lifting of Zimbabwe Democracy and Economic Recovery Act of 2001.

Despite 'smart sanctions' targeted to the ruling elite, there is evidence that majority of Zimbabweans supported land redistribution under Chimurenga 3. Symmetrical and seminal debates confirm that ordinary Zimbabweans explicitly supported their political leaders - even if majority of that populace suffered the most from draconian Western-imposed sanctions. It has been stated that Zimbabweans sanctions are multilateral in that they are being handled by several countries – USA, UK including the European Union. In other words, they are being driven by world economic blocks, because almost all western nations are participating including Australia and New Zealand. Targeted sanctions are aimed at individuals in receiving countries, but this affects the whole country in including individuals and groups like industrialists, Chamber of Commerce executives and those groups that are not particularly responsible. The foregoing creates victims within the innocent populace who serve to reinforce contradictions within the capitalist social structures. This situation is more prominent because those same targeted individuals in Zimbabwe are the ones heading strategic business consortiums, quisi-government organisations and parastatal organisations.

On the same wavelength, opposition politics never challenged or doubted the legitimacy of land reforms as they called for a forensic audit and transparency in the land distribution. In principle, there is consensus across the Zimbabwean population that equitable land distribution is a legitimate justification for dismantling injustices of coloniality and imperialism. What may appear to be a point of debate particularly in opposition politics is the way land was distributed after colonial master Britain reneged on Lancaster House constitutional provisions of 1979.

Marxist Sociological paradigm in Economic Sanctions

The subject of economic sanctions cannot be discussed comprehensively without nuancing the Marxist sociological paradigm. We attach new meanings in linking how capitalist relations has created new social relations for those countries fighting against exploitation of their resources through imposition of sanctions. Kuhn (1970) uses the term paradigm for purposes of evolving a new concept to explain the structure of scientific revolutions. The Marxist counters capitalist ideology in interpreting relations of production in receiving countries. For example, in case of Zimbabwe, such relations specifically changed as the country registered adverse GDP growth while industries started to close down during the peak of economic meltdown in 2008. Grinding the economy to a halt through economic sanctions sabotage was a strategy used by Western governments to prepare for the fall of ZANU PF revolutionary fall and the inevitable fall of Robert Mugabe in November 2017. I highlight effects of biting economic sanctions onto the civil and innocent population in Chapter 5 – *Counting the toll of Zimbabwe's Economic Sanctions: A Case Study of Zano Remba Housing Cooperative in Chitungwiza Township*. We are able to assess the lasting impact of sanctions on social and political relations in that housing cooperative estate.

Studies by Dobrianov (1986) illuminates on the alternative paradigm to Sociology by dwelling and situating Marxist Sociological paradigm on dialectical-materialist outlook. Thus, in the imposition of economic sanctions on Zimbabwe, we formulate principles of understanding concrete historical events that are imbedded in colonialism and neo-colonial relationships of Zimbabwe with Western countries. Colonialism means Zimbabwe 'belongs' to the West and any form of threats to change that status was met with fierce and punitive resistance through ZDERA of 2001. In that regard, I observe an abstract theoretical model for the sociological interpretation of how Zimbabwe managed sanctions through four social spheres:

a) The Economic Model through which Zimbabwe tried and succeeded in by-passing the impact of sanctions. Among other strategies and to raise much needed cash, the Zimbabwean government initiated the creation of parastatal organisations like Zimbabwe National Roads Administration (ZINARA) (August 2001); for road networks management including vehicle registrations, taxation, insurance and collections from tollgates. The government also implemented commercialisation of certain services like water and reticulation services through local authorities. It also created Zimbabwe National Water Authority (ZINWA) in 2001, a parastatal organisation which was whose mandate is to manage sustainable commercialisation and distribution of water provisions in Zimbabwe – thereby raising capital to fend off sanctions. The government of Zimbabwe also tightened revenue collection procedures by Zimbabwe Revenue Authority (ZIMRA) especially from private sector organisations and mining conglomerates through corporate tax following the enactment of Zimbabwe Democracy and Economic Recovery Act in 2001;

b. Social Model which was based on educating the public on the devastating impact of economic sanctions and how sanctions had brought hardships to the general populace of Zimbabwe. This raised citizens' levels of consciousness to a higher level in which Zimbabweans from all walks of life questioned the purpose of economic sanctions against implementation of land reform programme. As a result, while people suffered from a collapsing financial sector, the ruling party ZANU PF convinced the people of where economic hardships were coming from as rhetoric and demonization between the government of Zimbabwe and the West escalated to unprecedented levels. In Chapter 4, *Love and Infection: British coloniality and Imperialism – A Repository of Zimbabwe's illegal post-2000 Land Reform Sanctions* we explore social and high stakes of politics between Zimbabwe and the West;

c). Political Model in which President Mugabe used the creation of the opposition MDC as a product of the Western powers. At every opportunity, President Mugabe reminded the West that opposition MDC in Zimbabwe was a Western project designed to eliminate and replace ZANU PF as a liberation struggle party. This strategy gathered momentum, but the ruling party enacted repressive laws like Public Order and Security Act (POSA) of 2002 as weapons to manage and contain opposition politics. Mugabe also used his support in SADC and AU to garner regional support against Western imposed sanctions;

d. Spiritual Model in which Zimbabwe registered the highest number of Pentecostal churches in Africa between 2001 and 2018 in which Zimbabweans hit by poverty and economic frustrations sought divine intervention. We bear in mind religion as an "opium of the people", but many had hoped that spiritual inspiration would help them to escape from dire realities of poverty and deprivation entrenchment. This worked to the advantage of ZANU PF in some ways in that the party continued to lead a docile population that had no zeal and capacity to stage an uprising on their own as predicted by the West when they hit Zimbabwe with economic sanctions in 2001. In addition, Zanu PF enjoyed the grassroots support of leading Pentecostal church denominations like Zimbabwe Council of Churches (ZCC Mbungo), Ezekiel Guti's Zimbabwe Assemblies of God Africa, Apostolic Church of Johanne Masowe; and was massively propped up by huge financial donations from some of the religious institutions. Thus, from post-colonial Zimbabwe viewpoint all contemporary attempts to reveal the inner structure of their system of society including their culture are based on coloniality and historical materialism derived from Marxist sociology. This is so because it is reflected on their productive forces, relations of production, political superstructure and social consciousness.

Sanctions as a Capitalist Weapon and Social Relations in Zimbabwe

In Marxist sociological tradition, societies function on the basis of social relations and social activities in various polemical ends. That society becomes an expression of connections and relations between individuals in the context of production relations or systems of social relations. Under public law 107-99 of December 2001, S 494, the Zimbabwe Democracy Economic Recovery Act of 2001 establishes in its preamble, that the act "provide for a transition to democracy and to promote economic recovery in Zimbabwe". Before we establish the context and nature of sanctions relations, it is important to highlight that the statement of this legislative policy is established through *relationships and engagements*. The statement of policy is translated and implemented through *capitalist relations* and activities between multilayers of a capitalist system. Zimbabwe is in financial relations with international financial institutions that caters for multilateral development via the International Monetary Fund, (IMF). Zimbabwe is also in financial relations with Multilateral Development Banks namely International Bank for Reconstruction and Development, the International Development Association, International finance Corporation, the Inter African Development Fund, the African development Bank, the African development fund, the European Bank for Reconstruction & Development and the Multilateral Investment Guaranty Agency. Imposing economic sanctions on Zimbabwe meant that *connections and relations* between Zimbabwe and foregoing agencies social and economic ended abruptly – leaving a lot of financial projects inconclusive and hanging in the balance. The capacity for Western governments to break connections and relations without further consultations or conclusions, is in itself a symbol of capitalist diktat; based on unequal and exploitative relationships. Zimbabwe is being told in this unequal relationship that it will be connected back to financial and economic relations on the basis of meeting conditions dictated by western governments on financial relationships. This is how Western governments' foreign policy [on Zimbabwe] attempted to force Zimbabwe and influence reversal of the *Third Chimurenga* land reform programme.

How does the Government of Zimbabwe of Zimbabwe "renders itself ineligible to participate"[6] in IMF programmes as dictated by Britain and the United States of America? We look at economic and political relations of Zimbabwe's *Third Chimurenga* of land revolution

---

[6]http://www.congress.gov/107/plaws/publ99/PLAW-107publ99.pdf/Accessed/30July18

in terms of influence and impact on the continent: through the "costly" deployment of troops to the Democratic Republic of Congo. We are aware that when [especially Western former colony] country is ungovernable through Western sponsored civil wars and banditry, it becomes easy for them to exploit and loot its resources. DRC is a vast and rich country which Western governments are jostling to exploit in the post-Brexit and post millennium economic meltdowns. Being seen seeking to prop up the DRC on the basis of African benevolence is one reason why Zimbabwe had to suffer through imposition of sanctions and punitive measures. Seeking to disrupt and eliminate chaos in the DRC through maintenance of functional governance there and reaping potential economic windfalls carried a heavy penalty for Zimbabwe. Imposition of sanctions was a deterrent measure that South Africa and other African countries immediately complied with. The concept of establishing *social interaction* among African countries involves the establishment of certain relations that excludes or creates a buffer zone to Western imperialism.

References

Dobrianov (1986), 'The Marxist Sociological Paradigm', in *Developments in Marxist Sociological Theory: Modern Social Problems and Theory,* AG Zdravomyslov, Sage Publications Inc., London, United Kingdom.

Galtung, J. (1967), 'On the Effects of International Economic Sanctions: With Examples from the Case of Rhodesia', *World Politics,* Volume 19, (3), 378-416.

Hufbauer, G.C., Schott, J.J. & Elliott, K.A. (1985) Economic Sanctions Reconsidered: History and Current Policy, Institute for International Economics, Paterson Institute, USA, Found at: http://books.google.co.uk/Economic_Sanctions_Reconsidered .html?id+etyVmnPOrG8C&redir_esc=y

Kuhn, T. (1970), *The Structure of Scientific Revolutions,* Chicago University Press, USA

Mararike, M. (2018) 'Theoretical Locations of Mugabeism, Land "Terrorism," and Third Chimurenga Neo-Coloniality Discourse in Zimbabwe: A Rejoinder of a Revolutionary' Volume: 49 issue: 3, page(s): 191-211, Article first published online: March 20, 2018; Issue published: April 1, 2018, https://doi.org/10.1177/0021934717750328

McGillivray & Stam, A.C (2004) 'Political institutions, coercive diplomacy, and duration of economic sanctions', *Journal of Conflict Resolution, Sage Journals* **48 (2)** 154-172

Portela, C. (2010) European Union Sanctions and Foreign Policy: When do the work? Routledge-Taylor & Francis Group, Oxon, United Kingdom

Chapter 4

Rodinising Economic Sanctions: How Sanctions have Destroyed Zimbabwe

"The Devil is right at home. The Devil, the Devil himself, is right in the house. And the Devil came here yesterday. Yesterday the Devil came here. Right here. And it smells of Sulphur still today. Yesterday, ladies and gentlemen, from this rostrum, the president of the United States, [George W Bush] the gentleman to whom I refer as the Devil, came here, talking as if he owned the world. Truly. As the owner of the world."

Hugo Chavez,
Address to the United Nations General Assembly,
delivered 20 September 2006

Introduction

This Chapter evaluates the impact and economic decline of the Zimbabwean economy following unilateral imposition of economic sanctions through the US and UK-crafted Zimbabwe Democracy and Recovery Act of 2001. Implementation of economic sanctions is widely perceived to be part of retaliatory measures for land redistribution to Zimbabweans by President Mugabe from 2000. I take a closer examination of the country's micro-economic policies and their subsequent effects on the GDP and output in different sectors of the country's as the country struggled under the burden of economic sanctions.

Sanctions have a devastating impact on the general populace and I argue that they create unsustainable levels of underdevelopment, poverty and deprivation. I analyse how the country has systematically been deprived of financial aid – with all of its credit lines with international financial institutions blocked in order to effect socio-economic changes including regime change in Zimbabwe. I make detailed insights on how economic sanctions have militated against

Zimbabwe's capacity to repay its debts – resulting in sinking the country into underdevelopment and poverty. I also analyse historical and constitutionality of the Lancaster House Constitution as a framework that was meticulously designed to foster the status quo of white hegemonic interests - thereby perpetuating and preserving Western imperialism. In my thematic analysis, I deploy Walter Rodney's underdevelopment theory, highlighting that sanctions in Zimbabwe have caused widespread suffering, critical levels of poverty gaps, income inequality, underdevelopment through endemic corruption and high levels of mortality due to lack of medical facilities.

Key findings are that economic sanctions in Zimbabwe lead to increase of poverty gaps and deprived communities in townships and rural areas feel the most impact. In that regard, while sanctions have harmed vulnerable groups including women in rural areas, political leaders have negotiated their way out of targeted sanctions, restrictive measures and adverse conditions. I establish the impact of sanctions in financial services – highlighting why Zimbabwe failing to access capital or service its own financial debts and obligations.

Sanction, as a noun is a form of threatened penalty for disobeying laws and standing protocols aimed at deterring abuse. As a verb it conveys approval of action, implying both to 'allow, encourage' [7]and to 'push to deter'. The word 'sanction' is derived from a Latin word *sanctio*, meaning 'a law or a decree that is sacred or inviolable under penalty of a curse'. The noun is related to the verb *sancere* which means 'to render sacred inviolable decree'. The Latin verb can be used in its extended meaning 'to forbid' – since something that is forbidden lies in the power of an inviolable decree. It is the historical reconstruction and evolution of this word that has brought a paradigm shift in terms of its contextual application especially in socio-politico and post-colonial discourses.

---

[7]Houghton Mifflin Harcourt, (2006) More Word Histories and Mysteries from Aardvark to Zombi. Visited at:
https://www.google.co.uk/search?q=more+word+histories+and+mysteries+fro m+aardvark+to+zombie&rlz=1C1HLDY_enGB693GB698&oq=more+word+ histories&aqs=chrome.1.69i57j0.10950j0j8&sourceid=chrome&ie=UTF-8/
Accessed Mar 09, 18

'Sanctions' and 'Restrictive Measures' have a universal definition applicable to the context of social or political change. Both have the same objectives in that they have been used by the international community, notably the United States of America as tools designed to effect changes in behaviour or policies of targeted states. Smith-Hohn (2010) notes that restrictive measures are directed at specific persons or entities that threaten international security. Restrictive measures "do not force or engender collective punishment and they are not directed at the state" but target "a select group of the political elite without jeopardising the national economy" or 'exerting a negative impact on the humanitarian condition of the greater population". The question of whether such measures can be deemed "smart" remains in contention.

Proponents of economic sanctions like Drury (2005) argue strenuously that they are effective and unlike military action less debilitating – and therefore safer and cheaper in terms of human cost. Countries like Zimbabwe that have experienced over three decades of economic sanctions (First, after proclamation of Unilateral Declaration by the racist Ian Smith Regime 1965-1980) and second, after the historic land reform programme from 2001 to date) arguably with the same ideological warfare designed to inflict lasting impact in form of regime change. Political scientists like Portela (2010), Sandler & Hartley (2007) Mararike (2018) argues that the success of sanctions is based on motives aimed at employing foreign policies as blunt instruments used by dominant sender countries. 'Blunt' as a comparative form of speech is a direct reference to their uncompromising, unceremonious and brusque processes of; and nature of negotiation which is synonymous with pain and agony.

Research Questions

i. In what way has Zimbabwe been affected by economic sanctions / restrictions imposed by the International Financial Institutions (IFIs) and a marked decrease in Official Development Aid (ODA) entering the country? What is the impact?

ii. What are coordinated efforts by various western governments have been implemented to deprive and starve the country of financial aid and what has been the impact? Has such aid been used as weapons designed to effect both micro political change in the country; and macro regime change in Zimbabwe?

iii.   Did the morbid Lancaster House Constitution (LHC) of 1979 play a role in maintaining the status quo that protected settler 'white' farmers at the expense of 'natives' in post-colonial Zimbabwe? What contradictions can be derived from the fast-track Land reform Programme of 2000?

One of the principle objective of this paper is to measure both the impact and success on a target country level of analysis – outlining how such consequential damages of sanctions can be considered an index of success on the part of those deploying them.

Rodinisation as a Construct of Underdevelopment.

What is *Rodinism* as a doctrine and why is it important and applicable to Zimbabwe? Walter Rodney (1972) is a pan Africanist writer whose classic book *How Europe Underdeveloped Africa* focuses on European development models that are implemented at the expense of poor African nations. *Rodinism* is a doctrine that is also based on colonial struggles that commenced in especially in the wave of pan-Africanism in the 1960s. In simple terms, colonialism brought unequal relations of power and exploitation in that it was designed to create the ruling class and the underclass. *Rodinisation,* also describes a process of exploiting African and the so-called Third World countries (TWC) of their land and mineral ore resources. Subjugation of 'natives' by Caucasians is based on perceptions of unequal co-existence with Africans as their 'subjects' under the guise of white supremacy. A-typical characteristics of *Rodinising* a homogeneous people also entail deprivation and destruction of their cultural artefacts, disregard of their norms and values on whose existence is based. It also involves the indigenous population re-norming their cultural styles and beliefs – with religion having played a devastating but effective role in achieving objectives of upholding white values and supremacy over the colonised. The question of language also forms part of the said cultural norms and belief systems. What this means in colonial Zimbabwe and many parts of Africa is that those that have the power to conquer and vanquish 'natives' managed to drive them off their land and become colonial rulers. By examining the use of power and violence in the post-colonial discourse, Rodney deploys political relations of exploitation of men by men in his capitalist narrative of underdevelopment.

Power does not only mean direct control, but direct rule through institutionalisation of colonial structures of governance – the executive, judiciary and legislature. Those three State apparatus formed the government machinery of colonial Rhodesia that ruled and directly controlled all operations of imperialism through the Royal Charter. The net gains of colonialism, according to Walter Rodney, meant that 'natives' were consigned to structured labour and landless subjects existing in configurations of settler white rule.

In terms of international capitalist trading systems, Africa has contributed immensely in creating wealthier European nations. The reason for this is that imperialist settlers benefitted from resources exploited from that continent. According to Rodney, Europe also stands accused of creating humanly-made problems including unfair trading barriers and steep bilateral agreements that were enforceable through suppression and repression. Rodney's book is an economic analysis of how Europe engaged in unequal relationship across the African continent. *Rodinism* is therefore a philosophy based on fighting under development, deprivation and poverty. Thus, *Rodinisation* rests within African societies regaining their sovereignty through consciousness. It is about empowerment, liberation and freedom. The aspect of liberating the mind is pursued vigorously by Ngugi wa Thiong'o (1992) in *Decolonising the Mind* as part of self-consciousness. *Rodinisation* is part of resistance and movement which forms the Chimurenga liberation struggle political ideology in Zimbabwe.

Literature Review

According to McGillivray & Stam (2004) economic sanctions are '...an example of coercive [and cohesive] diplomacy designed to induce a target country to change some policy it would not otherwise...' (p. 156). This means that economic sanctions achieve their objectives through deliberate and systematic acts of destructive engagement as they employ what can be termed by victim countries as 'sabotage' in the interest of sender countries. It is necessary in this paper to ascertain whether or not sanctions are negative (punishment for deviance and dysfunctionality) or positive (as a measure of instituting reward for compliance)? Clyde, Hufbauer & Schott (1985) define 'sender countries' as [the] principal authors [or architectures] of sanctions episode while 'target country' denotes immediate object of the episode (p 10). Economic damage of a target country is achieved through the systematic reduction of customary trade, sudden withdrawal of financial relations and systems thereby causing maximum damage to the target country and its citizens.

The question of success or failure of sanctions as an instrument of foreign policy enforcement depends on perceptions: First, does the impact of damages caused by sanctions and the resultant suffering of vulnerable population constitute achievement? If that is the case, in whose interests is it achieved? In a comprehensive analysis on 1965 Rhodesian sanctions, Galtung (1967) observes sanctions objectives by stating that:

> "… it is not obvious that the same action or sanction can serve both purposes; in fact, modern penology does not seem to warrant much belief in punishment as a general method for making people comply. Punishment may have other effects, as when criminals are kept of the streets and isolated in prisons where their deviant actions are hidden from the general view and thus are less consequential to the outside world, but this is not the same as making them comply…" (p. 380)

This Chapter clarifies on the criterion of measuring successes and failures of sanctions. When are sanctions considered to be successful? Is that success measured in terms of their extent or degree of causing suffering of citizens affected by conflict borne out of international disconnect?

In an article entitled US sanctions designed to impede development of successful nations Russia clarifies what US sanctions are designed for.

"The main purpose of United States sanctions is to slow the progress of rapidly developing nations ...The USA is conducting its sanctions policy against the countries that are actively developing. This includes not only Russia, but also China, Iran and other countries..."[8]

For us to understand the origins of sanctions in Zimbabwe, we must trace the imperialist agenda. Zimbabwe decolonisation is part of the wider and gigantic imperialist configurations that swept through Europe in the 18th and 19th centuries. The German Chancellor Otto von Bismarck presided over *The Kongokonferenz* of 1884 to 1885, better known as the Berlin Colonial Conference. The words 'scramble' or 'partition' are very significant. From the Cambridge Dictionary – to scramble is to move or climb quickly but with difficulty, often using hands for help in order to compete for scarce resources. Deductive meanings imply desperation and competition for scarce resources. 'Partition' in the historical and colonial discourse is [often] used to deploy imperial maladies in sharing spoils... which boarders on mean and derogatory pathologies of robbing a group of nations of their independence. This creates enduring social formations of inequality.

Based on foregoing, scholars seek to underpin colonialism as a process or a condition, the coloniality of being as an identity tag and decolonisation processes as a question of subjectivity. At one other level, coloniality is characterised by patterns of power based on inequality.

Wider Implications: Historical epochs of the Southern African Struggles

As noted by Mararike & Mtapuri (2018):

---

[8] US sanctions designed to impede development of successful nations, says Russian Duma chief
Published time: 15 May, 2018 09:22 Edited time: 21 May, 2018 15:11, found at https://www.rt.com/russia/426745-us-introduces-sanctions-impede/accessed Feb 26 19/

"The Berlin Colonial Conference of 1884-1885 marked long dark days for the Scramble for Africa, in what was known as the new world order. It was about colonial domination, subjugation, exploitation of mineral and exploitative extraction of natural resources. Western Europe became principal beneficiaries of the newly 'discovered' wealth – pillaging and looting to their countries through exploitation, false pretences, deception and outright theft. The insidious process was complemented by subjective constructs of political, social, religious and cultural domination of indigenous populations or 'natives' as imperialism defined them in an unbalanced and parasitic framework of socio-economic relationships…" (p 1)

At the time that Rodney wrote his classic indictment, Zimbabwe was at the height of fighting Chimurenga two of liberation which ended with the Lancaster House Agreement and Constitution of 1979. Mozambique's FRELIMO party had fought a war of liberation from the colonial tentacles of the Portuguese. Angola gained its independence through the barrels of Mikhail Kalashnikov's AK47 in a treacherous war of Independence stretching from 1961–1974. Portuguese colonial rule was intractable and ruthless but was brought to its end by the People's Movement for the Liberation of Angola (MPLA). As noted by Brinkman, I. (2005) Angola is one of the richest countries in the world. It is no coincidence that a CIA-sponsored civil war ravaged this rich country from 1975 to 2002 – in another western crafted strategy designed to fight the Marxist-Leninist state of the Socialist republic of Angola headed by President Dos Santos. Angola's terrorist and regional dissident, Jonas Savimbi of National Union for the Total Independence of Angola (UNITA), was killed on 22 February 2002, in one of the fiercest battles with Angolan government troops along riverbanks in the province of Moxico.

At the time when Rodney was compiling statistics for How Europe Underdeveloped Africa, the Kliptown's South African Freedom Charter was 10 years old, having been promulgated on 25 June 1955. The Freedom Charter was to reposition the fight against pernicious apartheid and struggles against evil dispossession and racial discrimination of (African) South Africans in their own country. 'The Land Shall be shared among those who work on it' was indeed enshrined in Part 4 of the said Charter – which came to be another rally point against the inimical system of apartheid and its depredations.

In 1986, Britain in a state of denial about imposition of sanctions on South Africa, when the whole world stood up to eradicate roots of apartheid. England supported apartheid for their own economic benefits at the time! Be that as it may, - come March 16, 2018 - the storyline has since changed: In the words of the British Prime Minister, Theresa May - *'South Africa will face embargoes and sanctions from the UK, EU and USA if land is expropriated without compensation'*. It is possible that history repeating a full circle of itself[9]

Lest we forget, Namibia's double tragedy sends tremors in the minds of coloniality victims and prisoners of conscience: That country went through brutal, savagery, inhuman, barbarous, homicidal and unlawful sexual intercourse by being, as a virgin, colonised by Germany first through statutory rape – to become a colony known as *Deutsch-Südwestafrika* from 1884 to 1915. After the Second World War in 1945 and through the League of Nations, South West Africa went through a historical double mastectomy by being re-colonised by South Africa in 1945. South Africa was yet, itself, a colony created as a dominion of the British Empire in terms of the South Africa Act 1909. Miraculously, as like many African states, the country survived!

As documented by du Pisani (2007) Andimba Taivo-ya Toivo and Sam Nujoma became decorated and gallant guerrillas of the struggle against the evil spirits of Namibia's 'double occupation': My perception is that SWAPO war of liberation and total independence that followed saved both the colonial victim and the patient! At the time of writing this report, Namibia has a clear bill of health – fully recovered and now totally cleared of lethal imperialist gonorrhoea and syphilis by SWAPO! However, Namibia still bears horrific scars from its colonial surgical operations in that it still must resolve its land question.

---

[9] South Africa will face embargoes and sanctions from the UK, EU and USA if land is expropriated without compensation' at https://statesman.co.zw/south-africa-will-face-embargoes-sanctions-ukeu-usa/Accessed March 18

This is the background against which the whole of Southern Africa was *Rodinised*. *Rodinisation* is an anti-imperialist struggle on colonial occupation and subjugation, stagnant development and creation of unequal partners in development. It is about Caucasians obliterating an African race through genocide and war and its proxies. It is a fight and a struggle. It is about translating perceived inferiority of the African race and juxtaposition of another race by upgrading its superiority. *Rodinism* is about understanding of a colonial race defending its ethnocentrism and dogmas; it also is about capital gains and capital losses. It relates to the powerful exploiting those weakened by deprivation and poverty. It is about African people making historical landmarks through consciousness – a re-awakening of a people in order to claim their rightful place in history.

Statement of the Problem

According to Raftopoulous (2009) the ZANU-PF controlled parliament passed Constitutional Amendment 16 which maintained that compensation of white farmers was constitutionally a British government colonial obligation. In light of legislative pronouncements, imposition of economic sanctions has brought contradictions and controversies - not only in terms of legitimacy, but their actual benefits. There are some paradoxical interpretations in terms of the liability of compensation. The Conservative-led government of Margaret Thatcher acknowledged British liability while New Labour's Tony Blair rebutted liability when he came to power in May 1997. Such inconsistencies in British foreign policy in Zimbabwe led to protracted arguments about British imperialism generally in former colonies – with Zimbabwe viewed, to a large extent as a victim.

In light of the foregoing, there was no consensus on how the international community should handle Zimbabwe notably in terms of approaches to land reform programme. Another point of contention and contradiction is the disproportionate nature of land distribution in Zimbabwe which was skewed in favour of settler colonialists. Sims (2010) state that there were 4500 'white' commercial farmers occupying 11 million hectares. In statistical terms 90% of the total land in Zimbabwe was occupied by 10% of Caucasian origin, while 90% of 'natives' occupied 10% of the land – very often in arid Tribal Trust Lands (TTLs) designated to them by the colonial Rhodesia regime. Paradoxical interpretations on land reform narratives appear to confirm that 'white' settlers were keen to maintain the *status quo* under the skewed Lancaster House Constitution. This is against the background where thematic statement of the problem is embedded deeply in Lancaster House Agreement that was perceived to be legislative instrument and often viewed as reinforcement of British imperialism by nationalist leaders in ZANU PF.

As a result of land re-distribution, it was inevitable that there would be disruption in productivity. For example, Raftopolous (op cit) cites that between 2001 and 2005, agricultural output fell by 70% as the Caucasian farming population was decimated from 4500 farmers to just 500. Interestingly, even though perceptions differ on the productive capacity of new farmers, there is no consensus on numbers of farmers who migrated to neighbouring countries and to European destinations. However, what is evident is that economic sanctions imposed in 2001, pushed Zimbabwe into a pariah state – with investors pulling out and leaving projects uncompleted. It is quite clear that the situation in which investors from countries imposing sanctions proceeded to dis-invest and de-industrialise leading to economic collapse. Workers lost their jobs as they drifted into poverty.

Methodology

This qualitative research is grounded in theoretical framework of utilitarianism critical theory in that it formulates research questions designed to gather eclectic information and data from secondary sources of data. Sources of data include journal studies, position papers, research remits and statistics collected from the print media, newspapers and broadcast media. My methodology intensely employs the World Wide Web (www) in order to capture salient thematic frameworks on economic sanctions. Information from the National Archives of Zimbabwe (NAZ) contains and represents credible accounts of historical developments in relation to economic sanctions and vast amounts of information on British colonialism in Zimbabwe. I gather priceless information from USA secondary sources of data including government's websites, Office of Foreign Assets Control (OFAC) sites and legislative instruments notably from Department of the Treasury. The paper also relies extensively on information gleaned from historical monograms and diaries. These sources confirm the existence of neo-colonialism and imperialism in Rhodesia as part of a highly sophisticated and planned policy of Britain – that was designed to maintain her influence even after 'granting' Zimbabwe independence. Research tools include consultation and interface of data using thematic analysis in themes intertwined with discourse analysis of nationalist accounts.

Discussion: Sanctions as a capitalist weapon in Zimbabwe's Social Relations.

In Marxist sociological tradition, societies function on the basis of social relations and social activities in various polemical ends. That society becomes an expression of connections and relations between individuals in the context of production relations or systems of social relations. Under public law 107-99 of December 2001, S 494, the Zimbabwe Democracy Economic Recovery Act of 2001 establishes in its preamble, that the act "provide for a transition to democracy and to promote economic recovery in Zimbabwe". Before we establish the context and nature of sanctions relations later on in this paper, it is important to highlight that the statement of this legislative policy is established through *relationships and engagements*. The statement of policy is translated and implemented through *capitalist relations* and activities between multilayers of international capitalist systems. Zimbabwe is in financial relations with international financial institutions, catering for multilateral development via the International Monetary Fund, (IMF). Zimbabwe is also in financial relations with Multilateral Development Banks namely International Bank for Reconstruction and Development, the International Development Association, International finance Corporation, the Inter African Development Fund, the African development Bank, the African development fund, the European Bank for Reconstruction & Development and the Multilateral Investment Guaranty Agency. Imposing economic sanctions on Zimbabwe means that *connections and relations* between Zimbabwe and foregoing agencies social and economic ended abruptly – leaving a lot of financial projects inconclusive and hanging in the balance. The capacity for Western governments to break connections and relations without further consultations or conclusions, is in itself a symbol of capitalist diktat; solely based on unequal and exploitative relationships. The bottom line is that, as observed by Lam (1990), the cost of sanctions to the 'sanctioner' is 'negatively related to sanctions success'. This means that for sending countries, effectiveness of economic sanctions is measured by their disruption and destruction. The more negative and damaging sanctions are to receiving countries, the functional and positive they are considered to be by sending countries. Powerful countries may not care as long as foreign policy objectives are achieved.

The imposition of sanctions followed Zimbabwe's Land Reform Programme (LRP) which came into full force in 2001 under President Robert Mugabe. According to Raftopoulous (2009) the ZANU-PF controlled parliament passed Constitutional Amendment 16 which placed compensation of Caucasian farmers on former colonial Britain. This was also in line with provisions of the Lancaster House Constitution (LHC) from which Zimbabwean Constitution was derived from in 1979.

The constitutional development had far-reaching implications in that the ZANU-PF controlled government mobilised citizens and successfully framed the economic sanctions narrative within the context of neo-colonialism and imperialism. This paper looks at the impact of economic sanctions on the Zimbabwean populace in terms of entrenched poverty and underdevelopment across all sectors of the economy. As such it is imperative to make deep analyses of what is termed *"Rodinisation of Economic Sanctions"* in this paper. I debate potential and real consequences of sanctions and restrictive measures imposed by Zimbabwe Democracy and Economic Recovery Act of 2001.

Rodney's Statistics on Gross Domestic Product

GDP per capita is obtained by dividing the country's gross domestic product, adjusted by inflation – by the total population. In comparison with Rodney's statistics (The information is obtained from United Nations statistical publications, that applies to the year 1968) – this research provides fair representations of development indices and underdevelopment profiles as indicated by Gross Domestic Product of selected countries. It is important to note that, for purposes of illustrating differentials between Highly Developed Countries (HDCs) and (Less Developed Countries (LDCs) the study looks at comparative per capita data for 2016 of same countries that Walter Rodney looked at 50 years ago. The results are alarmingly perturbing in their similarities in terms of Countries Per Capita income in US Dollars in the year 2016.

In using data sets from World Bank sources, I take into consideration of the fact that Walter Rodney predicted that the gap of GDP by regional blocks (of developed and underdeveloped) countries will increase as developed countries grow richer. Rodney sums up that situations of widening gaps of poverty between HDCs and LDCs is a phenomenon based on the powerful countries exploiting poor and weaker countries especially in former colonies from Africa. Furthermore, at the time that Rodney was compiling per capita statistics, there was a belief that Africa will show stagnation or slow rates of growth particularly in colonies and ex-colonies due to Western induced wars. This was a European strategy for accessing cheaper resources from war-ravaged economies. Rodney predicted that international trade for underdeveloped countries, because of their over reliance on the export market from emerging markets like China and other former socialist countries – was possible to counter capitalism. Rodney did not explain how.

Comparative Data from 1968 versus 2016:

Countries Per Capita income in US Dollars (1968)
(From How Europe Underdeveloped Africa)

CANADA	*2.247*
USA	3.578
FRANCE (1967)	1.738
UNITED KINGDOM	1.560
AFRICA AS A WHOLE	1.400
CONGO	52
GHANA	198
KENYA	107
MALAWI	52
MOROCCO	185
SOUTH AFRICA	543
TANZANIA	62
UAR	156
ZAMBIA	225

Canada	*50 231.90*
USA	52 194.90
UK	75725.25
FRANCE	42013.29
AFRICA AS A WHOLE	1855.00 (2011)[10]
CONGO	404.50
GHANA	1513.50
KENYA	1455.40
MALAWI	300.30
MOROCCO	2892.80
SOUTH AFRICA	5274.50
TANZANIA	877.50
UAR	NIL
ZAMBIA	1269.60
ZIMBABWE	1029.10

Countries Per Capita income in US Dollars (2016)[11]

---

[10] Africa: gross domestic product (GDP) from 1995 to 2016 (in billion U.S. dollars) at https://www.statista.com/statistics/240665/gdp-of-africa/Accessed Mar 18

[11] Trading Economics at https://tradingeconomics.com/united-kingdom/gdp-per-capita/Accessed Mar 18

African Economic Data: The problems areas:

1. Resources Available to Measure National Income

The National Income Grid can be used to measure the extent of poverty and underdevelopment of a country. The main factor impacting on the quality of national income statistics across Africa is the capacity of national statistical offices and the resources available for them to follow best international practice to ensure comparability with other parts of the world. This is a global problem, but it is particularly serious across Africa because of the relatively higher proportion of the world's poorer nations that are situated in the continent. Rodney's question is: why are African countries part of the equator for under-development in the first place? How many times are we told that there is paucity of data or statistics are not available or missing? Why is that so?

2. Unreliable Data

Why is this inference to unreliable data important in this paper? Poverty and development measures of any country are based on statistics. In the absence of statistics, data created may not accurately represent reality. Secondly, there is a distinct possibility of making biased or skewed assumptions. According to the United Nations System of National Accounts (SNA), global standards are set by the United Nations for individual national accounts. However poorer countries generally report lower quality statistics because of the lack of resources available to national statistical offices. There are large differences in "official" GDP per capita across Africa although, as this report makes clear, the data are highly suspect and almost certainly under, rather than over, estimates of GDP per capita. Of the countries analyzed, 37 had a GDP per capita measured in PPP terms of below US$5,000 while 22, had national income falling below US$2,000 per capita. This compares with typical developed world figures of approximately US$50,000 per capita[12]. This is supported by Jerven (2013) in an extensive study of African economic statistics:

---

[12] The United Nations System of National Accounts (SNA) at http://unstats.un.org/unsd/nationalaccount/Accessed Mar 18

...in most African states the database for aggregating measures of income and growth are weak. For large shares of the economy we have little or no information and the figures involve a great deal of guesswork... (p. 84)

The problem is more serious than the shortcomings that can arise from individual national statistics offices feeding inaccurate data into the public domain. As a result of weaknesses cited above, there are often some serious discrepancies in the data on African economies published in international economic databases.

For example, Jerven (2013) notes that the UN reported annual national accounts for 45 sub-Saharan African countries between1991-2004, but it had only received data for less than half of the 1,410 observations, but for 15 countries no data had been received at all. The World Bank also provides data for African countries in constant and current prices even when no figures, accurate or otherwise, have been provided by national statistical offices of countries concerned. These are necessary adjustments for measuring, development, GDP, industrial growth or inflation. The result of weak back up information is that different international databases give different rankings about the size, growth rates through 'a method for filing the data gap'. Jerven (2013) describes this procedure as 'unclear' in terms of reflecting correct living standards of African economies. Schneider & Williams (2013), brings contesting arguments to these views by suggesting and recommending transformational economics – although, of course, this does not happen in a vacuum.

Zimbabwe's Debts: Root Cause of Underdevelopment

Jones (2011) identifies the origins and impact of Zimbabwe's debt:

"At independence in 1980, Zimbabwe inherited US$700 million of debt from the Rhodesian government; the result of UN sanction-busting loans to the white regime to buy arms during the civil war. This inherited, unjust debt was short-term and high interest; imposing a large repayment burden in the early 1980s just as drought struck. In the absence of significant grant aid to deal with the drought and fund post-civil war reconstruction, Zimbabwe relied on loans to buy imports. The country's large debt burden was created" (p. 6)

Other significant factors which constitutes a measurement of Zimbabwe's underdevelopment is lack of capacity to service US$750 million debts and repayment of leans after the spectacular failure of World Bank IMF Economic Structural Adjust Programme. Western governments 'bailing out' Zimbabwe were driven by corporate and economic interests in exploiting the country's mineral ore resources. According to the World Bank (2011) since 1980 Zimbabwe has been lent US$7.7 billion but repaid US$11.4 billion. The current debt stands at around US$11 billion

Aid has a symbiotic relationship with underdevelopment theories. Moyo (2009) adequately explores the question of aid by arguing that aid is responsible for the creation of structural weaknesses of underdevelopment specifically in Africa through underdevelopment and corruption. She also argues that the provision of aid in Africa has 'fostered dependency, encouraged corruption and ultimately perpetuated poor governance and poverty' (p. 3) What is evident in Moyo's (2010) theoretical framework is that aid is a capitalist strategy designed to keep recipient countries struggling with punitive repayments and high interest rate on some of the loans lent with strings attached. Sanctions came to Zimbabwe when the economy was already depleted as far back as 1980 through the Zimbabwe Conference on Reconstruction and Development. (ZIMCORD) that granted highly indebted loans when Zimbabwe did not have the capacity to pay them back. Zimbabwe had emerged from an expensive guerrilla warfare which in 1980 - technically with depleted capacity for long term growth and repayment of credit and loans. The Economic Structural Adjust Programme (ESAP) finished off Zimbabwe in that it was a complete disaster engineered by the World Bank. It is arguably correct to state that – against the said background, the impact of Zimbabwe's second phase of economic sanctions was felt almost immediately

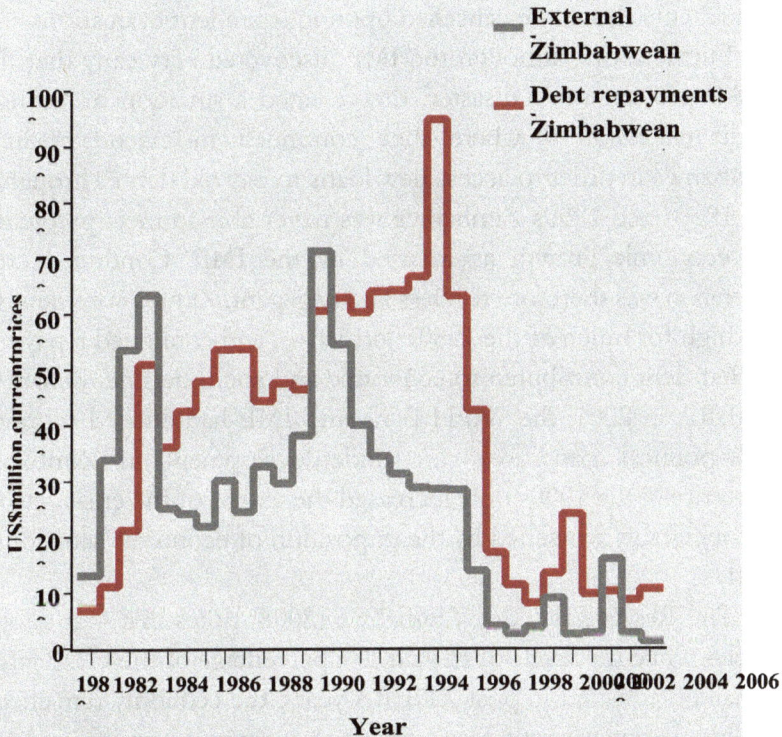

Foreign loans disbursed to Zimbabwe debt repayments, 1980-2009 (US$ million,

Adopted from Jones, T (2011) Uncovering Zimbabwe's Debt: The case for a democratic solution to the unjust debt burden, Debt Jubilee Campaign, London, UK. (p. 4)

The above is a representation of credit that was extended to Zimbabwe from 1980 to 2008. It is important to note that in 1980, Zimbabwe had a poor credit rating due to the debilitating effects of UDI-induced economic sanctions. Despite what was evidently a struggle in paying the odious debts and loans, the international community continued creating unjust debt, funding counter projects that arose from the failure of their flagship Economic Structural Adjustment Programme (ESAP) itself. Lenders were reckless in that they did not make efforts to the size of the debt. There was no consideration of how the country would raise repayments especially against the background of ecological factors like successive droughts. This situation ended up in burdening Zimbabwe in that it had to pay excessive interest rates and penalties for their reduced capacity for payment. Irresponsible lending by institutions entails that loan repayments should be cancelled upon independent evaluations.

Furthermore, although the IMF discovered very early that their ESAP project was a disaster, they created a situation of 'stringed' credit extension – where they continued to extend credit to Zimbabwe in order to access new loans to pay old debt. Throughout the 1980s and 1990s Zimbabwe was never able to meet predictions for economic growth as focused by the IMF. Continued credit extension was therefore reckless and negligent. Zimbabwe's debt was too high for much of the 1980s and 1990s, and continued repayment of that debt contributed to economic and social decline. Before the ZDERA in 2001, the World Bank and IMF had created economic and political conditions for underdevelopment in Zimbabwe. Austerity in the 1990s only increased the extent of the crisis – which was inevitably worsened by the imposition of economic sanctions in 2001

The Reserve Bank of Zimbabwe (2008) notes that – at another level – while the levels of net aid as a percentage of the GDP largely remained constant in post ZDERA years, the economy remained in decline as government faced financial constraints arising from the over 30% decline in GDP between 1998 and 2004. Thus, loan inflows 'declined an average of US$49.3 million between 2000 and 2006 – compared to the previous decade when an increase from an average of US 134.3 million in 1980s to US480.3 million in the 1990s.' The fact that, as noted, grant inflows declined significantly from 'an annual average of US$138 million in the 1990s to 39,9 million registered between 2000 and 2006' (p. 6) meant that the general populace continued to be marginalised into poverty as the economy declined into an acute recession. Moretti (2017) highlights that:

> …The consequences of this acute recession have been heavily felt by Zimbabweans, hit by increasing unemployment, declining incomes and erosion of public service provisions. The budget for social

expenditures, dropped from 15% of GDP in 2005 to 6% in 2009, leaving schools, hospitals and public facilities compromised... Poverty and deprivation has risen in urban areas, as government persistently struggles to pay civil servants on time due to dwindling revenues and a higher domestic and external debt of USD 11.2 billion. Businesses continue to close down due to low capacity utilisation, cash challenges and shrinking demand, as 95% of Zimbabweans are officially unemployed...

Because of the hostile economic sanctions environment, Zimbabwe has struggled to boost its social spending by seeking assistance under the Highly Indebted and Poor Countries (HIPC) The IMF and World Bank were among the first international finance organisation to cut credit lines in 2000s. Paradoxically, they make pronounced demands for Zimbabwe to clear its arrears as a prerequisite for further financial aid extension. According to "Humanitarian Needs Overview", UNOCHA, Zimbabwe, (2016) approximately 14 million Zimbabweans representing the total population, almost 3 million people are food insecure nationwide and an additional 1.3 million are at risk of slipping into food insecurity over the coming years. Further analysis carried out by the ZIMSTAT, confirm an upwards poverty trend, with more than 70% people living in deprivation.

According to the ZIMSTAT Poverty and Poverty Datum Analysis conducted in 2013 confirms that between 1995 and 2001 the poverty rate dropped from 75.5% to 70.9% - but has since risen in 2011 72.3% due to debilitating effects of economic sanctions on its population.

The Nature of Zimbabwe Economic Sanctions

The principal legislation regulating imposition of economic sanctions in Zimbabwe is the Zimbabwe Democracy and Economic Recovery Act 2001 (115 STAT. 963; 115 STAT. 965) and the Council Common Position (2002/145/CFSP) of 2002. This was amended in 2018 to incorporate three forms of sanctions formulated as ZDERA – in which Zimbabwe is prohibited from accessing credit for both

Government and the Private Sector. The Second provision is formulated as AGOA which restricts access of Zimbabwean products to the USA market; and third provision espouses OFAC provisions which regulate trade and financial transactions to and from Zimbabwe. OFAC adversely impacts on Banking as it places Zimbabwe on a 'High Risk Country' profile, resulting in most Zimbabwean banks losing correspondent banking relationships. OFAC provisions also affect Zimbabwe's financial institutions' capacity to access lines of credit that support its local industry. The biggest impact is financial because it limits access and movement of money in and out of a country thereby affecting the country's ability to trade and grow.

Economic sanctions imposed on Zimbabwe affect access to USA, UK and European markets for Zimbabwean companies. In the banking sector for example, the impact of restrictions has affected credit rating for Zimbabwean banks, their eligibility for loans and their liquidity position. It has also created banking relationships for Zimbabwean banks, - which ultimately has also affected jobs and the livelihood of ordinary Zimbabwean. Let me illustrate how:

i. Section 541.201 of the new regulations states in part: "(a) All property and interests in property that are in the US, that come within the US, or that are or come within the possession or control of any US person including any foreign branch of the persons, are blocked and may not be transferred, paid, exported, withdrawn or otherwise dealt in."

The US sanctions have prevented Zimbabwe from accessing international lines of credit including support from multilateral institutions. The regulations also prohibit transactions of any immediate family members or officials on the sanctions list or properties "owned or controlled by, directly or indirectly, the Government of Zimbabwe or an official or officials of the Government of Zimbabwe".

ii. Section 541.405 of the regulations also prohibits provision of services to Zimbabwe and the sanctioned officials. Reads S541.405: "The prohibitions on transactions contained in S541.201 apply to services performed in the US or by US persons, wherever located, including by a foreign branch of an entity located in the US (1) On behalf of or for the benefit of a person whose property and interests in property are blocked pursuant to S541.201 9 (a) or (2) with respect to property interests of any person whose property are blocked pursuant to S541.201 (a)." The regulations also bar US financial institutions from performing any "credit agreements, including but not to limited to, charge cards, debit cards or other credit facilities issued by a US financial institution to a person whose property and interests in property are blocked pursuant to S541.201(A)."

iii. The regulations under S541.701 also state that: "Any person who willfully commits, willfully attempts to commit, or willfully conspires to commit, or aids or abets in the commission of a violation of any license, order, regulation or prohibition may, upon conviction, be fined not more than $1 million, or if a natural person, be imprisoned for not more than 20 years or both."

Descriptive formulation of Impact of Economic Sanctions

The figures below appear inconsistent partly because of the numerous currency conversions that took place between 2005 to date. The Reserve Bank at that time removed zeros from the currency many times in an effort to manage thereby distorting micro-economic indicators. This partly explains skewed measures of GDP. There are other factors like how the effects of the disastrous Economic Structural Adjustment programme (ESAP) implemented in the mid 1990's hit industrial growth especially in the manufacturing sectors and heavy industries, decline of the agricultural sector due to farm occupations, decline in real wages of consumers, poor management of the economy including budget deficit due to unsustainable borrowing and shortages of foreign currency.

Economic Decline after Economic Sanctions in 2001:

Table 1: Selected Macroeconomic Indicators

Indicator	2000	2001	2002	2003	2004	2005	2006
GDP (current US$ million)	8,135.8	12,882.6	17,875.6	7,913.1	4,712.1	3,372.5	7,033.7
GNP	7,150.0	12,800.0	30,800.0	7,850.0	4,640.0	3,180.0	n.a.
Population	12,595.0	12,698.0	12,786.0	12,863.0	12,936.0	13,010.0	13,085.0
Current account balance (as % of GDP)	−0.4	−1.0	−2.6	−4.6	−5.6	−7.5	-4.0
Fiscal deficit, including grants (% of GDP)	−18.6	−7.0	−2.7	−0.2	−7.6	−6.1	−3.1
GNS per GDP (%)	11.1	7.0	4.9	−1.4	−3.2	−6.7	4.0
Gross of official reserves (months of imports)	1.5	0.6	0.7	n.a.	n.a.	n.a.	n.a.
GDP growth rates	−7.3	−2.7	−4.4	−10.4	−3.8	−6.5	−5.1
CPI inflation	55.6	73.4	133.2	365.0	350.0	237.8	1,216.0

Sources: **African Development Bank database; IMF**
(for balance-of-payments current account balance) – page 12

Concluding Remarks and Recommendations

In this Chapter, I have demonstrated that Zimbabwe was hard hit by economic sanctions which were imposed under ZDERA in 2001. While sanctions affected all Zimbabwean citizens in one way or the other, they tended to affect the poorest communities including the lower working class who lost jobs in massive retrenchments as companies were forced to close down. The situation was made worse by the fact that ZDERA sanctioned severed all financial links that Zimbabwe had with international financial institutions and banks. Banks have been routinely monitored and sanctioned for acting as conduit pipes for financial aid to Zimbabwe. Banks ran out of cash as ordinary people struggled to access their cash. The response from the government and particularly from President Mugabe was that economic sanctions are used as weapons designed to effect both micro political change in the country; and macro regime change in Zimbabwe. Furthermore, sanctions have been the basis upon which to draw conclusions of the western agenda aimed at destroying liberation political parties because they are perceived to be nationalistic – hence hard to negotiate neo colonial business and financial deals. Some of the contractions derived from the land reform programme include the emergence of corruption in land allocation, underutilisation of land leading to under production of crops – and in some cases leading to hunger and starvation. In response, government has had to sustain huge financial bills in food imports.

On a way forward, it is important to outline that there is the need to acknowledge the liberation agenda in any political settlement in Zimbabwe. In the history of mankind and of nations, liberation struggle and land issues are national values that form sovereignty. These are founding principles of the nation state of Zimbabwe on which its independence and nation state are based. Therefore, in addressing post-sanctions and governance issues in Zimbabwe, it is paramount to compromise settlement around historical and founding principles. Conflict resolution in Zimbabwe should not be emphasized on nationalist agenda at the expense of governance issues or vice versa as this is likely to be a protracted conflict. It must be made very clear that any settlement on Zimbabwe must never aim to remove ZANU PF from power. It must not evoke sentiments designed to neutralize the role of the liberation struggle because ZANU PF has a history of evoking nationalist sentiments especially when threatened particularly by imperialist interests. It must also aim to perfect the revolution through acknowledging the liberation struggle and governance.

References

Drury, A.C. (2005) Economic Sanctions and Presidential Decisions: Models of Political Rationality, Palgrave Macmillan Publishers, Hampshire, England. Found at:

https://books.google.co.uk/books?isbn=1403976953./Accessed July31.2018

Brinkman, I. (2005) 'A war for people Civilians, mobility and legitimacy in south-east Angola during the MPLA's war for independence, Ghent University Library, Found at http://handle.net/1854/LU-5816877/Accessed31July18

du Pisani, A. (2007), 'memory politics in Where Others Wavered: The Autobiography of Sam Nujoma My Life in SWAPO and my participation in the liberation struggle of Namibia', *Journal of Namibia Studies.* Vol **1** 97-107

Dobrianov, (1986), The Marxist Sociological Paradigm, in Developments in Marxist Sociological Theory: Modern Social Problems and Theory, AG Zdravomyslov, Sage Publications Inc., London, United Kingdom.

Galtung, J. (1967), 'On the Effects of International Economic Sanctions: With Examples from the Case of Rhodesia', World Politics, Volume 19, (3), 378-416.

Hufbauer, G.C., Schott, J.J. & Elliott, K.A. (1985) Economic Sanctions Reconsidered: History and Current Policy, Institute for International Economics, Paterson Institute, USA, Found at: http://books.google.co.uk/Economic_Sanctions_Reconsidered .html?id+etyVmnPOrG8C&redir_esc=y

Jerven, M. (2013), "Poor Numbers: How we are misled by African Development Statistics and what to do about it", Zed/Cornell University Press, London, United Kingdom

Lam (1990), 'Economic sanctions and the success of foreign policy goals: A critical evaluation', *Japan and the World Economy,* Volume 2, **(3),** September 1990, Pages 239-248, https://doi.org/10.1016/0922-1425(90)90003-B

Mararike, M. (2018) 'Theoretical Locations of Mugabeism, Land "Terrorism," and Third Chimurenga Neo-Coloniality Discourse in Zimbabwe: A Rejoinder of a Revolutionary' Volume: 49 issue: 3, page(s): 191-211, Article first published online: March 20, 2018; Issue published: April 1, 2018, https://doi.org/10.1177/0021934717750328

Mawere, M., Marongwe, N. & Duri, FPT., The End of an Era? Robert Mugabe and a Conflicting Legacy, Book Chapter

82

published in Mugabe Legacy, Bamenda, Langaa, Cameroon, Book Chapter 19, by Mararike, M and Mtapuri, O. (2018) *Mugabeism and the Struggle against Western Imperialism: Land Reform, Restitution and Post and (neo-) Coloniality Discourses in Zimbabwe.*

McGillivray & Stam, A.C (2004) 'Political institutions, coercive diplomacy, and duration of economic sanctions', *Journal of Conflict Resolution, Sage Journals* **48 (2)** 154-172

Moretti, V (2017). 'Zimbabwe in a dubious Battle: The Unexpected Consequences of Western Sanctions.' *Observatoire de l'Afrique australe et des Grands Lacs,* Ifri, Note no 18 of 2017, Found at https://www. OBS_Afrique Australe_Grands Lacs-R18-Zimbabwe in dubious battle The unexpected consequences of Western sanctions.pdf

Moyo, D (2010). Dead Aid: Why aid is not working and how there is another way for Africa Paperback. Bury St Edmunds, England

Moyo, D. 2009 'Why Foreign Aid Is Hurting Africa', The Wall Street Journal, WSJ.com, Found at https://web2.uconn.edu/ahking/Why%20Foreign%20Aid%20Is%20Hurting%20...pdf/accessed 26 Feb 19 https://www.wsj.com/articles/SB123758895999200083#print Mode

Ngugi wa Thiong'o (1992) Decolonising the Mind: the politics of language in the African culture, Zimbabwe Publishing House, Harare, Zimbabwe. Found at https://books.google.co.uk/books?isbn=9966466843/Accessed31July2018.

Portela, C. (2010) European Union Sanctions and Foreign Policy: When do the work? Routledge-Taylor & Francis Group, Oxon, United Kingdom

Raftopoulos, B. 2009. The crisis in Zimbabwe, 1998–2008. In B. Raftopoulos & A. Mlambo, (eds.) Becoming Zimbabwe: A History from the Pre-colonial Period to 2008, pp. 201–232. Weaver Press, Harare.

Reserve Bank of Zimbabwe, 'Impact of Sanctions against Zimbabwe', Documented Presented to the Pan-African Parliament, The Herald, 8 November 2008

Rodney, W. (1972) How Europe Underdeveloped Africa, Bogle-L'Ouverture Publications, London, UK

Sandler, T. & Hartley, K (2007) Handbook of Defence Economics: Defence in a Globalised World, Elsevier, Amsterdam, The Netherlands

Schneider, F and Williams, C. C., (2013), 'the shadow economy', *Institute of Economic Affairs,* Hobart Hobbs Printers, Westminster, United Kingdom

Sims, B. (2008) Restrictive Measures and Zimbabwe: Political Implications, Economic Impact and a Way Forward, IDASA at http://www.academia.edu/1861567/Restrictive_Measures_and _Zimbabwe_Political_Implications_Economic_Impact_and_a_ Way_Forward. Accessed 18 Feb 2019 16:27:18 GMT.

Smith-Hohn, J, (2010) "Zimbabwe: are targeted sanctions smart enough? On the efficacy of international restrictive measures," *Institute for Security Studies,* http://www.iss.co.za/uploads/4Jun2010.pdf

UNOCHA (2016). "Humanitarian Needs Overview", UNOCHA, Zimbabwe, 2016.

World Bank Report (2011), 'Challenges in Financing Education, Health and Social Protection Expenditures in Zimbabwe, Zimbabwe Public Expenditure Note, Poverty Reduction and Economic Management Unit, Africa Region, Report no.3, 2 February 2011, available at: documents.worldbank.org.

ZIMSTAT (2015). "Zimbabwe Demography and Health Survey", Zimbabwe National Statistic Agency (ZIMSTAT) Report, 2015. Available at: https://www.zimstat.co.zw.

ZIMSTAT (2013). "Poverty and Poverty Datum Analysis in Zimbabwe: 2011-2012", *ZIMSTAT,* April 2013, available at:

GDP per capita

Real levels rebased, 1997=100

— Zimbabwe — Sub-Saharan Africa

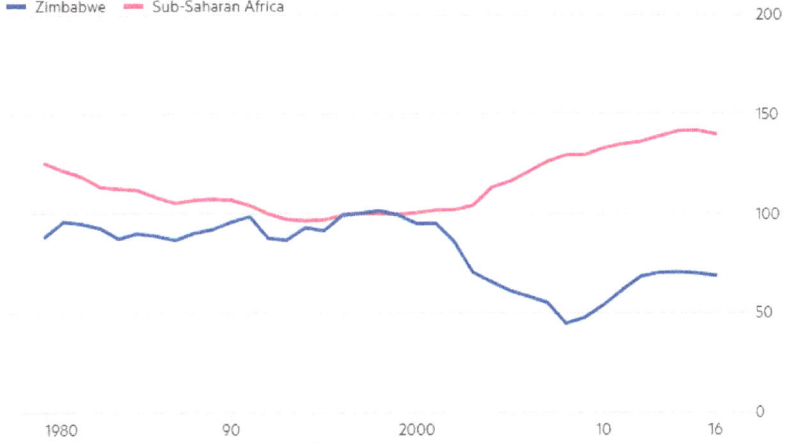

Source: Thomson Reuters Datastream, World Bank

© FT

GDP per capita

Selected countries, sub-Saharan Africa=100

■ 1997 ■ 2016

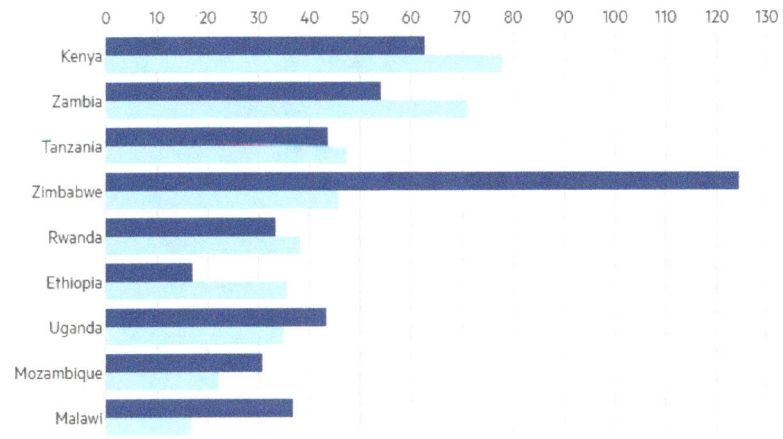

Source: Unctad

© FT

Trade balance

External balance on goods and services, % of GDP

■ Zimbabwe   ■ Sub-Saharan Africa

1987 89 91 93 95 97 99 01 03 05 07 09 11 13 15

Source: Thomson Reuters Datastream, World Bank
© FT

Zimbabwe's manufacturing output

Real level rebased, 1996=100

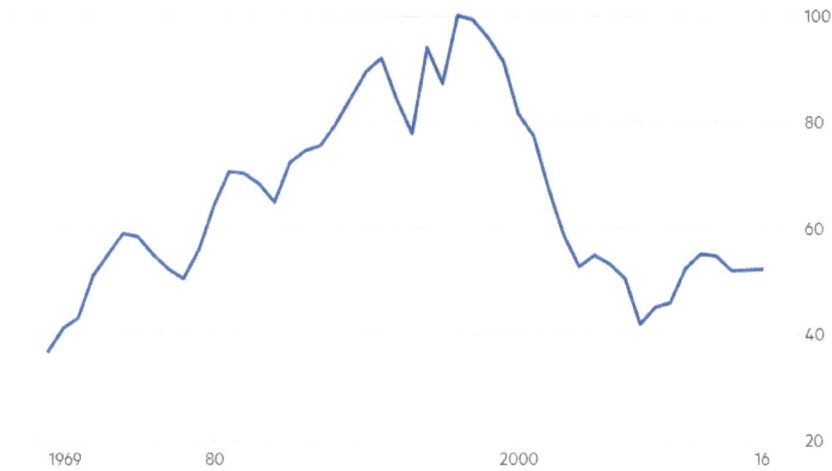

1969   80   2000   16

Source: Thomson Reuters Datastream, World Bank
© FT

Chapter 5

Love and Infection: British coloniality and Imperialism – A Repository of Zimbabwe's illegal post-2000 Land Reform sanctions

"A civilization that proves incapable of solving the problems it creates is a decadent civilization.

A civilization that chooses to close its eyes to its most crucial problems is a stricken civilization.

A civilization that uses its principles for trickery and deceit is a dying civilization."

Aimé Césaire

Introduction: Contextual Overview

In coloniality, imperialism and neo-colonialism spaces, the question of reclamation and restitution cannot be analysed conclusively without a historical brevity and intellectual acuity. For us to understand the origins of sanctions in Zimbabwe, we must trace the imperialist agenda. Decolonisation is part of the wider and gigantic imperialist configurations that swept through Europe in the 18th and 19th centuries. The German Chancellor Otto von Bismarck presided over *The Kongokonferenz* of 1884 to 1885, better known as the Berlin Colonial Conference. The words 'scramble' or 'partition' are very significant. From the Cambridge Dictionary – to scramble is to move or climb quickly but with difficulty, often using your hands to help you; to compete with other people for something there is very little of. Deductive meaning implies desperation and competition for scarce resources. 'Partition' is [often] used to deploy imperial maladies in sharing spoils... which boarder on the derogatory pathologies of robbing a group of nations of their independence. This creates enduring social formations of inequality.

Apparently, it is no remarkable coincidence that the conference bears the signature of Kongo (Congo) in its name, a country which euphemistically as Franz Fanon observed "...is shaped like a gun, and Congo is a trigger. If that explosive trigger bursts, it's the whole of Africa that will explode..."[13] The Conference was about partitioning Africa to share the spoils - a very generous but macabre reference to committing bloodshed, economic cannibalism, theft and armed robbery in a continent referred to by Conrad as outpost of the "Heart of Darkness"[14].

The story of British South African Police (BSAP) occupation of Southern Rhodesia is about love and infection. They descended on Rhodesia with their love and eyes set on gold and other mineral ores: - yes on the riches, gold, platinum, tin, rutile, coal, asbestos, diamonds...nickel. The settlers' love with thick-lipped African cannibals and savages came along with other evils that bedevilled the beautiful African people: evils of a higher magnitude - of theft, the bible, unpronounced but deliberate imposition of the settlers' unique brand of civilisation based on exploitation of man by man. It is correct that the 'love' from colonial kleptomaniacs and their scarecrows left a people infected with inequities of deprivation and exploitation. They left too, sceptic wounds borne of colonial venereal diseases or just VD, transmitted by imperial rapists! They loved the country. The infected the country.

This was followed by the illegal occupation of Zimbabwe in 1896 via the agency of a British South Africa Company (BSAP) led by Cecil John Rhodes. King Lobengula was forced to sign three Treaties – The Grobler Treaty (July 1887), Moffatt Treaty (February 1888) and Rudd Concession (March 1888) after which the Queen of England granted Cecil Rhodes a Royal Charter in October 1889 for exclusive mining rights for gold which had been 'discovered' in 1867 in *Matabeland*. The Pioneer Column of September 12, 1890 effectively sealed the deal for colonial occupation of then Southern Rhodesia (Zimbabwe). In effect, at that time 4,000 white, die-hard racist farmers monopolised most of the land while Zimbabwean masses

---

[13] Frantz Fanon: "Africa is shaped like a gun and Congo is the trigger" at http://www.theefedstudent/18/frantz-fanon-africa-is-shaped-lie-a-gun-and-c0ngo-is-the-trigger/, Accessed 24 Jan 18

[14] Joseph Conrad at https://www.scribd.com/document/369906987/Conrad-Imperialism/ Accessed 25 Jan 18

were compelled to eke out a miserable existence in the infertile native reserves known as Tribal Trust Lands. The 'natives' were consigned to reserves on marginal land, which were mostly in dry, infertile arid lands in ecological regions 4 and 5 of the country. Natives as they were derogatively called were subjected to slave labour and forced convert to Christianity for conformity.

Based on foregoing, scholars seek to underpin colonialism as a process or a condition, the coloniality of being as an identity tag and decolonisation processes as a question of subjectivity. At one other level, coloniality is characterised by patterns of power based on inequality. Scholars like Van Onselene (1976) state that 'power' is translated to inter-subjective relations of labour and productivity which he routinely referred to as *"Chibharo"*[15] or forced labour. Between 1891 and 1895 'Natives Reserves' for Africans later known as 'Tribal trust Lands were created marking the beginning of racial segregation and forced removals of families off their land.

In 1893, the first rebellion known as *Matebele* Uprising took place in protest of white occupancy and racially motivated removals of indigenous groups off their land. This was followed by the *First Chimurenga* of 1896-97 where natives were defeated by the military mighty of the settlers. What followed this was a raft of repressive legislative instruments designed to consolidate white colonial rule in Rhodesia.

Colonial Rhodesia was a depiction of Master/Servant dialect which contributes to the ontology of coloniality racism. Fanon (2008) draws on extremal expressions of coloniality in relation to racial subjectivity. These characteristics are adjuncts that British imperialism exhibited in their rabid colonial agenda in Zimbabwe.

---

[15] Chibharo is a Shona noun derived from a radical 'kubata chibharo' which means committing statutory rape. The symbolism of the use of Chibharo especially in Rhodesian mines is that men were rounded up against their will by the colonial regime and forced to work as wage labours. Exploitation of African cheap labour was rife and unchecked by the repressive regime of the day.

Zimbabwe: A Brief History of Economic Sanctions

The Rhodesian Sanctions 1965-1979[16]

The history of Zimbabwean economic configurations has three constellations in its historical epochs. First, the period of Pioneer Column of 12 September 1890 was the effective colonial occupation of Zimbabwe by white settlers. Rhodesia's Unilateral Declaration of Independence (UDI) in 1965 in a country that was not even their own was a defining moment for repression and white supremacy. The third *Chimurenga*, led by President Robert Mugabe gave birth to Zimbabwean Land Reforms that empowered landless blacks who land had been expropriated or even stolen from them by settlers.

According to the New York Times Magazine, Southern Rhodesia was established in 1923 as a British colony named for Cecil Rhodes, who made his fortune in consolidating diamond mines. By the 1960s, as much of Africa rapidly decolonized around it, the colonial government faced pressure from London to hold free elections and accede to majority rule.

> The colonial government refused [to capitulate]. In 1965 it renamed itself Rhodesia and broke from the United Kingdom with the express purpose of maintaining white rule. The new government was

---

[16] Historically, academics differ in terms of the Rhodesian cut off or end date for UDI sanctions. I argue that in Margaret Thatcher's memoirs titled The Path to Power, - when she came to power in 1975 - she was still dealing with residual effects of sanctions which formed the prelude to Zimbabwe Independence and after the Lancaster House Constitution of 1979. Rhodesia sanctions of the UDI era lasted till 1979 when Zimbabwe gained independence from Britain. It is correct to state that from independence in 1980, Prime Minister Mugabe dealt with sanctions-related economic problems [in the first decade of his rule] that the ZIMCORD Donor Conference had failed to resolve. It is important to correct that historical misalignment. Collateral events from the Internal Settlement in Rhodesia signed on 3 March 1978 – a constitution would be signed under the Zimbabwe-Rhodesia banner. "In August 1978 Congress passed an amendment requiring the President [of the United States] to lift sanctions by December 31 if Rhodesian government demonstrates willingness to negotiate at all party conference held under international auspices [of the Lancaster House Conference] page 163: See Bipartisanship & the Making of Foreign Policy: A Historical Survey, By Ellen C. Collier

led by Ian Smith, who declared that "the white man is master of Rhodesia. He has built it, and he intends to keep it … [17]

Without alluding to nitty gritty details of the Rhodesian dirty war in Zimbabwe in the 60's and 70's, we have always argued that war has hidden agendas. It may not be about casualties of that war which matters. What Blair termed 'the battle of hearts and minds' in Iraq was about winning the war at all costs without a heart or consideration for collateral damages including war civilian casualties. This is put in a different storyline in the above-mentioned *New York Times Magazine* story on white supremacy:

> Smith's government soon found itself at war with a black insurgency, fighting for representative government and self-rule. Many of the fighters received weapons from China or the Soviet Union. Rhodesia's government labelled them "communists" and "terrorists" … 'it's a complicated story,' said Gerald Horne, author of "From the Barrel of a Gun" and a professor of history and African-American studies at the University of Houston. … but of course, the apartheid side knew what sold in Washington, so they portrayed it as a battle against communism because it got pulses racing in the United States...

Communist propaganda was used to fight a war of ideological differences, a war in which thousands of Africans would be killed, while perpetrators of that war watched and laughed at the dramatic irony of it[18]. Southern Rhodesia was everything to do with imperialism, while Ian Smith's Rhodesia was everything to do with white supremacy! The gallant sons and daughters of Zimbabwe and those who perished at Nyadzonya and Tembwe mass massacres are not worried about the resurgence of white supremacy in 2018 [after the "fall" of Mugabe] and social media hash tags of "Make Zimbabwe

---

[17] Rhodesia's Dead — but White Supremacists Have Given It New Life Online by John Ismay, found at
https://www.nytimes.com/2018/04/10/magazine/rhodesia-zimbabwe-white-supremacists.html/accessed April, 11, 18
[18] New York Times Magazine article cited in (vi) above

Rhodesia Again" or "Be a Man Among Men," - Rhodesian Army recruiting slogan now used by hate and white terrorist groups.

In a two-page document titled "Rhodesia's Finest Hour" Ian Smith declared Independence from Britain on 11 November 1965 but dramatically declared full allegiance to the Queen[19]. The Prime Minister Wilson's British Labour government immediately dismissed Ian Smith's declaration of independence as illegal because the act was a direct rebellion against the Crown and the constitution. In the following year in 1966, The United Nations Security Council imposed mandatory economic sanctions designed to bring down Rhodesia's illegitimate government. By a vote of 11 to 0—with four abstentions, the council declared an international embargo on 90% of Rhodesia's exports, forbade the U.N.'s 122-member nations to sell oil, arms, motor vehicles or airplanes to the racist regime[20]. On 22 December 1966, Rhodesia left the Commonwealth to avoid expulsion.

Britain's policy of export of weapons to Rhodesia came to a halt, while British export of financial capital was banned. The purchase of Rhodesian tobacco, the country's main export, also stopped. Partners in the imperialist agenda joined hands as USA immediately supported the British sanctions - with embargoes on arms exports and sugar imports - and the UN called for all its members to implement economic sanctions in 1966. Godwin, Peter & Ian Hancock (1993), state that there were some 'facilitative loopholes' that allowed Rhodesia to gain advantages of recovery – for example' oil was not included in the first schedule of sanctions. Rhodesia was treated like a renegade break away colony. The goal of the sanctions was to undermine the stability of the Rhodesian currency, something which failed. It was also noted that Britain's continued to favour economic sanctions rather than use of military force and regarded Rhodesia as a British responsibility.

---

[19]
http://news.bbc.co.uk/onthisday/hi/dates/stories/november/11/newsid_26580 00/2658445.stm, Accessed Jan 09, 18
[20] http://content.time.com/time/magazine/article/0,9171,840760,00.html, Accessed Jan 10, 2018

Some of the goals of the sanctions were designed to put Rhodesia's economy under pressure, create dissatisfaction within its isolated white population, and thus pressure Ian Smith to negotiate terms acceptable to Wilson's British government. The United Kingdom's decision not to use military force against Ian Smith's regime was deliberate because it was designed to protect white hegemonic economic interests as a colony. However, sanctions against Rhodesia were a considerable failure in the sense that they failed to exert pressure on white minority regime, Rhodesia did not experience a fall in real wages and a rise in unemployment and inflation within the first 10 years of UDI. Ian Smith circumvented sanctions by creating a huge manufacturing base as the country continued to trade with South Africa, Portugal (colonizers of Mozambique and Angola), and South-West Africa – bastardized colony (illegally occupied then by a promiscuous colony of South Africa). Countries like Japan. Belgium and West Germany continued to maintain trade relations with Rhodesia thereafter[21].

In that period, sanctions failed to undermine the country's socio-economic structure or least create enough dissatisfaction among the Caucasians thereby abandoning Ian Smith as widely anticipated. If at all, on the other one hand, Rhodesia's sanctions strengthened the Marxist ideology of Mugabe's ZANLA and Nkomo's ZIPRA military wings of Zimbabwe who continued to fight against the deleterious regime for majority rule and total liberation of Zimbabwe. But Ian Smith held core beliefs of "Rhodesia Forever" / "Not in a thousand years" which was dangerous not just for mankind, but for the sons and daughters of Zimbabwe:

> Sometimes people hold a core belief that is very strong. When they are presented with evidence that works against that belief, the new evidence cannot be accepted. It would create a feeling that is extremely uncomfortable, called cognitive dissonance. And because it is so important to protect the core belief, they will rationalize, ignore and even deny anything that doesn't fit in with the core belief. (p. 18)
>
> [Franz Fanon, From "The Wretched of the Earth"]

---

[21] http://www.popularsocialscience.com/2012/10/19/the-fall-of-rhodesia/, Accessed Jan 09, 18

Ian Smith's mission and core belief to frustrate majority rule in Zimbabwe became the rallying point and battle cry for Zimbabwe's long-drawn-out armed liberation struggle[22]. In all walks of our liberation politics, here is what Zimbabwean cadres must know and embrace as part of the history of economic sanctions in Zimbabwe. I call this organogram "Mind Games of Rhodesia/Zimbabwe Sanctions".

---

[22] Full quotation denigrating majority rule read as follows: "I have said before, and I repeat, we are prepared to bring black people into our Government to work with us. I think we have got to accept that in the future Rhodesia is a country for black and white, not white as opposed to black and vice versa. I believe this is wrong thinking for Rhodesia. We have got to try to get people to change their line of thinking if they are still thinking like that. This is outdated in Rhodesia today. I don't believe in majority rule ever in Rhodesia… not in 1,000 years. I repeat that I believe in blacks and whites working together. If one day it is white and the next day black I believe we have failed and it will be a disaster for Rhodesia." Found at
https://imperialtraditionalist.wordpress.com/2016/04/22/was-ian-smith-racist/
Accessed 25 Jan 18

Sanctions Against Rhodesia (1965-79)	Sanctions Against Zimbabwe (2001-18)
Punitive for undermining/demeaning British Crown	Punitive for reclaiming and redistributing land to landless Zimbabwean peasants
Punitive on errand boy and prodigal son Ian Smith and his racist cabal: British mentality 'Rhodesia should not hang us up to dry in public shame'	Punitive on a ruthless dictator Robert Mugabe who dares challenge imperialist status quo by telling off his 'masters'
White on White racism (Part of Caucasian tribal wars)	Racist dimension on colonial subjects "If we tell to jump never ask us: How high should we jump Sir"
"The world is watching us" mindset: softly- softly approach is a face saver	The world must never know the truth! To Zimbabweans: "Mugabe is a ruthless dictator and despot. We will liberate you from your ZANU PF oppressors and tormentors."
Aimed at minimizing damages on Rhodesian Front, downplay their motive and effects to the advantage of colonial master	Aimed at thwarting "War of liberation and empowerment". Sanctions must achieve total obliteration of African liberation struggles for their quest for total independence
Britain to Rhodesia 'After all, you are our kith and kin – don't worry, we will rescue you in the end'	'Smart' Objective: We must create stooges in opposition politics who will do the dirty job of destroying their own country for us
Britain to Ian Smith: 'We are your liberators – let's delay majority rule'! 'No to majority rule!'	Europe: 'Let us destroy liberation struggle war heritage, legacy of black war politics, deface liberation parties and all their so-called revolutionaries.'
Refusal by white supremacists to pay restitution and reparations for land stolen from these buffoon natives. 'Not in a thousand years' mantra	Let Europe be on the watch out: we want to eliminate vehement refusals of our patronage by [Black] Zimbabweans. Their knowledge of imperialism and neo-colonialism through ideological consciousness is dangerous for the new world order.
"Blair keep your England"	"…And I keep my Zimbabwe"

It is important to note that for the better part of its governance, from 60s and 70's (the height of the liberation struggle) to the post-land reform era from 2001, Zimbabwe has endured a total of 32 years of Western crafted sanctions. Three quarters [almost two decades] of Zimbabwe's independence was dominated by economic sanctions. To establish the reasons for the transgression, one must ask questions like: Why is Zimbabwe being repeatedly hit by sanctions from colonial times to independence? Why is the West registering keen and unwavering interest in Zimbabwean politics and socio-economics? Why has the USA out-classed their British counterparts and out maneuvered all European countries by building the biggest embassy in Africa at 200 million dollars in the leafy suburb of Westgate in Harare, Zimbabwe? [23] The reasons are not hard to find. Elsewhere, it has been reported that "Shine starts to fade on Botswana's diamond dividend" citing that Botswana's Gross Domestic Product per capita would drop by 48% by 2030 when their diamonds are exhausted[24]. As admitted by the World Bank, the mission to exploit former colonies to the bone can never be clear as this:

> …Despite Botswana's economic growth, the country faces high levels of poverty and inequality, especially in rural areas and the southern part of the country. It is expected to make slow progress on poverty reduction over the medium-term, with poverty falling to approximately 16% according to the 2015/16 Multi-Topic Household Survey. Accelerating poverty reduction will require bold decisions that encourage greater private sector job creation, higher value-added agricultural production and services, credit expansion, and lower household debt. While Botswana's social sector expenditures have been generous, they have not yielded the impact one might expect.

---

[23] Construction of the US Embassy in Zimbabwe begins, found at – Construction Review Online
https://constructionreviewonline.com/2015/09/construction-of-a-us-embassy-in-zimbabwe-begins/Accessed April 07, 18: *Mr. Bruce Wharton the U.S. Ambassador to Zimbabwe said that the new compound will cost the American taxpayer a about $200 million. During a ceremony at the site in Westgate the ambassador said the new embassy would help open pathways for mutual respect and understanding between Harare and Washington, adding that it will also add to the flow of business and assets between the two nations.*
[24] The Guardian, 'Shine starts to fade on Botswana's diamond dividend.', found at https://www.theguardian.com/global-development/2016/jan/28/botswana-diamond-mines-tourism-transport-agriculture-karowe/ Accessed April 07, 18

Education expenditure is among the highest in the world —about 9% of GDP — and includes the provision of nearly universal free primary education, but - has not created a skilled workforce. Unemployment has remained stubbornly high at 17.7% and Botswana's income inequality is one of the highest in the world…

> From article entitled "The World Bank In Botswana", 'The World Bank partners with the government to promote private sector-led, jobs-intensive growth, strengthen human and physical assets, and support effective resource management', Found at The World Bank Website: https://www.worldbank.org/en/country/botswana/overview/Accesed19August18

Given the foregoing report from the World Bank, ten years from now when the West has completed the rout of exploitation of precious diamonds, the Batswana people will start asking of where tangible benefits of their stolen mineral ore. By that time, USA and Europe will be jostling for unequal trade and contracts for Zimbabwean diamonds where a $200 million embassy is nearly complete at the time of this report. Zimbabwe has unexploited fields of diamonds worth billions of dollars at *Chiyadzwa – Manicaland*, at *Bikita* and in *Chivi* District of *Masvingo* that the USA is curiously eying. The CIA is also aware of the existence of the late Roy Bennett's Charleswood Estate Farm in *Chimanimani, Manicaland*, which has bottomless reserves of diamonds[25].

Mugabe's policies of empowering blacks are the enemy of capitalism. Naturally the west will do anything to be in Zimbabwe first, unhindered! ZDERA is clearing booby traps and *zvimbambaira* or landmines for Uncle Sam (US) imperialism in Zimbabwe! Out of what many perceive to be desperation for normalization of relations with the west, ZDERA is a harbinger for neo-colonial market reforms designed to benefit foreign international companies through the creation of "favourable investment climate". Concessions

---

[25] The UK Times Newspaper: Obituary: Roy Bennett, Found at https://www.thetimes.co.uk/article/roy-bennett-obituary-jz7xbkz6s#/Accessed 15 May 18

97

guaranteed to foreign as part of FDI drive are abnormally skewed in favour of western exploitation of Zimbabwean resources.

The Post Chimurenga 3 Economic Sanctions 2001 -

Views from Fowale (2010) about the "Sanctions Road Map" quoted by Hove (2012) are very important in tracing their planning milestones and timing. It is no remarkable coincidence that the chain of events in this sanctions agenda appears to have been set in motion by Tony Blair's election to office on 2 May 1997. Armed with his ambitious co-called Ethical Foreign Policy, Blair entered his premiership and identified Africa as "scars on the conscience of the world" and planned a "Marshall Plan for Africa". The cornerstone agenda also involved his regime change in Zimbabwe – that of removing President Robert Mugabe from power using military means. Blair said "...the world does not have to wait until they see how African governments react to power hungry leaders [like Mugabe] and referred to Nigeria as a "troubled corner of the continent". Blair talked publicly and unashamedly about "disillusionment in Africa that could provide fertile breeding ground for a new generation of terrorists" and took an aim at Zimbabwe's "flawed presidential election" scheduled for 2003. One of the central tenets of his government's foreign policy spearheaded by the then Foreign Affairs Secretary of State, Robin Cook was to institute good and "ethical" governance in Africa, a project which he kick-started by alleging that Nigeria was "plundering petrol dollars" through endemic corruption and mis-governance[26].

In his emotive Labour Conference Speech of 2001, Blair had referred to "murderous group of gangsters who threatened its democratically elected government and people" in Sierra Leonne. About Zimbabwe he had elliptically talked of presiding over a "deal" that involved "...true democracy, no more excuses for dictatorship,

---

[26] Full text: Tony Blair's Speech (Part One) found at http://www theguardian.com/politics/2001/oct/02/labourconference.labour6, Accessed January 5, 18 Blair confronts 'scar on the world's conscience' found at http://www.theguardian.com/world/2002/feb/07/politics.development. Accessed January 5, 18

abuses of human rights, no tolerance of bad governance from the endemic corruption of some states [sic], to activities of Mr Mugabe's henchman in Zimbabwe...Proper commercial, legal and financial systems... The will, with our help to broker agreements for peace and provide troops to police them..."[27] Blair's 2001 Labour Conference speech set the tone to what was to prove to be intricate and truncated phase in Zimbabwe-British relations, culminating in the imposition of what was widely viewed by Africa Union as 'punitive' economic sanctions. By the time Tony Blair embarked onto the impossible mission of his African Renaissance journey, Africa Union (AU) was on high alert, after having been rattled by his bad mouthing, blunt, undiplomatic and despicable attitude on Africa and its leadership.

In an article entitled *'Rhetoric without responsibility: the attraction of 'ethical foreign policy'*, Chandler (2003) provides an apt recapitulation of Blair's spectacular failure of his foreign policy and noted that "...the gap between rhetoric and responsibility lies in the fact that policy can be declared a success with little regard to policy outcomes, as there is no formal accountability to non-citizens abroad, while problems can be on the actions of other people or their governments..." Thus, Blair's overzealous interventionist and gradualist ethical approach proved a disaster for the new world order as he eventually took Britain into an unsanctioned and illegitimate war in Iraq.

According to Tendi (2014) 'Mugabe thus formed a negative perception' of Labour in 1965 when the Labour leader defended irredentist Rhodesia's regime's Unilateral Declaration of Independence (UDI). Tony Blair's New Labour lacked appreciation and significance of the history of the Lancaster House negotiations on land. We deploy the thesis that there was double coincidence in historical epochs of Labour tenures of office. First, when sanctions were first imposed on Rhodesia in 1965, it was Labour's Harold Wilson government (1964 to 1974; then 1974-1976) that initiated the whole raft of sanctions. Tony Blair's New Labour (1997-2007) was the chief architect of the second and current wave of deadly sanctions. Labour's dark hand of history remained ominous particularly for President Robert Mugabe throughout his rule (1980-

2017). Yet as historians argued, if military options had been considered, Rhodesia would have been prevented from the 50 000 genocides where civilians lost lives. On second ahistorical 'do good' approach exhibited in Short's 1997 letter Mugabe[28] reaffirmed his

---

[28] Zimbabwe - Claire Short's Letter Nov 5th 1997

5 November 1997
From the Secretary of State
Hon Kumbirai Kangai MP
Minister of Agriculture and Land

Dear Minister

George Foulkes has reported to me on the meeting which you and Hon John Nkomo had with Tony Lloyd and him during your recent visit. I know that President Mugabe also discussed the land issue with the Prime Minister briefly during their meeting. It may be helpful if I record where matters now rest on the issue.

At the Commonwealth Heads of Government Meeting, Tony Blair said that he looked forward to developing a new basis for relations with Commonwealth countries founded upon our government's policies, not on the past.

We will set out our agenda for international development in a White Paper to be published this week. The central thrust of this will be the development of partnerships with developing countries which are committed to eradicate poverty, and have their own proposals for achieving that which we and other donors can support.

I very much hope that we will be able to develop such a relationship with Zimbabwe. I understand that you aim shortly to publish your own policies on economic management and poverty reduction. I hope that we can discuss them with you and identify areas where we are best able to help. I mentioned this in my letter on 31 August to Hon Herbert Murarwa.

I should make it clear that we do not accept that Britain has a special responsibility to meet the costs of land purchase in Zimbabwe. We are a new Government from diverse backgrounds without links to former colonial interests. My own origins are Irish and as you know we were colonised not colonisers.

We do, however, recognise the very real issues you face over land reform. We believe that land reform could be an important component of a Zimbabwean programme designed to eliminate poverty. We would be prepared to support a programme of land reform that was part of a poverty eradication strategy but not on any other basis.

I am told Britain provided a package of assistance for resettlement in the period immediately following independence. This was, I gather, carefully planned and implemented, and met most of its targets.

Again, I am told there were discussions in 1989 and 1996 to explore the possibility of further assistance. However that is all in the past.

If we look to the present, a number of specific issues are unresolved, including the way in which land would be acquired and compensation paid -

unfavourable view of the [Labour] party. The letter addressed to the Minister of Agriculture, Kumbirai Kangai in part read as follows:

> I should make it clear that we do not accept that Britain has a special responsibility to meet the costs of land purchase in Zimbabwe. We are a new Government from diverse backgrounds without links to former colonial interests. My own origins are Irish and as you know we were colonised not colonisers. [29]

It is at that point that demonization discourses between the two countries took off the ground, with Zimbabwean leadership being assertive on anti-British and anti-Blair style of propaganda which helped Mugabe to win the 2003, 2008 and 2013 elections. The anti-sanctions bashing trump card worked to the advantage of Mugabe

---

clearly it would not help the poor of Zimbabwe if it was done in a way which undermined investor confidence.

Other questions that would need to be settled would be to ensure that the process was completely open and transparent, including the establishment of a proper land register.

Individual schemes would have to be economically justified to ensure that the process helped the poor, and for me the most important issue is that any programme must be planned as part of a programme to contribute to the goal of eliminating poverty. I would need to consider detailed proposals on these issues before confirming further British support for resettlement.

I am sure that a carefully worked out programme of land reform that was part of a programme of poverty eradication which we could support would also bring in other donors, whose support would help ensure that a substantial land resettlement programme such as you clearly desire could be undertaken successfully. If is [sic] to do so, they too will need to be involved from the start.

It follows from this that a programme of rapid land acquisition as you now seem to envisage would be impossible for us to support. I know that many of Zimbabwe's friends share our concern about the damage which this might do to Zimbabwe's agricultural output and its prospects of attracting investment.

I thought it best to be frank about where we are. If you think it would be helpful, my officials are ready to meet yours to discuss these issues.

Yours sincerely

Claire Short

[29] (A full letter by Short, 'how it all started', appears in New African Magazine, of March 2002). See Claire Short One bad letter with long lasting consequences, at New African Magazine at http://www. Newafricanmagazine.com/ Accessed Jan 5, 18

who immediately saw that the goal posts had shifted by the imposition of targeted and economic sanctions by the West[30].

The question of restitution and responsibility for land financial packages was a constitutional matter which had been agreed viva voce at Lancaster House Conference in 1979. The Conservative governments followed that by way of land restitution in the late 80s. According to Alexander (2006) it was not in dispute that the Conservative government had provided financial support for a successful initial phase of Zimbabwe land reform during the 1980s.

Short's letter was analysed by the ZANU PF government who perceived its contents as downright condescending and objectionable. Her allusions to her personal experience of being an Irish added impetus and credibility to accusations of racism and patronage. Short's stance created the impression of spirited attempts to absolve imperial Britain form colonial obligations. She was accused of perceiving Zimbabweans as subjects of the empire. Her 'diverse' background as defined in colonial configurations was a strategy designed to limit and neutralise the racial banalities of racist Britain. It remains paramount to state that the above historical interface had a defining role in Zimbabwe's post Chimurenga 3 land reform led by Mugabe and the imposition of sanctions by the Western governments.

In November 1998, the International Monetary Fund (IMF), imposed unpublicised sanctions under the instigation of Britain. The International Development Secretary who had attended the Land Donor Conference and publicly accused President Mugabe of using aid money to fund his corrupt regime. In consultation with American counterparts at the World Bank and Britain, despite earlier pledges

---

[30] Soni Rajan a London Based Consultant on International Development employed by ODA at the time of Claire Short's infamous letter recounted that "it was absolutely clear from the attitude of her [Claire Short] staff towards my recommendations that Labour Strategy was to accelerate Mugabe's unpopularity by failing to provide him with funding for land redistribution...they thought that if they did not give him the money for land reform his people in the rural areas would start to turn against him. That was their position, they wanted him out and they were going to do whatever they could to hasten their demise" From "In the Name of Democracy – New African Magazine at http://www.newafricanmagazine.com/in-the-name-of-democracy/, Accessed Jan 5 18

and commitments to support Land Reform Rehabilitation Phase 2, (LRRP11) at the said same conference, imposed a wide range of unpublished sanctions. Immediately after that, the British Foreign Secretary announced a regime change agenda for Zimbabwe, citing the rule of law as obstacles to the democratisation processes in Zimbabwe.

Robert Mugabe is a tyrant who has crippled Zimbabwe. He has oppressed its people. Degraded its constitution and vandalised its economy. Millions of Zimbabweans face famine, their basic freedoms are denied and 80% are unemployed. Mr Mugabe's continued wreckage of country is a brake on economic development and an affront to hopes for democratic renaissance in sub-Saharan Africa...

This faceless allegation was countered by what a South African commentator termed "Labour Imperialism"[31]:

...while the record of all British governments with regards to Rhodesia and Zimbabwe is shameful, that of Labour governments is particularly so... During the Lancaster House Constitution of 12 December 1979, the Thatcher Conservative government did all it could to protect the privileges of white minority Rhodesia. The Lancaster House Constitution under which Rhodesia gained its independence barred the newly elected government of Zimbabwe from effecting any changes in the ownership of land for a period of 10 years. Land was sold based on willing seller willing buyer principle which led to a tragedy of good intentions. ... [John] Major honoured part of the deal to fund for land distribution to landless peasants. On taking office in 1997, Labour, contrary to conventions of international rule of law, reneged on land undertakings...The Zimbabwe government above all the towering of its leader Robert Mugabe has earned the wrath of imperialism and has set a precedent which could prove very infections indeed and spread to other parts of Africa, notably South Africa... Imperialism does not seek freedom, it seeks domination...

---

[31] Zimbabwe: Imperialism's attempts at regime change in the name of concern for human rights found at http://www.lalkar.org/article/1091/zimbabwe-imperialism-attempts-at-regime-change-in-the-name-of-concern-for-human-rights. Accessed January 5 18

In September 1999, IMF completely suspended its support for economic adjustment and reform in Zimbabwe. The International Development Association, heavily influenced by Britain and the World Bank, suspended all structural adjustment loans to Zimbabwe, leaving a trail of disaster for their unfinished projects in Zimbabwe. No one highlights that the financial ruin of financial pull out had to be paid by Zimbabwe as loans where rescheduled, with interest rates recalculated to cushion the principal costs of disbursing finance. The impact of this was that it further marginalised communities in rural areas into extreme ends of poverty by depriving the same communities of access to basic services like food and nutrition, health services and adequate medical facilities. Communities in rural areas who bore the sharp brunt of liberation struggle by supporting Mugabe's ZANU PF were targeted under this strategy. The same communities were known to be backbone supporters of Robert Mugabe's ZANU PF. We can see why the USA was apprehensive about putting up a war to fight innocent and defenceless peasants who became immediate victims.

The timeline for fixing Zimbabwe into submission is quite clear, well thought and logical: In March 2001, the US Senate passed the Zimbabwe Democracy and Economic Recovery Act. There is evidence of British's massive contributions in that piece of legislation as they worked hand in glove with various non-governmental organisations and the opposition Movement for Democratic Change on the ground in Zimbabwe to cripple Zimbabwe. This resulted in Zimbabwe being denied access to all international credit lines and loans, thereby effectively grounding the country to a halt. The bill put a condition and called for Zimbabwe to withdraw its military forces from the Democratic Republic of Congo (DRC) – where democratic order would have prevented western powers from plundering massive mineral ore reserves from that country. [Refer to images of a gun-shaped Africa and a trigger above] There is evidence that it is easier for international capital and imperialism to loot from a country that is lawless than one that is governable. The DRC, according to imperial capital vultures, must not be a stabilized democracy because it then becomes difficult to pillage and loot.

In May 2001 the International Development Agency (IDA), an arm of the World Bank (WB) that funds some of poorest communities under financial aid agreements, suspended all forms of financial aid lending's to Zimbabwean communities, leaving communities desperate in accessing basic medical care, drugs and medication. This was followed immediately in 2001 when Britain cancelled an aid package to Zimbabwe worth US 5 million dollars. Zimbabwe, set to be expelled from the commonwealth, left the group in 2002, citing that the commonwealth was a badge of imperialism hence nothing to be proud of by belonging to that group. In 2003 the US government froze all the assets of seventy-two government officials alleged to be linked with undermining democratic processes in the regime change agenda. Tony Blair went on another unsuccessful crusade to lobby the UN Security Council to indict President Robert Mugabe in the International Criminal Court of Justice in The Hague. The year 2005 saw George Bush signing Executive Orders that expanded the number of government officials affected by economic sanctions including 39 financial institutions. In an analysis of the Zimbabwean crisis and International response, Chan & Primorac (2007) imply that 'the space of silence' appeared to have backfired as Mugabe then at that point seized the opportunity to tighten his grip on power. He mobilised his country against western crafted sanctions and conscientised ordinary Zimbabwe people against the West.

Research Questions

Using in-depth qualitative research techniques of semi-structured interviews, the following research questions shape the context of Zimbabwean post-land reforms economic sanctions:

i.   What is the impact of western crafted imposed on Zimbabwe through the enactment of the Zimbabwe Democracy and Recovery Bill of 2001? Can we measure the genocidal damage of the punitive measures on the population of Zimbabwe; and if so, how and what is measurable? To date, there has not been specific case studies that highlight the extent to which western governments connived under Tony Blair to deprive most Zimbabweans of quality of life, access to financial support capital and aid, access to affordable primary health care drugs and medication

ii.   What is the nature of the sanctions that were imposed on Zimbabweans? What did they comprise of? How were they implemented in mainstream economic structures controlled by western governments? Using case studies of money transfer companies registered and operational in the United Kingdom specialising in the transfer of funds mainly to Zimbabwe by Zimbabweans based in there, I conduct semi -structured interviews with company representatives. Interviews help to establish the volume of business transactions and difficulties encountered by the company to adhere to 'restrictive measures' imposed by the government of the United Kingdom. Sub-questions are designed to establish the nature of UK government contact and involvement with those financial companies; through an array of standing instructions and legislative instruments. What surveillance is in place for companies dealing business with Zimbabwe? What do companies in business relationships know about sanctions and restrictive measures? I explore the fears to disclose information, fear for retribution by the British government.

iii.   What information are companies obliged to collect from their clients conducting business in Zimbabwe through them? How is it collected and how do the companies use such information at the level of British and European Union (EU) governments. How does the companies in question account to the UK government for its business associations and deals with Zimbabwean financial institutions? For example, are there any financial caps and limits imposed on the companies in respect of volumes of 'acceptable' or legally set limits? What are such limits? How do they impact on them? What sanctions, penalties and tariffs do they incur in the event of breaches?

iv.   Is it possible for some companies based in the UK and dealing with Zimbabwean bound financial throughput, to quantify what can be perceived as losses of business by the financial sector or government of Zimbabwe? What exactly is going on this sector regarding handling of Zimbabwean bound transactions? What is the severity of the sanctions? What are the implications in terms of operational challenges?

Literature Review – a brief of key themes

The subject of economic sanctions is wide. Academicians and scholars approach the subject from different contextual and theoretical perspectives. According to Weiss (1999) sanctions have invariably been used as a foreign policy tool designed to subjugate former colonies into compliance and submission to imperial demands. In his scholarship expose on sanctions Helms (1999) points out of Washington's 'sanctions madness' which has become an 'epidemic' that defeats the original purposes they serve. There has been growing misgivings about their consistency and transparency as detected by Conlon (1995), Von Braunmuhl, C & Kulessa, M (1995). Other intellectuals like Jing et al (2003), van Berggeijk (1989) raise serious questions and concerns on the benefits of sanctions in view of aggravated and sustained civilian suffering they cause. Muler & Muler (1999) note of tribulations exerted on innocent populations as powerful states disproportionately settles scores with weaker nation states. According to the Institute of International Economics, imposition of unilateral sanctions has spectacularly failed at 34% for 16 cases studied from 1914 to 1990. Current figures from World Finance postulate the success rate to be as low as 20-30%. Cashen (2017) observes failure of economic sanctions imposition dating back to 432 BC when the Athenian Empire levied unsuccessful economic sanctions against neighbouring Megara State which consequently failed[32].

The question of effectiveness of sanctions has drawn a lot of asymmetrical arguments in terms of how and under what conditions sanctions work. U-Jin Ang et al (2007) submits that in sanctions repertoire and narratives, there had not been systematic analysis on the role and salience of sanctions, their effectiveness and their effect. In a Select Committee on Economic Affairs 2nd report of Session 2006-07 entitled "The Impact of Economic Sanctions. Volume 1

---

[32] Cashen, Emily 2017 http://www.worldfinance.com/special-reports/the-impact-of-economic-sanctions. Accessed Jan 2, 18

Report" The British House of Lords, under Chapter 7, Section 109 highlights that:

> ...economic sanctions used in isolation from other policy instruments are extremely unlikely to force a target to make policy changes, especially where relations between the states involved are hostile more generally...
>
> ...even when economic sanctions are combined effectively, with other foreign policy instruments, on most occasions they play subordinate role to those other instruments. Economic sanctions can be counter-productive in a variety of ways, including when more vigorous cohesion in the form of force is needed but is forestalled by those making inflated claims for the value of sanctions as an alternative. Sanctions can also be counter-productive when what is required is much greater emphasis on economic, diplomatic and security incentives...furthermore, when the use of economic sanctions for this purpose is proposed, serious consideration should be given to the possibility that their overall effect will be counter-productive, even in symbolic terms... (p. 35)

What is important in the above clause is "where relations between the states involved are hostile". That qualification calls for the closer analysis of the nature of post-independence and especially post land reform relations between Britain and Zimbabwe. In 1997, New Labour government came to power. Difficulties in foreign policy relations, colonial baggage and neo coloniality are documented by Miyagawa, M. (1992), Herbst (1991), Lewis (2008), Raftopolous (2009), Ndlovu-Gatsheni (2009), Sithole (2015), Alexander et al (2017)

Theoretical Repository of Zimbabwean Sanctions

What does the following statement from the then Assistant Secretary of State Chester Crocker to the US Congress at a hearing in June 2001 mean?

'To separate the Zimbabwean people from Zanu-PF, we are going to have to make their economy scream, and I hope you, senators, have the stomach for what you have to do'[33]

The cumulative effect of evilness in politics tends to negate the concept of humanity. It reinforces how dare devils celebrated the suffering of the poor and dispossessed Africans. That evilness inevitably culminated in a *coup d'état* in which Robert Mugabe was deposed in November 2017. What must be made clear is that it was a long run with good old guerrilla Robert Mugabe as he put up a fierce struggle in which imperialism and stooges lost in the process.

Studies by McGillivray & Stam (2004), Bolks, & Al-Sowayel, (2000) and focus on effectiveness of international economic sanctions as a tool for coercive diplomacy. Coercive success or failure of international sanctions is limited because it is practically impossible to tell how long they should last to achieve substantive goals. In the case of the US sanctions against Cuba, they remained in place for decades under which the Cuban health delivery system developed to be one of the best models in the world. One reason why sanctions are withdrawn is when they succeed in bringing about change in policy or leadership in the target state. After Robert Mugabe proceeded to win two more elections after the imposition of sanctions through Zimbabwe Democracy Act and Recovery Act of 2001, Western diplomacy had no idea of how else they should handle him. The opposition Movement for Democratic Change (MDC) in Zimbabwe was in disarray as ZANU PF still commanded a lot of grassroots support especially in rural areas. The fact that in November 2017, Mugabe was succeeded by [his] Vice-President, Emmerson Mnangagwa – who rose to Presidency from the same ZANU PF party - does not signify in any way, a regime change agenda, but perpetuation of same philosophical ethos represented by the party. In his inaugural address President Mnangagwa has

---

[33] Putting Urban Legends to rest: What Chester Crocker actually said about Zimbabwe in 2001: February 13, 2012 article by Charles Ray, United States Ambassador to Zimbabwe (December 9, 2009 – August 2012 Found at: https://asnycnowradio.wordpress.com/2012/02/13/putting-urban-legends-to-rest-what-chester-crocker-actually-said-about-zimbabwe-in-2001/Accessed May 05,18

indicated at government policy level that Zimbabwe land reform will not be reversed but reformed to fit contextual changes of capacity building and optimal food security through high productivity. In his Acceptance Speech delivered by the new President at his inauguration on 24 November 2017, he specifically said that:

> … Dispossession of our ancestral land was the fundamental reason for waging the liberation struggle. It would be a betrayal of the brave men and women who sacrificed their lives in our liberation struggle if we were to reverse the gains we have made in reclaiming our land...
>
> ...as we go into the future, complex issues of land tenure will have to be addressed both urgently and, to ensure finality and closure to the ownership and management of this key resource which is central to our national stability and to sustained economic recovery. We dare not prevaricate on this key issue...[34]

Although this was not what the British expected, President Mnangagwa referred to total decoloniality of Southern Africa, hinting in the process, that South Africa was next in line. The ordinary citizens of Zimbabwe are imbued with self-consciousness and belief - a mutation of ZANU PF core beliefs. Said "Cde Muzvinavhu" (Lateral meaning: "rightful owner of land")

> … An important assertion on our land reform. We entrenched our land reform in our new constitution. Our President is spot on. The reprisal from the West did not dampen our revolutionary spirit, when sanctions were applied to punish us. Today we walk with our shoulders and heads up, while we take measures to improve its utilization. We are celebrating our Independence with dignity. It is heartening that our brothers and sisters in South Africa have now come to this important verge of land reform... They will learn from our takes and mistakes, but the bottom line is the necessary land reform to give credence and dignity to their freedom from satanic apartheid. A neo

---

[34] President Munangagwa's inauguration speech in full, The Chronicle. http://www.chronicle.co.zw/president-mnangagwas-inauguration-speech-in-full/; Accessed Jan 2, 18

apartheid economy in S Africa without land reform is anathema in Africa....

[Taken from 'Our land is for Zimbabweans: President': 38th Independence Celebration found at https://www.herald.co.zw/our-land-is-for-zimbabweans-president/Accessed April 18

Commitment to the liberation struggle of Zimbabwe remains the cornerstone of the ruling ZANU PF government:

"Many of our comrades, brothers and sisters perished in this war, but in the end the spilling of blood of our sisters and brothers brought us this independence... we should cherish, defend it. *Never again should we allow our land to be occupied by foreigners.* The burden of defending our land, passing on the patriotism in our blood is upon us to pass on to generations to come."[35]

In their theory of leadership turnover and democratisation, Bueno de Mesquita et al. 2002 discuss leadership renewal as a component considered for reversal of sanctions policy. They note that while turnover of leadership in sender states may occur, it may not necessarily lead to reversal of policy, (as has been the case in Cuba, Iran, North Korea) but withdrawal of sanctions is likely to occur following a leadership change in the target state. Based on the same predilection, here are some hypothetical conditions for Zimbabwe for sanctions withdrawal:

i   Mugabe who was the targeted leader for both targeted and economic sanctions has gone – US and the European Union is likely to lift the sanctions on the premises of encouraging what they term 'a new Zimbabwe' based on dictated democratic reforms. By removing sanctions, the US and European Union are likely to claim victory based on claims that they created the right and conducive conditions of economic hardships in which a 'soft' *coup d'état* took place resulting in the overthrow of Mugabe in November 2017. Thus,

---

[35] Our land is for Zimbabweans: President found at https://www.herald.co.zw/our-land-is-for-zimbabweans-president/Accessed April,18 18

sanctions worked to eject "a brutal dictator" from power. In fact, the "dictator" was so unpopular in his own country to a point where "he was expelled from his own party that he formed in the 60s"!

ii   The timing of coercive diplomacy and duration of sanctions (of almost 20 years) are symbiotically linked to leadership changes in both sender and target countries. For example, in the UK, Tony Blair (1997-2007) who put sanctions in palace together with USA's George Bush (2001-2009) have gone, Gordon Brown (2007-2010) replaced Tony Blair, David Cameron (2010-2016) replaced docile Gordon Brown, Theresa May (2016 to date) replaced David Cameroon. In the USA, Obama (2009-2017) replaced George W Bush while Donald Trump (2017 to date) is the current incumbent. There have been changes within the EU states that ratified imposition of sanctions on Zimbabwe: In France, Jacques Chirac (1995-2007) was replaced by a crony Nicholas Sarkozy (2007-2012), Francois Hollande (2012-2017) took over from a cranky Sarkozy, and Emmanuel Macron (2017 to date) is the current French President. Macron has a completely different agenda for the new world order. German Chancellor Markel congratulated the new President of Zimbabwe on his inauguration in November 2017. Current Spanish Prime Minister Mariano Rajoy Brey, has led since 21 December 2011. Thus, according to Bueno de Mesquita et al (2002) "Different Leadership typically represent different interests and therefore a leadership change in sender countries is likely to change foreign policy and diplomatic coercion" (p. 155). These changes are likely to influence a seismic shift in policy towards Zimbabwe's economic sanctions policy. Already, at the time of writing this report, there is a new thinking regarding Zimbabwean sanctions as individual countries side step them to pledge bi-lateral relations with Zimbabwe[36].

iii   As argued by Smith (1999) and Kaempfer & Lowenberg (1988), domestic politics in both sender and target nations are likely to drive the application or withdrawal of sanctions. Western countries are competing for exploitation of mineral ore resources

---

[36] Australia ready to engage Zimbabwe: Envoy: The Herald at
http://www.herald.co.zw/australia-ready-to-engage-zim-envoy/, Accessed Jan 5, 18

from Zimbabwe. This comes against a background where Zimbabwe registered considerable success in its "Look East" policy through multilateral trade deals with China. According to McGillivray (2004), if a new leader represents different interests, a leadership change in the target state could lead to a change in policy that initially aggravated the sender state, causing the withdrawal of sanctions. President Munangagwa is from a liberation struggle background of ZANU PF military wing, [We bear in mind that the obliteration of liberation struggles political parties in Southern Africa by western democracy is an ongoing agenda which falls outside this sanction research remit for now] - and hence [his] ideological interests may not be homogenous to opposition politics as supported by the West. International capital will dangle sweeteners to influence positionality and status quo. A week after the inauguration of President Munangagwa in November 2017, British Foreign Secretary, Boris Johnson released a press statement: "...Britain could take steps to stabilize Zimbabwe's foreign currency system and extend a bridging loan to help it clear World Bank and African Development Bank arrears, but such support depends on democratic progress..."[37] Although British's economy is in tailspin because of Brexit, we bear in mind of political mind games that former colonies use to influence or assert foreign policy and authority in their domination of small states.

iv Leadership turnover in either the sender or target state can lead to the end of sanctions, but it does not necessarily mean that it will. There is evidence that President Mnangagwa who came to power in November 2017 has struggled to meet the conditionalities for lifting of economic sanctions because the bar is being lifted. The goalposts are being shifted using the criterion of meeting democratic reforms as dictated by the West. What is the standard definition of 'free and fair elections'? If elections do not fall in the favour of those advocating for sanctions and those backed by the West, what are the implications in as far as fair play is concerned? It is only when the new leader draws support from different political groups that

---

[37] Johnson: UK support for Zimbabwe linked to democratic progress...ewn.co.za at Http://ewn.co.za/2017/11/29/johnson-uk-financeial-support-for-zim-linked-to-democratic-progress, Accessed Jan 2, 18

leadership change is expected to change affect sanctions policy. As the situations stands, the ruling ZANU PF government remains in variants with opposition policies – for example, on key aspects of governance including land reform programme policy. Although some key opposition figures have resisted embracing the new Zimbabwe government, there is evidence from some opposition MPs that they support efforts by the new government[38] Furthermore, domestic political institutions have a role in mediating the effect that leadership change has on sanctions duration. This is precisely because the nature of domestic political institutions (like the army, political affiliations, Church Leadership or institutions of higher learning) determines political interests.

Zimbabwean Economic Sanctions Package – 2001-2018

Zimbabwe Democracy and Economic Recovery Act of 2001, 115 STAT 962, Public Law 107-99, 494 came into law on 21 December 2001 for purposes of "...providing for a transition to democracy and to promote economic recovery in Zimbabwe..." It was part of the Statement of Foreign Policy of the United States aimed at

"… Supporting the people of Zimbabwe in their struggle to effect peaceful democratic change, achieve broad-based and equitable economic growth and restore the rule of law..."

In it, the law barred transaction of financial businesses and credit lines of International Financial Institutions including the International Money Fund (IMF) that had supported Zimbabwe financially in multilateral development projects including reconstruction.

Section 4 of the act stipulated that the Act would regulate and support for democratic transition and economic recovery through identification of economic mismanagement, undemocratic processes

---

[38] This is based on informal interview conducted with an opposition MP for Sunningndale, Ms Margaret Matienga who praised the new Mnagagwa vision for political and economic change. The MP said the Finance and Economic Planning Minister's Budget was 'exceptionally good in that it is realistic and achievable'.

including the costly deployment of Zimbabwean troops to the Democratic Republic of Congo (DRC). 4 (a) (2-5) involved statements for suspended projects by IMF, International Development Association, new lending for development projects and disbursement of funding for ongoing projects under previously agreed loans, credits and guarantees to the Government of Zimbabwe

Other Restrictions under 4 (b) (1-2) Under "Recovery" include Bi-lateral and multilateral debt relief, Multilateral Financing Restrictions, premised on 'good governance' conditionality. Restoration of the rule of law that related direct to the land reform programme including "respect for ownership and title property, freedom of speech and associations, end to the lawlessness, violence and intimidation sponsored, condoned or tolerated by government of Zimbabwe and the ruling ZANU PF party or their supporters or entities" The Act also set out conditions for presidential and national elections. The Act also stipulated land reform commitments of the government of Zimbabwe, citing that government was to commit itself to "equitable, legal and transparent land reform programme" in line with the resolutions of the International Donors' Conference and Resettlement in Zimbabwe of September 1998.

Section 5 focuses on "Support for Democratic Institutions, the free Press and Independent Media and the Rule of Law" while Section 6 focus on sanctions "on the actions to be taken against individuals responsible for violence and the breakdown of the rule of law in Zimbabwe" This section mandates the US government to consult with the European Union and member states including Canada and "appropriate foreign countries" that trade with Zimbabwe.

Under 6 (1-4) The Act gives the provision for member states to identify and share information regarding individuals responsible for the breakdown of the rule of law, politically motivated violence and intimidation in Zimbabwe; identifying assets of the said individuals held outside Zimbabwe; implement travel and economic sanctions against those individuals and their associates and families. It is against the background of the provisions of this section that the Federal Register, Part 3 Volume 70 No. 226 of 2005 was implemented through the Presidential Executive Order 13391 on pursuance of Section 6 (1-4) of the Zimbabwe Democracy and Economic Recovery Act of 2001. The Presidential Order, which Blocks property of additional persons deemed to be undermining democratic processes or institutions in Zimbabwe, was renewed by George Bush in 2005 and Obama on his election in 2009 and re-election in 2012 and has since been renewed by Donald Trump in 2017. The order containing documented individuals who are perceived to be influential in Zimbabwean politics is filed under Reference 71204 of the Federal Register. This Order forms the basis of what is now commonly referred to as "Smart" or "Targeted" Sanctions on specific individuals and their entities in Zimbabwe.

EU involvement in Zimbabwean Sanctions: An Outline of the Law

Zimbabwean sanctions are a package that was crafted by Britain and roped to the United States for drafting of the legislation and overall implementation. This is because of two factors: In its imperialist dealing, Britain does not want to be seen to be on the forefront of touting punitive measures like sanctions and embargoes. Because of the vicious nature of British coloniality and imperialist abuse, Britain has terrible records and relationships with almost all its former colonies. In international relations and public records, Britain does not want to be perceived in bad light and has notably struggled with image problems in atonement of its deprecating sins and heinous crimes committed in former colonies.

Even at the height of South Africa's apartheid in the 70s and 80s, Britain, a famous but reluctant denier was hesitant to dismantle apartheid through punitive measures and sanctions as their Margaret Thatcher maintained that sanctions would hurt the South African economy. Although this was about maintaining imperialism and white supremacy, Britain rather stayed quietly in the background and pretended that all is well in terms of foreign policy articulation and elaboration. Instead, it was the Western World that condemned apartheid the most in the end - while Britain maintained peculiar silence on applying sanctions to decimate apartheid-ruled regime of South Africa. There is a lot of pretentious attitude especially in matters perceived to be controversial, unpopular and imperialist in policy.

The British are good at using the tactic of hitting very hard, for that matter even below the belt – from behind the curtains – surreptitiously 'unnoticed' as it were. In the case of Zimbabwean sanctions, Britain remained 'smart' by making their demands from behind the curtains to have its former colony stitched up in the public gallery 'by the USA'. It is well-known that the land dispute was between Britain and Zimbabwe as many political theorists' struggle to link the USA to British neo-colonial agenda. Those who understand the texture of symbiotic partnership in conspiracy and evil designs can easily interpret USA-UK enduring links. But elsewhere, we have heard of the US-British 'special relationship' from the post-second world war of 1945's Marshall Aid Plan to George Bush-Tony Blair invasion of Iraq in 2003.

Here is the background of links in the web of alliances and coalitions:

The European Commission, European Union, Restrictive measures (sanctions) in force (Regulations based on Article 215 TFEU and Decisions adopted in the framework of the Common Foreign and Security Policy) are used as part of legal instruments shared on common security measure of the EU. The relationship is that:

> Article 215 of the Treaty on the Functioning of the European Union (TFEU) provides a legal basis for the interruption or reduction, in part or completely, of the Union's economic and financial relations with one or more third countries, where such restrictive measures are necessary to achieve the objectives of the Common Foreign and Security Policy (CFSP).

This works in synergy with other provisions of the EU law in terms of restrictive measures in force.

> The legislative measures based on Article 215 TFEU and those based on the relevant provisions of the Treaty establishing the European Community (in the years prior to 1 December 2009: Articles

60 and 301) and the relevant CFSP Decisions and (prior to 1 December 2009) Common Positions, including those which merely provide for measures for which no specific Regulation was made, such as restrictions on admission.

Under EU restrictive measures in force, Countries affected are listed under Table of Contents which includes Zimbabwe. Under Zimbabwe, the following terms and conditions are specified in EU Law:
http://eurlex.europa.eu/LexUriServ/LexUriServ.do?uri=OJ:L:2011:042:0006:0023:EN:PDF

see: CORRIGENDA Corrigendum to Council Decision 2011/101/CFSP of 15 February 2011 concerning restrictive measures against Zimbabwe (Official Journal of the European Union L 42 of 16 February 2011);

COUNCIL Notice for the attention of the persons, entities and bodies to which restrictive measures provided for in Council Decision 2011/101/CFSP apply (2011/C 49/03) COUNCIL OF THE EUROPEAN UNION;

NOTICES FROM EUROPEAN UNION INSTITUTIONS, BODIES, OFFICES AND AGENCIES COUNCIL Notice for the attention of the persons, entities and bodies to which restrictive measures provided for in Council Decision 2011/101/CFSP, as amended by Council Decision 2014/98/CFSP, and in Council Regulation (EC) No 314/2004 as amended by Council Regulation (EU) No 153/2014 concerning restrictive measures against Zimbabwe apply (2014/C 48/02); NOTICES FROM EUROPEAN UNION INSTITUTIONS, BODIES, OFFICES AND AGENCIES COUNCIL Notice for the attention of the persons, entities and bodies to which restrictive measures provided for in Council Decision 2011/101/CFSP, as amended by Council Decision (CFSP) 2015/277 and in Council Regulation (EC)

No 314/2004 concerning restrictive measures against
Zimbabwe apply (2015/C 62/02);

NOTICES FROM EUROPEAN UNION
INSTITUTIONS, BODIES, OFFICES AND AGENCIES
COUNCIL Notice for the attention of the persons, entities
and bodies to which restrictive measures provided for in
Council Decision 2011/101/CFSP, as amended by Council
Decision (CFSP) 2016/220 and in Council Regulation (EC)
No 314/2004 concerning restrictive measures against
Zimbabwe apply (2016/C 61/03);

As amended or implemented by:
> http://eur-lex.europa.eu/legal-
> content/EN/TXT/PDF/?uri=CELEX:32014D0098

> Notice to listed persons, entities and bodies (OJ C 48,
> 20.2.2014, p. 2)
> http://eur-lex.europa.eu/legal-
> content/EN/TXT/PDF/?uri=CELEX:32016D0220&from
> =EN

> http://eur-
> lex.europa.eu/LexUriServ/LexUriServ.do?uri=OJ:L:2004:0
> 55:0001:0013:EN:PDF

see: IV (Notices) NOTICES FROM EUROPEAN UNION
       INSTITUTIONS, BODIES, OFFICES AND AGENCIES
       COUNCIL Notice for the attention of the persons, entities
       and bodies to which restrictive measures provided for in
       Council Decision 2011/101/CFSP, as amended by Council
       Decision 2014/98/CFSP, and in Council Regulation (EC)
       No 314/2004 as amended by Council Regulation (EU) No
       153/2014 concerning restrictive measures against
       Zimbabwe apply (2014/C 48/02)

IV (Notices) NOTICES FROM EUROPEAN UNION INSTITUTIONS, BODIES, OFFICES AND AGENCIES COUNCIL Notice for the attention of the persons, entities and bodies to which restrictive measures provided for in Council Decision 2011/101/CFSP, as amended by Council Decision (CFSP) 2015/277 and in Council Regulation (EC) No 314/2004 concerning restrictive measures against Zimbabwe apply (2015/C 62/02);

Notice for the attention of the data subjects to whom the restrictive measures provided for in Council Regulation (EC) No 314/2004 concerning certain restrictive measures in respect of Zimbabwe apply (2015/C 62/03);

IV (Notices) NOTICES FROM EUROPEAN UNION INSTITUTIONS, BODIES, OFFICES AND AGENCIES COUNCIL Notice for the attention of the persons, entities and bodies to which restrictive measures provided for in Council Decision 2011/101/CFSP, as amended by Council Decision (CFSP) 2016/220 and in Council Regulation (EC) No 314/2004 concerning restrictive measures against Zimbabwe apply (2016/C 61/03);

Notice for the attention of the data subjects to whom the restrictive measures provided for in Council Regulation (EC) No 314/2004 concerning certain restrictive measures in respect of Zimbabwe apply (2016/C 61/04);

Addendum to Council Regulation (EC) No 314/2004 of 19 February 2004 concerning certain restrictive measures in respect of Zimbabwe (1) Statement concerning the Council Common Position renewing restrictive measures against Zimbabwe and the Council Regulation concerning certain restrictive measures in respect of Zimbabwe.

As amended or implemented by:

COMMISSION REGULATION (EC) No 1488/2004 of 20 August 2004 amending Council; Regulation (EC) No 314/2004 concerning certain restrictive measures in respect of Zimbabwe

COMMISSION REGULATION (EC) No 1367/2005 of 19 August 2005 amending Council Regulation (EC) No 314/2004 concerning certain restrictive measures in respect of Zimbabwe;
I (Acts whose publication is obligatory)
COUNCIL REGULATION (EC) No 1791/2006 of 20 November 2006 adapting certain Regulations and Decisions in the fields of free movement of goods, freedom of movement of persons, company law, competition policy, agriculture (including veterinary and phytosanitary legislation), transport policy, taxation, statistics, energy, environment, cooperation in the fields of justice and home affairs, customs union, external relations, common foreign and security policy and institutions, by reason of the accession of Bulgaria and Romania;

COMMISSION IMPLEMENTING REGULATION (EU) No 145/2013 of 19 February 2013 amending Council Regulation (EC) No 314/2004 concerning certain restrictive measures in respect of Zimbabwe;

II (Non-legislative acts) REGULATIONS COUNCIL REGULATION (EU) No 517/2013 of 13 May 2013 adapting certain regulations and decisions in the fields of free movement of goods, freedom of movement for persons, company law, competition policy, agriculture, food safety, veterinary and phytosanitary policy, transport policy, energy, taxation, statistics, trans-European networks, judiciary and fundamental rights, justice, freedom and security, environment, customs union, external relations, foreign, security and defence policy and institutions, by reason of the accession of the Republic of Croatia;

REGULATIONS COUNCIL REGULATION (EU) No 153/2014 of 17 February 2014 amending Regulation (EC) No 314/2004 concerning certain restrictive measures in respect of Zimbabwe and repealing Regulation (EU) No 298/2013 (Notice to listed persons, entities and bodies (OJ C 48, 20.2.2014, p. 2)

(Non-legislative acts) REGULATIONS COUNCIL REGULATION (EU) 2015/1919 of 26 October 2015 amending Regulation (EC) No 314/2004 concerning certain restrictive measures in respect of Zimbabwe

(Non-legislative acts) REGULATIONS COUNCIL REGULATION (EU) 2016/214 of 15 February 2016 amending Regulation (EC) No 314/2004 concerning certain restrictive measures in respect of Zimbabwe

COMMISSION IMPLEMENTING REGULATION (EU) 2016/218 of 16 February 2016 amending Council Regulation (EC) No 314/2004 concerning certain restrictive measures in respect of Zimbabwe

NOTICES FROM EUROPEAN UNION INSTITUTIONS, BODIES, OFFICES AND AGENCIES COUNCIL Notice for the attention of the persons, entities and bodies to which restrictive measures provided for in Council Decision 2011/101/CFSP, as amended by Council Decision (CFSP) 2016/220 and in Council Regulation (EC) No 314/2004 concerning restrictive measures against Zimbabwe apply (2016/C 61/03);

Notice for the attention of the data subjects to whom the restrictive measures provided for in Council Regulation

122

(EC) No 314/2004 concerning certain restrictive measures in respect of Zimbabwe apply (2016/C 61/04)

Through the EU legislation, all countries affiliated to the European Union are mandated to implement sanctions, manage the suspension of the freezing of funds and economic resources about certain natural and legal persons, entities and bodies Council Regulation under (EU) 2015/1919 (OJ L 281, 27.10.2015, p. 1. They are mandated to monitor information on data concerning listed persons, entities and bodies in Zimbabwe - that can be included in the list of persons, entities and bodies (freezing of funds and economic resources) Council Regulation (EU) 2016/214 (OJ L 40, 17.2.2016, p. 1) Furthermore, EU legislation requires member states to identify list of persons, entities and bodies benefitting from the suspension Commission Implementing Regulation (EU) 2016/218 (OJ L 40, 17.2.2016, p. 7) as read with Notice to listed persons, entities and bodies (OJ C 61, 17.2.2016, p. 2) Notice to data subjects (OJ C 61, 17.2.2016, p. 3) - which outlines list of persons, entities and bodies involved and targeted in the freezing of funds and other economic resources.

Characteristics of Sanctions Trajectories

History deploys Mugabe as a liberator and a dictator (Meredith 2009). Some Zimbabweans define him as a founder and destroyer of the revolutionary ZANU PF party. For others, he is a nationalist and a statesman (Martin & Johnson 1981), (Sithole 2014). Many also find him to be a despot and tyrant (Godwin 2010). Political dispatches portray him as an extremist, shrewd and stubborn politician - of existentialist and abstract narratives (Moorcroft 2011). What is common unitary theme in monolithic patriotism, ontological African revolution renaissance of land redistribution - is Mugabe's *'ego conquiro'* in defining what Maldonado-Torres (2007) terms 'the coloniality of being'. The "being" is characterised his direct rhetoric mantra, a weapon that he exploits to full capacity when he was discharging and debunking barren ideological mind-set of Tony Blair's New Labour government.

High Politics and High Moral Ground:

Having said that, we wish no harm to anyone. We are Zimbabweans, we are Africans, we are not English. We are not Europeans. We love Africa, we love Zimbabwe, we love our Independence. We are working together in our region to improve the lot of our people. Let no one interfere with our processes. Let no one who is negative want to spoil what we are doing for ourselves in order to unite Africa.

We belong to this continent. We do not mind having and bearing sanctions banning us from Europe. We are not Europeans. We have not asked for any inch of Europe, any square inch of that territory. So (Tony) Blair, keep your England and let me keep my Zimbabwe.

Economically, we are still an occupied country, 22 years after our Independence. Accordingly, my Government has decided to do the only right and just thing by taking back land and giving it to its rightful indigenous, black owners who lost it in circumstances of colonial pillage. This process is being done in accordance with the rule of law as enshrined in our national Constitution and laws. It is in pursuit of true justice as we know and understand it, and so we have no apologies to make to anyone.

[President Robert Mugabe: Address to the World Summit on Sustainable Development, Tuesday 3 September 2002]

High Rhetoric, Drama and High Demonization

Let Europe keep their homosexual nonsense there and live with it. We will never have it here. The act [homosexuality] is not humane… Any diplomat who talks about homosexuality will be kicked out. There is no excuse and we won't listen to them.

[President Mugabe: Independence Speech 18 April 2014]

Personality cult and Personalisation

Mr President, clearly the history of the struggle for our own national and people's rights is unknown to the president of the United

States of America. He thinks the Declaration of Human Rights starts with his last term in office! He thinks he can introduce to us, who bore the brunt of fighting for the freedoms of our peoples, the virtues of the Universal Declaration of Human Rights. What rank hypocrisy!

Mr President, I lost eleven precious years of my life in the jail of a white man whose freedom and well-being I have assured from the first day of Zimbabwe's Independence. I lost a further fifteen years fighting white injustice in my country.

Ian Smith is responsible for the deaths of well over 50,000 of my people. I bear scars of his tyranny which Britain and America condoned. I meet his victims every day. Yet he walks free. He farms free. He talks freely, associates freely under a black Government. We taught him democracy. We gave him back his humanity.

He would have faced a different fate here and in Europe if the 50,000 he killed were Europeans. Africa has not called for a Nuremberg trial against the white world which committed heinous crimes against its own humanity. It has not hunted perpetrators of this genocide, many of whom live to this day, nor has it got reparations from those who offended against it. Instead it is Africa which is in the dock, facing trial from the same world that persecuted it for centuries.

Let Mr. Bush read history correctly. Let him realise that both personally and in his representative capacity as the current President of the United States, he stands for this "civilisation" which occupied, which colonised, which incarcerated, which killed. He has much to atone for and very little to lecture us on the Universal Declaration of Human Rights. His hands drip with innocent blood of many nationalities.

[President Robert Mugabe: Speech at the UN General Assembly, 26 September 2007]

Logarithm of Punitive Measures

Total breakdown of Zimbabwe British relations can be summed up in one of Mugabe's daring speeches at the burial of his sister at the National Heroes Shrine on 1st August 2010:

...To hell with European and Americans! We say hell! Hell! Hell! With them. They will not decide who will who is going to lead the people of Zimbabwe!

... Europe and America want to keep these odious sanctions. We are still being treated as if we don't own this country. They want to tell us, do A, B and C of that, remove so-and-so and they are now saying Mugabe must go first...Whoever told them that their will is above that of the people of Zimbabwe?

The only white man you can trust is a dead one.

Our party must continue to strike fear into the heart of the white man, our real enemy...!

Methodology – Guidance on Selection Criterion of Research Companies for research

Qualitative methods are descriptive and inferential - in other words, data obtained must be interpreted through evidence. I use the qualitative approach for this research to investigate how Britain and the EU implemented sanctions following the enactment of the Zimbabwe Democracy and Economic Recovery Act (2001) as amended in 2018. I also gather evidence of how UK financial watchdogs robustly monitors companies and individuals in financial traffic to Zimbabwe. It is the prerogative of this research to check on whether money transfer companies hold data on customers who circumvent restrictive measures and sanctions in their financial dealings with Zimbabwe. I investigate whether there are companies who have bypassed financial systems deliberately or unknowingly; [and how] they incur penalties for such acts.

For this study, I use a unison of sampling techniques. By using *purposive* sampling, we are defining the *macro* financial composition of the business environment. First, we specify our requirements by sampling companies involved in money transfer business to Zimbabwe. Their global financial environment is part of an economy sector with major players, investors and markets. From the other end of the sectorial spectrum, Zimbabwe is part of that market. Second, at *micro* levels, we specify how such UK-based companies operate.

How are money transfer companies and their agencies monitored for breaches on ZDERA? They must comply not only with UK financial sector regulations but with EU and OFAC regulations specifically on implementation of Zimbabwean sanctions. How do they do that? Thus, although companies may not necessarily transfer funds [only] to Zimbabwe as a destination, we seek to establish functional remit and compliance with statutory requirements as demanded by EU member states subjectively on money laundering and economic sanctions.

The second phase of my sampling procedures involves selection of companies through *internet sources of secondary data*. Financial companies and money transfer agencies must be fit for purpose in reflecting research themes for this study. Thus, using bench marks of *known research criteria* - highlighted in above-mentioned sampling procedure, we search for *specific* companies that are involved in business financial transactions – money transfers Zimbabwe. For example, we narrowed research criterion by searching for money transfer companies based in the United Kingdom. Results were refined even further as *'UK-London Money Transfer Companies to Zimbabwe'*. On definition of capsule key words, I *google* internet search engine to find companies based [only] in London, UK. [Google: "UK London Money Transfer Companies to Zimbabwe"][39] yielded 108 000 results in 1.12 seconds. It is from the [www] *World Wide Web* returns on google search engine that I randomly selected on London-based companies to conduct interviews. Follow up by telephone enquiries with Company Customer Services Departments was established for interview facilitation.

As highlighted by Brynan (2007) semi-structured interviews are probably the most employed in qualitative research. This is so because they are effective in gaining greater interest and flexibility in terms of probing for more information. This important point is also emphasized by Santakokos (2007: 248) who contends that *'there are no*

---

[39]https://www.google.co.uk/search?rlz=1C1HLDY_enGB693GB698&ei=d Ja4WtTfAYTisAfVoLeoAw&q=UK-London+Money+Transfer+Companies+to+Zimbabwe&oq=UK-London+Money+Transfer+Companies+to+Zimbabwe&gs_l=psy-ab.12...11197.836955.0.840486.1.1.0.0.0.0.787.787.6-1.1.0....0...1c.2.64.psy-ab..0.0.0....0.rxqUK1WI0uc

restrictions on the wording of questions, order of questions or on how interview schedule is structured...' In my view as an interviewer, the structure of my interviews is flexible – in terms of application and conceptualization of Zimbabwean economic sanctions. This enables free-flowing narratives that are designed to reflect accurate data obtained direct from respondents.

Based on drawn *Interview Schedules*, (Appendix 1), I conduct 20 interviews with company *spokespersons* in selected vehicle companies of this research. All companies are based in London. We avoid use of proper designations or titles in transcripts, submissions or findings in line with ethical considerations of protecting subjects of this research. Interviewees are referred to as 'Spokesperson[s] rather than divisional directors. Branch managers, chief executive etcetera to maintain anonymity. There are some companies that allowed the researcher to interview two or more of its executives working or heading different business units. I distinguish as 'Spokesperson 1 or Spokesperson 2'. This term is gender neutral and helps eliminate bias or discrimination.

Anonymizing Research

To protect the identity of companies I worked with in my research, certain information on each company was redacted, omitted, altered or totally removed from my transcripts and qualitative data gathered. This anonymized companies in terms of identity of strategic operational affiliates. Any similarities of certain information in terms of corporate missions and statements - by wording and contextual texts are purely coincidental. In addition, background information has not been 'copied and pasted' from company sources or their websites. Information used in this research has been properly and legitimately obtained by the researcher with consent and legal guidance. Identities of company directors and employees have been protected in line with Data Protection Act 1998's eight (8) principles[40].

---

[40] The principles are a code of good practice for processing personal data. Expanded information on each of the principles is available in Schedule 1 part 2 of the Act.

Data is used exclusively and specifically for purposes of this research. I observe research protocols enshrined in the ethical codes of conduct for a research of this nature including copyright laws and rules on plagiarism. I fully subscribe to legislation on information gathering and sharing in the UK and in Zimbabwe including The Official Secrets Act 1989 (c. 6) is an Act of the Parliament of the United Kingdom that repeals and replaces section 2 of the Official Secrets Act 1911, thereby removing the public interest defence created by that section. We are mindful and cognizant of the terms of reference and conditionality of the US OFAC (https://www.treasury.gov/resource-center/sanctions/Programs/pages/zimb.aspx) and those of the UK Information Commissioner Office at https://www.gov.uk/government/organisations/information-commissioner-s-office, Data Controller found at

---

Schedule 1 part 2 of the Data Protection Act

First principle - Personal data shall be processed fairly and lawfully and shall not be processed unless at least one of the conditions in Schedule 2 is met and in the case of sensitive personal data, at least one of the conditions set out in Schedule 3 or either of the two Statutory Instruments below is met.

Schedule 2

Schedule 3

Statutory Instrument 417/2000

Statutory Instrument 2905/2002

Second principle - Personal data shall be obtained only for one or more specified and lawful purposes and shall not be further processed in any manner incompatible with that purpose or those purposes.

Third principle - Personal data shall be adequate, relevant and not excessive in relation to the purpose or purposes for which they are processed.

Fourth principle - Personal data shall be accurate and, where necessary, kept up to date.

Fifth principle - Personal data processed for any purpose or purposes shall not be kept for longer than is necessary for that purpose or those purposes.

Sixth principle - Personal data shall be processed in accordance with the rights of data subjects under this Act.

Seventh principle - Appropriate technical and organisational measures shall be taken against unauthorised or unlawful processing of personal data and against accidental loss or destruction of, or damage to, personal data.

Eighth principle - Personal data shall not be transferred to a country or territory outside the European Economic Area, unless that country or territory ensures an adequate level of protection for the rights and freedoms of data subjects in relation to the processing of personal data.

https://www.dataprotection.ie/documents/forms/NewAGuideFor DataControllers.pdf. We take note of UK Economic Sanctions Guidelines on Zimbabwe at

http://www.legislation.gov.uk/uksi/2017/754/contents/made including S.I. 2009/847; amended by S.I. 2013/472, 2014/383 and 2017/560. I also note specifications of The European Union Financial Sanctions (Amendment of Information Provisions) Regulations 2017 as read with 2006 c.46. Section 1210 was amended by S.I. 2008/565, 2008/567, 2008/1950, 2012/1809 and 2013/3115 on Zimbabwe (Financial Sanctions) Regulations 2009. As a researcher, I also remain informed of implications of Money Laundering legislation and information Governance protocols relating to companies involved in money transfer business - including corporate companies' and their affiliates as espoused at

https://www.gov.uk/topic/business-tax/money-laundering-regulations/latest.

www.legislation.gov.uk/ukpga/1998/29/schedule/1

I use the following research instruments to collect information. Data obtained helps to some of the research questions and overall research objectives of this study.

a. Research tool (i) - Interviews

I use semi-structured interviews to collect data from host companies for my fieldwork research. I have attached Interviews Schedule Guide for semi structured interviews in the addendum. Interviews are semi-structured to allow room to discuss peripheral and collateral issues that often arises when collecting quantitative data from fieldwork. I am aware that a rigid structure of questions is likely to be inhibitive especially in eliciting for more information related to themes of my research. As noted by Burns (1999: 118) "Interviews are a popular and widely used means of collecting qualitative data." This allows room for further clarifications if needed.

b. Research tool (ii) - Desktop Research Sources of Data:

The following UK legislation and regulations are specific in their complementary functions in implementing Zimbabwean Sanctions. The requirements of the UK anti-money laundering regime are set out in:

- The Money Laundering, Terrorist Financing and Transfer of Funds Regulations 2017 (SI 2017 No. 692)[41]
- The Proceeds of Crime Act 2002 [42](as amended by the Crime and Courts Act 2013[43] and the Serious Crime Act 2015)[44]
- The Money Laundering Regulations 2007 (SI 2007 No. 2157)[45]
- The Terrorism Act 2000 [46](as amended by the Anti-Terrorism, Crime and Security Act 2001[47], the Terrorism Act 2006[48] and the Terrorism Act 2000 and Proceeds of Crime Act 2002 (Amendment) Regulations 2007)[49]

Research Findings

Because of the combative nature of this research, we digress from making theoretical allusions based on regression analysis and number crunching. We desist from simplified observations of quadratic or polynomial equations, data tabulations, the "yes "and "no" tick boxes - neither are we obsessed with upper percentiles and statistical integers. We formulate salient findings from semi structured interviews as follows:

Findings from Semi Structured and In-Depth Interviews:
(a) All respondents interviewed stated that there is no limit in terms of what individuals or organisations can repatriate to Zimbabwe as cash. There is no written instruction or standing orders regarding cash transfer restrictions destined for Zimbabwe. All Interviewees said that are involved in repatriation of cash to Zimbabwe from local businesses, non-governmental organisations, private individuals and other agencies. However, they all cited a very complex process in terms of requirements that must appear on the *"Schedule of Drawdown"*. Cash donations or aid must be verifiable in

---

[41]http://www.legislation.gov.uk/uksi/2017/692/pdfs/uksi_20170692_en.pdf
[42] http://www.legislation.gov.uk/ukpga/2002/29/contents
[43] http://www.legislation.gov.uk/ukpga/2013/22/contents/enacted
[44] http://www.legislation.gov.uk/ukpga/2015/9/contents/enacted
[45] http://www.legislation.gov.uk/uksi/2007/2157/pdfs/uksi_20072157_en.pdf
[46] http://www.legislation.gov.uk/ukpga/2000/11/contents
[47] http://www.legislation.gov.uk/ukpga/2001/24/contents
[48] http://www.legislation.gov.uk/ukpga/2006/11/contents
[49] http://www.legislation.gov.uk/uksi/2007/3398/contents/made

terms of sources for funds and how that cash has been moved from account to account. Money transfer agencies are expected to follow a very stringent process of establishing the source of funding and senders are required to justify their cash in terms of accountability and traceability. Companies intending to place funds for transfer must show proof of authenticity via submission of Certificates of Incorporation, their schedules of directors and trustees, consultancy and managers for verification. If necessary, notarial documents have been demanded by the system for amounts of £20 million or more including access to books of accounts. Money transfer agencies believe that it is difficult and complex processes that deter financiers from dealing with Zimbabwe because some of them do not want to be traced. Respondents believe that, as a result, Zimbabwe as a country and their beneficiaries have lost millions of pounds in the two decades of economic sanctions.

(b) All Money Transfer Agencies (MTA's) confirm that they work with electronic systems designed to detect all recipients of funds transferred to destination by wire. While the said system does not discriminate in terms of nationalities of recipients or their geographical location, there is evidence from interviews that several Zimbabwean individuals and firms on the OFAC sanctions list have been barred from receiving cash through formal money transfer channels from the United Kingdom. 17 out of 20 money transfer companies confirmed that they have received *"Activity Reports"* indicating *"holds"* for transactions destined to some Zimbabwean companies or individuals on the sanctions list. If money is being transferred direct from a Bank through a MTA to a sanctions-listed recipient in Zimbabwe, the system flags up the transaction – thereby disabling the intended transfers. 15 out of 20 companies confirmed that money donations flagged up were destined to alleviate the ravaging effects of drought, cyclones or hurricanes that hit Zimbabwe at a time that the country had formalised the use of the US Dollar as its currency from 2009.

(c) One interviewee whose MTA operates worldwide – including in Zimbabwe where they run MTA under the RBZ lamented the biting effects of sanctions on Zimbabwe finance market:

> ...Zimbabwe cannot receive direct aid money because lines of finance have been cut; the banks in Zimbabwe cannot borrow money from European Banks like they used to do. Credit facilities have been cut off by European Investment Banks and the African Development Bank. The Banking sector in Zimbabwe is aware of the hostile European financial markets and has been seeking funding from more friendly banks in former Eastern Bloc Countries including from Turkey and Romania. The cost of borrowing European money and propping it up with local surrogate money is unsustainably high. Unfortunately, all aid and financial transactions have got to pass through banks and Zimbabwe has been marginalised by financial embargoes preferred in 2001. That is bad... and these guys do not have a conscience or a heart for the suffering majority in Zimbabwe...

One interviewee talked about the punitive nature of capitalism and capital accumulation:

> ... Our organisation was hit by a spate of fines. We are expected to verify the underlying source of funds always. We need to know of the activity that generates specific transactions to Zimbabwe. We are instructed to trace "dirty money" ... drug money, funds going to terrorist organisations and tax invasion funds that may end up in Zimbabwe and other third world countries. This must be supported by evidence that detail sources of funding...
>
> ... In the past, we have had individuals breaking down chunks of finance by sending money from our different world-wide agencies. In the process, our auditing failed to pick *systems failures* resulting in us incurring heavy fines. We are expected for example to pick up paper trail for suspicious funds and activities sent from our different world-wide branches to European recipients - let's say funds for dialysis machines meant for shipment to Zimbabwe. In short, we have paid a heavy price as an organisation...

Another respondent completed their interview by teasing out snippets and observations that illustrate adversity of sanctions and their inauspicious effects as they continue to take a huge toll on the financial money market in Zimbabwe:

> ... Zimbabwe as a country, has not only suffered financial prejudice but struggled in terms of sanctions-related losses in 'goods and services'. .... You must bear in mind that during the run up to changes in governments in November 2017, Europe had increased the sanctions regime quietly and sanctions were even deeper than you think... ...even huge financial institutions and banks were caught and fined in the process. All those cases are a clear loss due to sanctions. The fact that banks are deterred from conducting what would be otherwise normal business means unquantifiable losses at country level...

(d) All respondents confirmed that they are severely monitored and asked to submit reports for suspicious monetary transfer activities for transactions picked up by monetary authorities. They made references to company briefings and meetings specifically designed to meet compliance to statutory regulations.

Schedule of Interviews Conducted with MTAs in London, UK: Nov 2017 – Apr 2018			
Company	Interview with Spokesperson 1	Interview with Spokesperson 2	Remarks
MTA 1	1	1	Same Company
Save Money Transfer Agency (Pvt) Ltd	1	0	
MTA 2	1	0	
MTA 3 (North London)	1	0	
MTA 4 (Central London)	1	0	
MTA 5 (Kilburn High St)	1	1	Same Company
MTA 6 (Edgeware)	1	0	
MTA 7 (Hendon)	1	0	
MTA 8 (Tolworth)	1	0	
MTA 9 (Hendon)	1	1	Same Company
MTA 10 (Brent)	1	0	
MTA 11 (Slough)	1	1	
MTA 12 (Surrey)	1	0	
MTA 12 (Crayford)	1	0	
MTA 13 (Wimbledon)	1	1	Same Company
MTA 14 (Wembley)	1	0	

Findings: Fusing Desktop Research Sources of Data and Interviews.

i   Statutory Intstument 2017 (692) Financial Services, The
Money Laundering, Terrorists Financing and Transfer of Funds
(Information on the Payer) Regualtions (2017) obliges money
transfer companies and fiancial services to collect certain information
from their customers for purposes of financial management and
regulations of their operations. MTA 1 confirm that, like any other
transfer of business in the UK, they are reminded and regulary
monitored by the Financial Services Authority for compliance with
the said regulatory provisions.

These regulations prescribed for purposes of satisfying Sections
168 (4) (b) (appointment of persons to carry out investigation in
practical cases) and 402 (1) (b) (power of the FCA to investigate
proceedings for certain other offences) of the Financial Services and
Markets Act (2000 (a). Money Transfer Companies are all corporate
entities incorporated under the binding laws of the United Kingdom.

ii   MTA 5 Kilburn High Street, "Spokesperson 1" pointed out
that the company is required, by virtue of its operations, to adere to
the capital requirements directive 2013/36 EU of the European
Parliament and the council of 26 June 2013 in which the law grants
access to the acitivity of credit institutions and the prudential
supervision of credit instituins and investing firms amending
Directive 2002/87/EU and repealing Directive 2006/48/EC and
2006/49/EC (b).

...the interpretation is that the Principal registration (Money
laundering terrosist Financial Transfer of funds (Information on the
Payer) Regulation 2017) requires us to compile data of all persons
engaged in money transfer and verify whether there is evidence of
persons on the Zimbabwean Sanctions list who are part of any money
transfer business...

... For purposes of dealing with our Zimbabwean customers and
those countries under Sanctions, we are constantly reminded through
financial regulatory authorities of provisions that fall under Part 3
"Customer One deligence" in which robust measures of verification of
our customers should be implimented. Additional customer due
deligence relates to risk assessment of customers sending money to

Zimbabwe, establishing sources of that money and lines of transmissions relating to the movement of that money...

On a related note, we make observations to the following comments:

> ... What this implies it that funds transferred by persons dealing business with Zimbabwer fall under the guidelines issued the European Supevisory Authorities under Article 17, 18.4 and 48.10 of the fourth money laudnering directive. The involvement of European Supervisory Authorities is consistent with the imposition of sanctions on Zimbabwe under the provisions of US initiated and EU-sanctioned Zimbabwe Democracy and Economic Recovery Act 2001... [Transcript from MTA 13 Wimbledon, "Spokesperson 2" January 2018]

iii Under paragraphs (1) (f) and (2), a person is considered engaging in financial activitiy on an occasional or very limited basis if the following conditions are met:

(a) the person's total annual turnover in respect of financial acitivity is limited in respect of financial acitivity does not exceed £100.000.00

(b) the financial activitiy is limited in relation to any customer is no more than one transaction exceeding £1000 whether transaction is carried out in a single operation or a series of operations which appear to be linked.

(c) the financial activity does not exceed 5% of the person's total annual turnover.

(d) The financial acitivity is ancillary and directly related to the person's main activity.

Said one MTA based in North West London:

> ... we use these guidelines to risk assess our customers transacting business through us with Zimbabwe financial institutions. What is important is that we are required to update our records and register of recipients of financial transfers and obviously we do not transact Zimbabwean companies listesd on sanction schedule. Penalties are

severe: you can check on penalties levied to major financial institutions in Zimbabwe for violations of Zimbabwean sanctions Regulations. Penalties are all stipulated in the OFAC Regulations passed in the United States...

[Transcript from MTA 7 Hendon, "Spokesperson 2" January 2018]

iv There is evidence from information obtained from Save Money Transfer Company (Pvt) LTD that the company is statutorily obliged to take appropriate steps to identify and assess risks of money laundering. The information takes into account risk factors relating to customers, the countries and geographical areas in which they operate from, products services including transactions and activitiy channels - "... we are required to trace each transactions and report irregular transactions to authorities at once once identified..."

Another notable observation from interviews is that:

... policies controls and procedure expectations require us to maintain policies, controls and procedures and these are open to inspections when required to do so by the Financial Services Authorities. One records must reflect customer due dilegence as expounded in the principal legislation; must be reliable in terms of accuracy of data. We flag up cases of huge transactions of £10.000.00 and above , unusual patterns of transactions like urgency or frequency, we stand to be guided by the FCA directives or guidelines issued by any other supervisory authority approved by the Treasury. These regulations and guidelines are open to inspection by our customers...

[Transcript from MTA 8 Tolworth February 2018]

We use Part 3 "Customer Due Deligence" Chapter 1 of the said Principal legislation, is used to apply a raft of measures as outlined in the legislation. Money Transfer Agencies risk assess by verifying the following:

(a) identification of the customer or the customer's beneficiary owner, noting any changes.

(b) any transactions which are not reasonably consistent with relevant person knowledge of customer.

(c) any changes in the purpose or intended nature of the relevant persons relationships with the customer.

Measures to eliminate risk include identifying the customer and verifying their details under 28(1) (3) (a) - where customer is a body corporate the relevant person must obtain and verify:

(i) the name of the body corporate

(ii) its company number or other registration number

(iii) the address of its registered office.

For all financial companies, besides being checked on their coprporate body consitution/articles of association or governing documents, they are required to check on full names of [any] board of directors members and be able to identify all senior persons responsible for the operations of business entities.

The above requirement obtains because some of board members are listed on the OFAC sanctions list. Save Money Transfer Company (Pvt) LTD confirmed that upon flagging up they cancel business transactions. They confirm to cancellation of business with some Zimbabwean enities deemed to be associated with political figures on the sanctions list. Business losses are said to be worth over £50 million.

v   As to the screening process, Money Transfer Agencies pointed to all the information regarding civil penalties process being outlined in OFAC regulations governing Zimbabwean Sanctions programme. This information is corroborated by MTA 9 Hendon, "Spokesperson 1":

> ... It is mandatory for financial institutions and banks to follow 31 C.F.R. part 501. The guidelines published under George W Bush on November 9, 2009, as OFAC legislated regulations are published as Appendix A to part 501 Economic Sanctions Enforcement Guidelines – in line with 74 Fed. Reg. 57,593 (Nov. 9, 2009). These are mandatory documenting civil penalties and enforcement information as outlined by the USA on its OFAC's Web[50]. The company explained that the rules apply across the board at international level and they are heavily

---

[50] http://www.treasury.gov/ofac/enforcement.

policed always for enforcement. If such regulations affect huge corporations like Barclays Bank International and Commercial Bank of Zimbabwe (CBZ) – major banks operating in Zimbabwe, then it follows that the rules are applied uniformly across the financial sectors, with referenced communications generated by enforcement authorities to corporate financial organisations involved. What this means is that every financial institution or company involved in transnational business with Zimbabwe, including ours is bound by International law and we receive standing instructions to that effect.

[Transcript from MTA 9 Hendon, "Spokesperson 1" March 2018]

vi   Thus, for all Money Transfer Companies, it is a requirement that they are expected to have full knowledge for all its customers – whether corporate or individuals who appear of scheduled lists. "We work with the list from OFAC". They do so by directly verifying with persons or companies identified on the U.S. Department of the Treasury's Office of Foreign Assets Control (OFAC) on the list of Specially Designated Nationals and Blocked Persons (the "SDN List"). All companies maintained electronic records that they update from time to time in line with successive US Presidential Decrees. MTA 4, London Central, noted that in certain situations, there has been difficulties in identifying those persons as some of the family members or spouses are not documented. Thus, it becomes a situational problem to identify or verify any connections of persons of similar surnames under schedule headed "Blocking Property of Additional Persons Undermining Democratic Processes or Institutions in Zimbabwe." This not only creates uncertainty, but inevitable loss of business. It is not possible to quantify such losses as that information is categorised and protected at corporate level.

vii The interviewer was unable to access information on failed transactions and levels or nature of business by desktop research because of the sensitivity or classification of such information. That gamut of information is not on the websites because it is classified – in short, it is not displayed on public domains. The knock-on effect in terms of figures varies from company to company. What appears to be clear through company operational reports is that there is evidence to support observations on the crippling effect of sanctions to business and finance sectors in Zimbabwe.

According to the Reserve Bank of Zimbabwe January 2018 Monetary Policy Statement 'Enhancing Financial Stability to Promote Business Confidence[51]', sanctions, especially involving trade finance, interrupt trade, and ultimately constrain the economy's foreign currency generating capacity, as well as economic activity in general. Sanctions have also had adverse and downstream social and economic effects on the Zimbabwean economy's key sectors. Most of these effects have manifested themselves in shortage of foreign currency, resulting in the country accumulating external payment arrears and failing to import critical supplies. Sanctions cause massive deinstitutionalisation, deindustrialisation, falling productive capacity in domestic economy that results in a shift to the left, decrease in aggregate supply of goods and services. To that extent, cost push inflation rises with marked depreciation of the bond note – all which have impact on rising unemployment and an increase on national debt.

I asked the following cluster of questions using probing strategies - to check on the existence, application, parameters, comprehension and conceptualisation of sanctions at international level: *What is the nature of the sanctions that were imposed on Zimbabwe? What did they comprise of? How are you as a corporate company instructed to implement and maintain sanctions? What difficulties do you encounter in adherence to 'restrictive measures' imposed by the government of the United Kingdom through Zimbabwe Democracy and Economic Recovery Act of 2001? How has the UK government been involved with your financial company on implementing Zimbabwean sanctions?*

This is a summary of information transcribed from data obtained from MTA 8, Tolworth, in South West London:

...The Zimbabwe Democracy and Economic Recovery Act (2001) is the guiding legislation which sets out terms and conditions of our operations as a company in money business. Although "Economic Sanctions" is a broad term used to define punitive measures taken or

---

[51] Reserve Bank of Zimbabwe January 2018 Monetary Policy Statement 'Enhancing Financial Stability to Promote Business Confidence' found at http://www.rbz.co.zw/monetary-policy.html/ Accessed March 18

imposed by the Western governments especially the UK after Zimbabwe's land reform programme in 2000, we consider four key areas - namely Trade, Targeted, Financial, and Undeclared sanctions. All four aspects involve trade and financial restrictions on in terms of how we conduct business with various entities and individuals involved in targeted state. Sanctions also create barriers and obstacles that result in loss of business on our part. Loss of business is realised at two levels – namely due to untranslated business by listed entities of individuals linked to entities. On another note, losses may be aggregated to penalties levied on businesses found to be in breach of sanctions by dealing with Zimbabwean companies on sanctions list. Dealing with sanctions involving the latter is perceived as a construction of circumvention - what is commonly referred to as 'sanctions bursting.

MTA 14 in Wembley explained:

... as a financial company involved in money exchange and transfer, we have experienced situations where we have felt that our inability to transact with some Zimbabwean entities through money transfers, impacts negatively on the Zimbabwean financial outlook because it obstructs financial flows and capital desperately needed by both capitalist and vulnerable groups in that country. For example, we have been victims of investigations on specific transactions coming from individuals in the diaspora. These investigations often take long to resolve and by the time they are completed, our customers will have moved on possibly to other money transfer agencies [while we are still busy refunding money]. Examples of cases that have been intercepted include transactions of sums between £2000.00 and £10 000.00 [or more] meant for building materials and school fees, hospital charges, funeral costs, schools construction and in some cases agricultural production...

MTA 12 in Crayford highlighted difficulties in the sanctions regime imposed by western governments especially on Zimbabwe:

.... We also note that sanctions impede financial flows such as aid. As Zimbabweans settle in higher corporate positions in the UK, there are some who are sending aid in form of money to their individual constituencies. Such aid is used to sink boreholes in rural areas, buy school text books or medical equipment for local clinics. That funding is also subjected to greater scrutiny because the British Government wants to know of its sources. The net effect of the sanctions vetting system is that it reduces foreign exchange flows to Zimbabwe – adversely affecting especially the poor recipients. Bridging loans through external remittances are meant to reduce and alleviate poverty especially in rural communities. The sanctions regime currently in place is cruel and unfriendly because it reduces access to external remittances from Zimbabwean diaspora communities...

One spokesperson at Save Money Transfer (Pvt) Ltd with previous experience for working in NGOs in Zimbabwe noted that:

> ...In terms of undeclared sanctions, we have several Charity Organisations and Non-Governmental Organisations started by Zimbabweans. Although these are not on the scope of the Zimbabwe Democracy and Economic Recovery Act of 2001, they tend to be affected because they are involved in financial transactions and there are certain limits permitted under existing UK legislation. They are expected to produce credible paper trail that satisfy FSA requirements. The net effect - even at a small scale - is that sanctions constrain the economy of Zimbabwe's foreign currency in terms of its generating capacity and economic activities in the country...
>
> [Transcript from Save Money Transfer (Pvt) Ltd Spokesperson]
> January 2018]

viii It is worth noting that one of the difficult areas of challenge in respect of processing international transactions to Zimbabwe under the current sanctions regime is specified in Part 4, paragraph (3) ("the third party") in line with customer assiduous measures outlined in 28 (2) to (6) and (10) for compliance purposes. Said MTA 3 Spokesperson in North London:

> ...this is important because third party persons domiciled out of the UK intending to shift or send finances and aid are subject to the requirements of the UK national legislation through statutory

instrument 692 Financial Services Money laundering, Terrorist Financing and Transfer of Funds (Information on the Payer) Regulations 2017. Additionally, anyone seeking to transact international financial business from an EU state through the UK is subject to this principal legislation. We, therefore, do not rule out attempts [by the country, interest groups and individuals] to avert sanctions by third party channels. The major problem is that this is strategy comprehensively monitored at EU and UK country levels for compliance purposes. Compliance in terms of Part 4, (39) (3) (b) (1-4) as read with (4), (5) and (6) is a pre-requisite under UK FSA and Treasury regulations...

MTA 4 Spokesperson from Central London highlights that:

... the implications are that it is practically impossible for third party Zimbabwean nationals to go undetected by the system mainly because of the manner of implementation, laborious and detailed records keeping systems, verification and multi organisation levels surveillance systems initiated by the UK treasury and OFAC. Multi organisation policing is also achieved at international statutory levels through the US-initiated Zimbabwe Democracy and Economic Recovery Act (2001).

... in a huge way, sanctions imposition, management and their multinational administration have worked in a spectacular way to the detriment of the Zimbabwean economy. Although we cannot disclose specific figures for fear of retribution and to protect our business, the network system has 'prevented' or 'thwarted' huge financial transactions destined to Zimbabwe from being processed. Some of the funds are meant to alleviate shortages of drugs in poor rural hospitals and some are meant to buy medical equipment – basic equipment meant to help poor and vulnerable communities in Zimbabwe. We do have that all in our records...

Observations:

i.   How were sanctions imposed on Zimbabwe in the first place? Following Chimurenga 3 from 2000, Zimbabwe case was taken to the United Nations Security Council originally to seek military intervention. Because of the composition of the UN Security Council, USSR and China refused to veto that UN Security Council Resolution on Zimbabwe. Britain quickly cobbled sanctions option which was taken up for alleged human rights abuses [mostly against white farmers]. The UN Security Council adopted the 'less devastating' option (as opposed to military intervention). This was approved by the European Union. This means is that Zimbabwe must approach its devil masters through the EU for lifting of odious sanctions. Whether the Munangagwa-led government will accept US-EU terms and conditions remains a matter for intense debate.

ii.   Brexit is an acronym coined by the David Cameroon-led Conservative government based on the results of the referendum on June 23, 2016 to leave the European Union. The term means "British exit" is based strictly on legislative and economic guidelines of leaving the EU, a regional Trade Agreement (RTA) body of 29 countries. The regional block eliminates trade barriers and bureaucracy for ease of doing business through harmonization of laws, movement of goods and people across continental Europe for its member states. The European Commission based in Brussels presides over the harmonization of the single monetary currency, the euro for this block although Britain chose to be out of the euro zone when it was introduced in 1999. Leaving the EU has adverse implications for Britain in terms of World Trade Organisation (WTO) obligations as stated in the General Agreement of Trade in Services (GATS), ushers limited investment opportunities and a strain on the UK export market. Restricted access to the EU is likely to force the UK to look for alternatives by strengthening imperialistic organisations like the Commonwealth of Nations.

iii.   Because of the rich mineral ore resources that Britain and preys on and pilfers, Zimbabwe remains a strategic but unequal partner in international capital. In the book entitled *"War on Want: The New Colonialism – Britain's scramble for Africa's energy and mineral resources",* Curtis (2016) notes that:

> ...the continent of Africa is today facing a new colonial invasion, no less devastating in scale and impact than that which it suffered during the nineteenth century. As before, the new colonialism is driven

by a determination to plunder the natural resources of Africa, especially its strategic energy and mineral resources. At the forefront of this 'scramble for Africa' are British companies actively aided and abetted by the UK government...

... Under the guise of the UK helping Africa in its economic development, (a mere continuation of the colonial paternal narrative), $134 billion has flowed into the continent each year in form of loans, foreign investment and aid. However, the British government has aided and abetted the extraction of $192 billion from Africa mainly in profits by foreign companies, tax dodging and the cost of adapting to climate change.

iv.   Specifically, on Zimbabwe, the following facts by Curtis (2016) are precisely valid:

... Anglo American corporation which operates in South Africa and Zimbabwe controls 200 million ounces of platinum and produces 40% of the world's newly mined platinum and operates Unki platinum mines in Zimbabwe, it owns 50% interest in the Mimosa Mine on a 50/50 share agreement with Anglo platinum, Amplats, Caledonia Mining Corporation incorporated in Canada for Gold Zimbabwe owns 49% in the Blanket Gold Mine in the South West, which produces an average of 192 000 ounces of gold. The remaining 51% is owned by Zimbabweans, In Mwana Africa PLC (Asa Resource Group PLC) incorporated in the UK, Zimbabwe owns 85% of Fred Rebecca Gold Mine which contains vast resources of the Hunter Road Nickel deposits resources and the company is exploring and developing Makaha Gold deposits. It has 75.4 % interests in Bindura Nickel Corporation which owns and operates Shangani and Trojan nickel mines which produced $102 million worth or mineral ores in 2014 despite economic sanctions constraints. Premier African Minerals BVI is incorporated in the British Virgin Islands. Zimbabwe has two projects exploring rare earth, wolframite. Sable Mining Africa incorporated in the BVI is developing the Lubu Coal Project in the North West of Zimbabwe covering 19 236 hectares which contains 786 tonnes and has an interest in Lubibi Coal projects in the west covering 16 545 hectares with resource base of 1 billion tonnes. Vast Resources incorporated in the UK mines gold where Zimbabwe has 50% interest in Breckridge Investments Ltd (a joint venture between Vast Resources and Grayfox Investments) – which holds 100% interest in the Pick Stone Peerless Gold Mine and mining claims surrounding former Giant Mine. The Zimbabwean mine contains 3.56 million ounces of Gold... [Data compiled from pages 35-69]

The above list of foreign owned and mostly British owned companies is not exhaustive.

v.　Sanctions will be removed for two reasons – first to facilitate ease of exploitation and extraction of resources which benefit Britain the most; second – to counter threat of competition from Eastern Bloc Countries, including China and Russia who are traditional friends of Zimbabwe in its struggle against British colonial and oppressive rule. Britain wants to consolidate its grip on Zimbabwean resources under smokescreens investment opportunities.

vi.　At another level, there is an ideological warfare between the west and former socialist block countries. Britain perceive the later negatively as they claim that China and Russia be a new front for imperialism and economic windfall - without shedding an iota of blood or firing a single bullet in Zimbabwe.

vii.　In the historical analysis of Britain foreign policy, we bring to the fore that Britain is not new to Brexit. Brexit (23 June 2016) is a modernised form of Splendid Isolation which dominated British war time history in the 19th Century. Following the Crimean war (1853 - 1856) under Prime Minister Lord Palmerston (1855-1858), Britain voluntarily entered isolation from 1902 to 1939, for pursuing economic interests and expansion of its empire. This was regulated by colonial boundaries, spheres of influence and power, trade routes and markets, tariffs and treaties that propped her government in maintaining the balance of power.

viii.　Although the forms of economic relationships at that time vary, splendid isolation was an attempt to protect the British Empire by keeping out of European affairs. If we fast forward to March 29, 2017 when Britain triggered Article 50 of the Lisbon Treaty (2007) (a2009) to exit the European Union: the pattern is the same as Britain seeks to engage its own trading alliances by strengthening her position with its weakened former colonies. It is a fact that the less developed and over-exploited former colonies notably in Africa have emerged worse off in terms of capital accumulation and globalisation at the turn of the millennium. Against that setting, Zimbabwe remains a target for re-colonialization and neo-colonization.

Economic Sanctions and Corruption

On another related note, I argue that the arbitrary imposition of sanctions in Zimbabwe created other socio economic and political problems that sank the country to the abyss. Specifically, corruption was and still is on the rise particularly within the upper echelons of power, the elite and petit bourgeois in Zimbabwe. Lines of argument are that corruption tends to fester and spread in a country when it is going through crisis situations like sanctions - including austerity measures, recession, inflation and regime change. Said the Presidential Spokesman George Charamba:

"... I think there must be consideration of the fact that most of the cases occurred at a time when the economy was in a tumultuous state, and what we are considering as misbehaviours, unlawful behaviour on the part of body corporates were in fact existential choices at the time [of the height of economic sanctions calamities in Zimbabwe][52]

We gather evidence that during the height of Zimbabwe economic sanctions in 2008, politicians and those who had access to finance siphoned millions of dollars of their and state money into offshore accounts. Stephen Chan, a professor of world politics at the School of Oriental and African Studies at the University of London, said anti-corruption drives rarely succeed:

"...Any country with many people at senior level suspected of corruption will mean that corruption is part, not just of the system of government, but the culture and structure of government..."

---

[52] The Daily Newspaper, Mnangagwa's anti-graft blitz loses steam, Found at: https://www.dailynews.co.zw/articles/2018/05/30/mnangagwa-s-anti-graft-blitz-loses-steam/Accessed 31 May 18

"...There is a transition period where government just won't work if all corrupt people are purged — as there will not be enough people left. Also, in Zimbabwe, the ruling elite is a tight group, bound by party ties, kinship ties, and liberation ties. Everyone knows how to steal, and everyone knows someone who will know how to turn the heat down if they are caught ..."[53]

For example, Zimbabwean politicians, top brass and private individuals were implicated in the Panama scandal in March 2016. Other high-profile names who are mentioned in the leaked Panama Scandal documents include Saudi Arabia's King Salman, the former Emir of Qatar, Sheikh Hamad bin Khalifa Al Thani, and the King of Spain's Aunt, Infanta Pilar de Borbon and the British Royal family.

For executives from Zimbabwe to fit in that category royals and elites, there is one thread of interpretation we can derive: either their dealings in the scandals were very sophisticated or their windfall was massive[54] . See also *Paradise Papers: Tax Haven of Super Rich including the Queen [of England] Exposed: Huge data leak reveals how monarch's private estate invested millions in funds based in Bermuda and Cayman Islands*[55]. It is surprising that sophisticated Zimbabweans are among the super-rich competing for their fair share of corruption spoils in offshore scandals! But the reality is that high incidences if corruption in Zimbabwe are linked to the way the Zimbabwe government was trying to manage sanctions in a process known as sanctions bursting. The post-Mugabe government is involved in retrieving some of the dirty money which is stashed away in offshore account while the rural

---

[53] The Daily Newspaper, Mnangagwa's anti-graft blitz loses steam, Found at: https://www.dailynews.co.zw/articles/2018/05/30/mnangagwa-s-anti-graft-blitz-loses-steam/Accessed 31 May 18

[54] Duchess of York named in Panama Papers scandal, Found at http://royalcentral.co.uk/other/duchess-of-york-named-in-panama-papers-scandal-59016/Accessed 18 May 18

[55] Paradise Papers: Tax Haven of Super Rich including the Queen [of England] Exposed: Huge data leak reveals how monarch's private estate invested millions in funds based in Bermuda and Cayman Islands. Found at: https://www.independent.co.uk/news/uk/home-news/paradise-papers-tax-haven-secrets-the-queen-appleby-law-firm-offshore-finance-a8039041.html/Accessed 18 May 18

population is bleeding in poverty. See[56] for government efforts in cleaning up the sanctions induced corruption[57]. The Panama papers that implicated former cabinet ministers and other executives linked to the ruling party was a tip of an iceberg. President Mnangagwa summed the depth of sanction-induced corruption:[58]

Zimbabwe published a list of more than 1,800 individuals and companies last week that the government said illegally transferred money abroad, including several who appear in the Panama Papers.

The list was the result of a three-month amnesty that allowed companies and individuals to return money to the country without prosecution. The list named those who had not done so.

In announcing the results, President Emmerson Mnangagwa said that $826 million – more than half of an estimated $1.42 billion stashed outside Zimbabwe – was not returned during the 90-day amnesty period.

"The authorities have no other recourse to cause these entities and individuals to respond, other than to publicize the names of the entities and individuals so that the concerned parties take heed of the importance of good corporate governance," Mnangagwa said in a statement[59].

---

[56] Zimbabwe-Governance-Externalisation Zimbabwe: Mnangagwa names and shames alleged forex looters Found at: http://apanews.net/en/news/zimbabwe-mnangagwa-names-and-shames-alleged-forex-looters/Accessed 18 May18

[57] Zimbabwe's President Emmerson Mnangagwa on Monday named and shamed over 1,800 companies and individuals who have ignored a government directive to return more than US$825 million allegedly stashed away in offshore accounts. Mnangagwa revealed that individuals and companies had by the amnesty deadline returned over US$591 million.

[58] OFFSHORE SECRECY:
Zimbabwe's List of Alleged Offshore Offenders Includes Panama Papers Shell Companies
Zimbabwe President Emmerson Mnangagwa says there is still $826 million stashed offshore, as the country names and shames those it believes illegally transferred money abroad. Found at https://www.icij.org/investigations/panama-papers/zimbabwes-list-of-alleged-offshore-offenders-includes-panama-papers-shell-companies/Accessed 18 May 18

[59] International Consortium of Investigative Journalists. Found at

Back at home, it is a fact that the existence of the OFAC list that specify persons on sanctions embargoes was also used differently and corruptly to bypass sanctions measures in place. One such "opaque dirty and corrupt deal" was the procurement of aircrafts for the national airline – Air Zimbabwe which is alleged to have been fronted Ex-President Mugabe's son in law:

> Simba, [Chikore] you are quite correct, people are smart enough and will know the truth eventually. However, for now I request you and the two ministers of State, i.e. Chinamasa [Finance] and Gumbo [Transport], stop making fools of yourselves [by] trying to sanitise this otherwise extremely dirty project [Corrupt procurement of Zimbabwe Airways aircrafts]. If this project was legitimate and above board, why was it done like a sting operation and not straight forward?
>
> ... We know that sanctions have been used in many cases to [justify and] siphon funds from the treasury through claims and as a cover up. If at all they were effective sanctions, why where there so many companies and individuals alleged to have siphoned money out of the country on a list provided?
>
> ... So, let us stop lying and come out clean on this issue. If there had been no change of government... would you have said this hog wash you are now singing? We are not fools, and the government must stop trying to sanitize this nonsense. I thought they were trying to clean up their image as well as that of the country...!
>
> [Comments from SHIBOBO April 22, 2018] [60]

The broader role of sanctions bursting strategies appears to be set in deep measures perpetuated in corrupt deals. National opposition-inclined press outlines the sanctions bursting as a smokescreen under which corruption festered. The following allegations tell of a difficult story in Zimbabwean socio-economics of economic sanctions:

---

https://www.icij.org/investigations/panama-papers/zimbabwes-list-of-alleged-offshore-offenders-includes-panama-papers-shell-companies/Accessed 19 May 18

[60] The Standard: Mugabe's Son-In-Law bears his soul. Found at: https://www.thestandard.co.zw/2018/04/22/mugabe-son-law-bares-soul/Accessed 18 May 18

"... It only took [Finance Minister] Chinamasa to come to his defence when he said the Zim Airways project had been kept off the radar as a sanctions-busting measure. A closer look at the initial purchase agreement, however, for the planes, tells a different story. Documents show the sanctions-busting story is a smokescreen as the purchase agreement openly indicates government bought the airliners on behalf of AirZim. This suggests the sanctions-busting narrative was a convenient smokescreen to cover their tracks..." [61]

Whatever the narratives and expiations, I argue in this Chapter that with the hardening of socioeconomic conditions in Zimbabwe at the height of economic sanctions in 2008, so did the increase of corruption and externalisation of funds. Economic sanctions brought about the culture of by passing formal financial channels of doing business. It brought about the collapse of the financial market and brought poverty to the poor. The argument that economic sanctions tends to affect the poor – those disempowered rural communities who have very limited options – holds rationale and credibility.

Conclusion

As a step towards repealing ZDERA, conclusions from Zimbabwe Council of the European Union Brussels, 22 January 2018 (OR. en) 5169/18 COAFR 8 CFSP/PESC 19 adopted the following key resolutions at its 3591st meeting held on 22 January 2018[62]. Note that the 'position' means adopting a wait and see attitude designed to give Western European and the US space in which to regroup. The West continues to work with opposition cabals in the cast of 'political figures' and 'civic groups' in Zimbabwe – in finding devious ways of dismantling powerful ruling party ZANU PF.

---

[61] The Independent: AirZim saga: Tale of half-truths, lies and deception. Found at: https://www.theindependent.co.zw/2018/05/18/airzim-saga-tale-half-truths-lies-deception/Accessed 24 May 18

[62] Zimbabwe: Council adopts conclusions in light of ongoing political Transition at http://www.consilium.europa.eu/en/press/press-releases/2018/01/22/zimbabwe-council-adopts-conclusions-in-light-of-ongoing-political-transition/ Accessed 29 Jan 18

It is within that political space where strategies pertaining to how opposition would win elections with the full backing of the west will be thrashed out. "If opposition loses then elections are not free and fair". "If ZANU PF wins the elections, then they have rigged them". It is also an opportunity to re-look at ZDERA with a view to amend and possibly not abolish it. The toxic Act is likely to be abolished in the [unlikely] event of ZANU PF going out of power.

1. The ongoing political transition in Zimbabwe creates high expectations among all Zimbabweans. It can open the way to a full return to the Rule of Law, within a constitutional framework and under civilian rule, allowing for the preparation and implementation of much-needed political and economic reforms.

2. The EU reaffirms its availability to engage constructively with the new authorities including through a structured political dialogue, with political actors across the spectrum, and with civil society, based on a mutual commitment to shared values focused on human rights, democratic principles and the Rule of Law. It will do so in coordination with African and international partners.

3. The upcoming electoral process will be an essential step. The EU welcomes the commitment of the authorities to hold elections in line with the constitution and underlines the importance that the conditions are in place to allow those elections to be peaceful, inclusive, credible and transparent. The EU would consider favourably electoral observation, provided that the required conditions are fulfilled and that an invitation from the Government of Zimbabwe is received.

4. The EU welcomes the stated intention of the Zimbabwean authorities to deliver economic reforms in Zimbabwe, aiming at supporting job creation, growth and sustainable long-term development, and reaffirms its willingness to support the planning and implementation of much-needed structural changes and the promotion of good governance. In this context, the EU will support the authorities in establishing as soon as possible a constructive re-engagement with international financial institutions based on a clear and time-bound economic and political reform programme.

5. The EU stands ready to review the whole range of its policies towards Zimbabwe at any moment to consider the progress achieved in the country.

Adoption of the key resolutions is a step towards procedures mentioned in observations above. According to the in-depth structured interview with a spokesperson at Save Money Transfer (Pvt) Ltd, the United Kingdom may move faster to normalize relations with a former colony because it is within its interests under Brexit:

> ... establishing as many bi-lateral relations as possible will create a buffer zone aimed at driving competing forces from the East. Presently, Zimbabwe is crowded space, a battleground where western countries are competing for breathing space. Because of the extent to which the Zimbabwe economy has been [deliberately] battered by years of unrelenting economic sanctions, it is possible to perceive Zimbabwe as a desperate regime begging hat in hand for investments ... but reality is that western countries, especially the UK is under extensive pressure to claw back lost ground over the past two decades. Zimbabwe must use that as a bargaining trump card. The new government must come up with a tangible economic agenda designed to manage not only the post Mugabe era, but imperialism and neo-colonialism.

References

Alexander, J, McGregor, J & Tendi, B.M. (2017) 'The Transnational Histories of Southern Africa Liberation Movement: An Introduction', *Journal of Southern African Studies,* **43 (1)** 1-12

Alexander, J. The Unsettled Land: State Making and The Politics of Land in Zimbabwe: 1983-2003, Oxford, James Curry, 2006

Blair, T. (2001a) Speech at the Labour Conference, 2 October 2001, *The Guardian,* 3 October 2001.

Bolks, S.M & Al-Sowayel, D. (2000) 'How do economic sanctions Last? Examining the sanctions process through duration' *Sage Journals Political Research Quarterly,* **53 (2)** 241-265

British House of Lords Select Committee on Economic Affairs 2nd report of Session (2006-07), "The Impact of Economic Sanctions. Volume 1 Report" 1-154

Bryman, A. (2001) Social Research Methods, Oxford University Press, UK.

Bueno de Mesquita, B, & Silverston, R. 2002 'War and the survival of political leaders: a comparative study and regime type and political accountability', *American Political Science Review,* **89 (4)** 841-855

Burns, A. (1999). Collaborative action research for English language teachers. Cambridge: CUP

Chan, S & Primorac, R. (2007) Zimbabwe in Crisis: The International Response and the Space of Silence, Routledge, Taylor and Francis Group.

Chandler, D. (2003) 'Rhetoric without responsibility: the attraction of 'ethical' foreign policy, *British Journal of Politics and International Relations,* **5 (3)** 295-316

Chimbange, A, Mukenge, C, Mutambwa, J (2013) 'Image Repair: An Analysis of President Robert Gabriel Mugabe's Rhetoric Following Sanctions on Zimbabwe' *Microthink Institute, International Journal of Linguistic,* **5 (1)**

Conlon, P (1995) 'The UN's questionable sanctions practice', *Aussenpolitik, German Foreign Affairs Review,* **46 (4)** 327-338

Fanon, F (1961). *The Wretched of the Earth,* Grove Press Publisher.

Fanon, F (1952) *Black Skin White Masks,* Pluto Press, London, United Kingdom

Fowale (2010) quoted in Zembere, M. (2014) 'An Evaluation of the Impact of Economic Sanctions on Science, Teaching and Learning at Secondary Level in Zimbabwe's Mbire District of Mashonaland Central', *Educational Journal* published on line on 11 August 2014, p. 1-7, at http: www.sciencepublishinggroup.com/j/edu, doi 10 11648/j.edu.20150405.12

Godwin, P (2011) *The Last Days of Robert Mugabe,* Picador

Godwin, Peter & Ian Hancock (1993). *Rhodesians Never Die: The Impact of War and Political Change on White Rhodesia,* c. 1970–1980. Oxford: Oxford University Press

Helmes, J. (1999) 'What sanctions epidemic?' *Foreign Affairs*, **78 (1)** (2-8)

Hove, M.H. (2012) 'The debates and impact of sanctions: The Zimbabwean Experience', *International Journal of Business and Social Science*, **3 (5)** 72-84

Jing, C, Kaempfer, W.H., Lowenberg, A.D. (2003) 'Instrument choice and effectiveness of international sanctions: a simultaneous approach', *Journal of Peace and Research* **40 (5)** 519-535

Kaempfer, W.M & Lowenberg, A.D, (1988), 'The theory of international economic sanctions: a public choice approach', *The American Economic Review*, **78 (4)** 786-793

Lewis, R. (1980) 'From Zimbabwe-Rhodesia to Zimbabwe', *Round Table* **(70)** 6-9

Maldonado-Torres, N 'On the coloniality of being'. *Cultural Studies*, **21:2-3**, 240-270 (2007)

Martin, D & Johnson, P. (1981) *The Struggle for Zimbabwe*, Faber and Faber, London and Boston.

Meredith, M. (2009) *Mugabe: Power plunder and the Struggle for Zimbabwe's future*, Public Affairs

Miyagawa, M. (1992) *Do Sanctions work?* Macmillan, London, Great Britain.

Muller, J & Muller, K. (1999) 'Sanctions of Mass Destruction', *Foreign Affairs*, **78 (3)** 43-53

McGillivray & Stam, A.C (2004) 'Political institutions, coercive diplomacy, and duration of economic sanctions', *Journal of Conflict Resolution, Sage Journals* **48 (2)** 154-172

Moorcroft, P, (2009) *Mugabe's War Machine: Saving or Savaging Zimbabwe*, Kindle Edition at Amazon.co.uk

Ndlovu-Gatsheni, S.J. (2009) 'Making sense of Mugabeism in Local and Global Politics: 'So Blair, keep your England and let me keep my Zimbabwe'. *Third World Quarterly*, **30:6,** 1139-1158, DOI: 1080/-1436590903037424 (2009)

Onsleen, V. (1976) *Chibharo: African mine labour in Southern Rhodesia*, 1900-1933, Pluto Press.

Raftopolous, B & Mlambo, A.S (Eds) *Becoming Zimbabwe: A History of Zimbabwe from Pre-colonial Period to 2008*. Weaver Press. Harare

Raftopolous, B (2009) 'The Crisis in Zimbabwe 1998-2008' ResearchGate at http://www.researchgate.com/282076567_The _Crisis_in_Zimbabwe_1998-2008_Brian_Raftopoulos/ Accessed Jan 29, 18

Sarantankos, S (2007) *Social Research* Paperback.

Sithole, T (2015) 'A Fanonian reading of Mugabe as a colonial subject', *Mugabeism?* 217-236

Smith, A (1999) 'A high price to pay: the costs of US economic sanctions policy and the need for process-oriented reforms' *UCLA Journal of International. & Foreign Affairs, Hein On Line.org*, 325 at http://www.heinonline.org/hol/landingPage?handle=hein.jour nals/jilfa4&div=17&id=&page=/Accessed April 07 18

Smith, D., Simpson, C & Davis, I. (1981) *Mugabe,* London, Sphere Books,

Tendi, B-M (2014) 'The Origins and Functions of Demonization Discourses in Britain-Zimbabwe Relations (2001-)' *Journal of Southern African Studies* **40 (6**) 1251-1269 (2014)

Van Berggeijk, P.A. (1989) 'Success and failure of economic sanctions', *Kyklos* **42 (3),** 385-404

Von Braunmuhl, C & Kulessa, M (1995) 'The impact of UN sanctions on humanitarian assistance activities, *Berlin Gesellschaft fur Communication management Interkultur Training*

Weiss, T.G. (1999) 'Sanctions as a foreign policy tool: weighing humanitarian impulses', *Journal of Peace Research* **36 (5)** 499-509

Williams, Chancellor, (1987) *Destruction of Black Civilization: Great Issues of a Race from 4500BC to 2000AD,* Third World Chicago Press, USA

Appendix 1

SEMI-STRUCTURED INTERVIEW SCHEDULE:
ZIIMBABWE ECONOMIC SANCTIONS IN THE UK

1. Are there any limits imposed on your organisation in terms of funds that that you can remit to Zimbabwe?

2. What are the legal requirements under Zimbabwean international sanctions regime and Zimbabwe for transmitting money?

3. What type of clientele group and business customers have you served – in terms of repatriations transfers of funds to Zimbabwe?

4. What systems are in place for money transfer surveillance to Zimbabwe or other countries on economic sanctions and embargos?

5. Have you been caught us in systems for sending /transfers of funds to individuals or organisations the OFAC sanctions list?

6. What sanctions penalties have you incurred for [attempting] transactions on the Red Flag list?

7. Can you tell me more about your activity reports and clearance for transfers destined to Zimbabwe?

8. How are you monitored by British Financial Services Authority and other watchdogs on sanctions bursting and [other] illegal activities?

9. Can you quantify losses incurred by Zimbabwe companies/ specific organisations and individuals because of economic sanctions?

10. What is your opinion on the outlook of Zimbabwe sanctions in terms of the way they are monitored and implemented?

Thank you very much indeed for taking your time to attend to this interview.

∞∞∞∞∞∞

Chapter 6

Counting the toll of Zimbabwe's Economic Sanctions: A Case Study of Zano Remba Housing Cooperative in Chitungwiza Township

...intellectuals have a special contribution to make to the development of our nation, and to Africa. And I am asking that their knowledge, and the greater understanding that they should possess, should be used for the benefit of the society of which we are all members

Julius Kambarage Nyerere,

General Overview of Sanctions-induced Poverty in Zano Remba Housing Cooperative (ZRHC)[63]

After implementation of ZDERA in 2001, poverty in Zimbabwe was crucially defined by the class system and high levels of deprivation. The working class, most of whom lost jobs in heavy industries and the manufacturing sector because of sanctions were the hardest hit. Loss of their incomes meant that they were pushed into lower classes of the Zimbabwean society as defined – among

---

[63] Zano Remba is a Lateral translation which means "Plan for a Home". Zano Remba was a plan devised to provide the poor and vulnerable with roofs above their heads, especially at a time when those groups had been hard hit by economics sanctions at the time. Some argue that at a time that ZANU PF support was whittling down because of sanctions-induced unpopularity and economic decline at the time. Zano Remba was therefore said to have been devised as an electioneering strategy devised to woo back its traditional core supporters. The fact that the project was sanctioned at Zanu PF political party level meant that it was not apolitical. Lines of argument also involve housing policy statements – the fact that Urban Development Corporation (UDCORP), an arm of the government meant formulation and implementation of policy at government level. What is evident in this project is the part of the Government of Zimbabwe's responsiveness to Western-imposed economic sanctions by supporting families with subsidised accommodation at the time. Provision of affordable accommodation, no matter how basic remains one of the cornerstones of poverty alleviation and capacity building.

other things – by levels of education, location of residence, quality of their accommodation, employment status, access to health care systems or health delivery services and general living standards.

From a Marxist perspective, the class system of every society is directly linked to mode of production as defined as a component in superstructures of relations of production. Loss of jobs due to sanctions alters the income base at individual family levels. If the head of a family is unable to earn a living from economic infrastructure they are associated with, this adversely impacts on that family in terms of how that family negotiates and processes its own survival. Importantly, it compromises on the capacity to afford and service inevitable overheads like school fees, transport money, food including access to clean water or medical facilities. Unemployment also alters the balance in terms of quality of life and material conditions and family standards. In ZRHC, my research looks at disposable incomes, earnings and savings of family households whose heads lost jobs because of economic sanctions imposed on Zimbabwe.

One of the indices of sanctions-induced poverty can be found in examining living standards, sanitation and outlook of the area as *relational* to adverse economic conditions. Although there are those *who have* in Chitungwiza in general, the question of living standards, including outlook of environs, amenities and facilities tends to *descriptively* place people within some kind system of stratification. Houses constructed inside parts of graveyards may not be due to poor planning by Local Authority but poverty of the mind in the lines of the quality of people who end up in such positionality. Thus, in ZRHC, poverty is stratified alongside classes and sub-classes as evidenced by subjective quantum of relations. Looking at relations, this research looks at interface of income generating resources and assets. For example, capacity to generate extra income from letting rooms or the whole house is dependent upon one's capacity to build or completing its capacity its construction in the first place. According to Wright (2002) the concept of class is both characteristic of both Weberian and Marxist traditions of social theory:

...geographical location, forms of discrimination anchored in inscriptive characteristics or genetic endowments... Locations, discrimination and genetic endowments may, of course, still figure in the analysis of class. They may, for example, play an important role in explaining classes... [with] the definition of class centring on how people are linked to those income-generating assets... (p 838) [Like the functional aspects of the core houses in ZRHC]

The crux of ZRHC case study in terms of devastating sanctions may also be positioned in the concept of class closely linked to causes of inequality not only in social class, but economic opportunities. This often generates conflicts and contradictions. For example, because of the scarcity of housing stands as a resource, there was a tendency for rival groups or bogus housing cooperatives mushrooming to 'annex' or 'invade' semi-completed houses thereby generate conflict. Those common contractions have inherent tendencies to pit same class of people against each other in pursuit of opportunities of exiting poverty. There criminal cases in respect of rivalry and illegitimate gangs in Zano Remba headed by corrupt Ward Councillor[64] at Chitungwiza Magistrates Courts illustrates attrition generated by rival groups in pursuit of limited resources[65]:

---

[64] The Herald, Land baron cashes in on desperate home-seekers at https://www.herald.co.zw/land-baron-cashes-in-on-desperate-home-seekers/Accessed 03/18 In all the cases cited in this reference, the Plaintiffs were fighting the Chitungwiza City Council through one of its Councillors, a one Calisto Masango - who, for political interests was allegedly corruptly and illegally distributing stands and making double allocations of houses to desperate home seekers. Councillor is alleged to have used his strong position and strong local authority connections to issue out fake lease agreements in a desperate bid to gain votes from opposition groups rivals and anti-ruling party faction.
[65]
http://ir.msu.ac.zw:8080/xmlui/bitstream/handle/11408/2530/FINAL_DESS ERTATIONMASHINGAIDZE%20.pdf?sequence=1&isAllowed=y

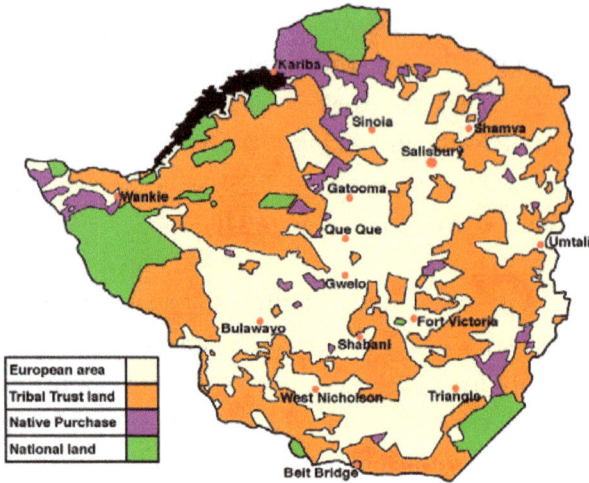

Patterns of Land Distribution by Race: 1980

ZDERA is part of the thesis of the 'The Black World at Crossroads' (p 309). That great work by Williams is a powerful narrative which focuses on the destruction of Black civilisation – which for Zimbabwe's Munhumutapa Empire, was an agenda running through the year 1450 when the Great King Mutota who presided over the present-day Zimbabwe and vast areas of Southern and Central Africa died. In this thesis Williams writes:

> Yet I did just that when I wrote that "the whites are the implacable foe, the traditional and enemy of the Blacks." The compelling reason for publicly putting this declaration in its historical context is clear: The necessary re-education of Blacks and a possible solution of racial crises can begin, strangely enough, only when Blacks fully realize this central fact in their lives: The white man is their Bitter Enemy. For this is not the ranting of wild-eyed militancy, but the calm and unmistakable verdict of several thousand years of documented history. Even the sample case-study of ten black states in this work shows that each and every one of those states was destroyed by whites. Facing this reality does not call for increasing hatred or screaming and utterly futile denunciations. Far from it. For all these shouting emotional outbursts

162

by Blacks are in themselves indications of weakness, because they becloud the mind and prevent the calm and clear thinking that is absolutely required for planning if the race is to be saved from final destruction. "Destruction" is not too strong a term here. Only fools will be unable to see that the race is again being hemmed in, surrounded by its enemies, and cannot survive forever under what might be called a state of gradual siege... (p.318)

When Robert Mugabe took up the armed struggle in the 60s to 1980 – he was fighting to liberate his people. He was fighting against neo colonialism and imperialism. He was fighting against those who had murdered and wiped out a whole civilization to for the settlers and foreigners to plunder their wealth. This is documented by Caucasian writes including Ranger (1900) Martin (1980) Beach (1979). I highlight the historical developments in strip down form without necessarily elaborating, making amendments or qualifications as I state facts as they are. I seek to clarify the characteristics of evil constructions of settlers rather than provide defence of our forbearers and politicians in defending their empires. I do not focus on means used to defend the 'empire' suffice to say that the battle to destroy Zimbabwe began in early civilisations.

Zimbabwe is the ultimate transformed empire which has been at the centre of attention and a victim of its mineral resources. Mudenge (1988) Mufuka (1983) Chigwedere (1980) develop the powerful Zimbabwean history of the Monomotapa Empire.

When then ZANU PF party decided to take up land reform programme – not as a battle, but as Chimurenga Three war, what theoretic motivations can we derive from these brave acts? Was that part of re-educating the people – probably a continuation of war time vigils or 'pungwes' that helped to boost morale and educate the masses in Chimurenga Two? Was Mugabe a lone ranger in the castellation of the organisation of African Unity (OAU) then? Who was he educating? Was he concertizing war veteran cadres to fight against the 'bitter enemy'? When, according to the Reserve Bank of Zimbabwe (2006) Zimbabwe was '*begging, kneeling and sweating in sweltering to gain access to the Global Fund to fight against Malaria, TB and HIV/AIDS*' – was it not an act of 'deliberate final destruction' of black civilisation in Zimbabwe? What is the implication of the IMF and World Bank cutting off aid desperately needed at *Murambinda Hosptial* in *Buhera*? In a Reserve Bank of Zimbabwe (Ibid) document entitled *The Effects of Economic Sanctions on Zimbabwe*, it is clearly stated under the heading *'Impact on the Poor and Vulnerable'*:

> Regrettably sanctions imposed on the country over the past seven years have resulted in the drying up of project finance and balance of payments support. This negative development has had far reaching effects on the majority of the people and manifested itself through the following economic evils – Denial of medication to the unborn child; poor rural folks unable to grind their maize meal; school children not able to go to school; transport system grounding to a halt; workers walking to work because of fuel shortages and black outs due to electricity outages...' (p. 2)

Is the above part of the state of gradual siege aimed at decimating a generation?

A view from the Rooftop: Sanctions as an anachronism of Poverty

The identification and measurement of poverty raises a lot of statistical problems of complexity. Researchers and academics remain ambivalent on the accuracy of measuring poverty in absolute or relative terms. I use ZRHC to identify dimensions of poverty in relative terms. Thus, the research establishes a framework for poverty reduction especially in urban settings by proposing solutions and recommendations at policy formulation levels. I also use the same model to analyse key constructs of poverty and their impact on the quality of life in households in this vast housing cooperative estate.

Why is this approach important? This is so because it enables the researcher to make distinctions between proximate causes of poverty, for example, lack of housing as an index and causal problem. I use purposive sampling procedures in this qualitative research to build upon themes on data management – most of which is obtained through questionnaires. In data analysis, I look at key elements of measuring poverty in the assessment of relative needs of families of different sizes and composition. I draw upon the relative deprivation model to examine the characteristics and poverty levels in ZRHC. This situational analysis helps to put records straight and clearer in terms of shortcomings relating to scarcity of data. I summarise by providing an overview of government initiatives on poverty alleviation strategies under the Zim-Asset Programme adopted by Zimbabwean government for implementation from 2013 to 2018.

Fiegehen, Lansley and Smith (1983) defines poverty as the "insufficiency of basic needs" or being in a state of "insufficiency of earnings [to] obtain minimum necessities for maintenance of merely physical efficiency" (Townsend 2001). The World Bank (2002) defines poverty as a state "of not having enough today in some dimension of well-being". The concept of poverty has many facets including dual labour market radical theories, sub culture of poverty, Marxist perspectives, Functionalist explanations of inequality and poverty and, of course, Foucault's power relations in the context of poverty and human action.

This chapter looks at the sub-culture of poverty as a concept derived from a variety of anthropological, sociological and eugenic studies expressed by Lewis dating back to the 60s. The premise of using this model is that ZRHC is a sub-culture of poverty within the wider population sample under Chitungwiza Town Council. Since the establishment of ZRHC in the 1990s, it has grappled with acute poverty levels and deprivation. Some of these important issues are referred to in findings.

Because of problems of corruption and political patronage in the allocation of stands, the cooperative has perpetuated a cycle of relative deprivation which has left families and households struggling in poverty. In that respect, this study draws upon three broad concepts which underline poverty. These are - *subsistence* as an empirical concept of real wages necessary in households to maintain life and economic efficiency (Fiegehen 1983); *normative value* which focus on what is "adequate or reasonable" in terms of household resources; *relative deprivation* because of inequality and comparison (Runciman 1966)

Literature Review: Theorising Poverty and Relative Deprivation

I make an overview of five dimensions of poverty, namely income, consumption, access to health, education and empowerment. World Bank (ibid) confirms that urban poverty is often characterised by "cumulative deprivation". This is a situation in which one dimension of poverty is often the cause of, or contributor to another dimension. Studies by Moser, Gatehouse and Garcia (1996b) provide urban context of poverty and vulnerability (the vulnerable face risk of falling into poverty); while the poor rely on cash economy in dangerous environments, for example, settling in wetlands or polluted areas. Such circumstances have an impact of poverty management.

The World Bank v2. (2002) confirms that vulnerability is closely linked to asset ownership as a measure of security of households. The fewer the assets held by the household, the greater their insecurity. Assets include labour (employment), access to health and education, skills (level of education) and productive assets. ZRHC is also looked at in terms of ownership of immovable property/house. This aspect enables the study to assess impact of poverty in livelihoods.

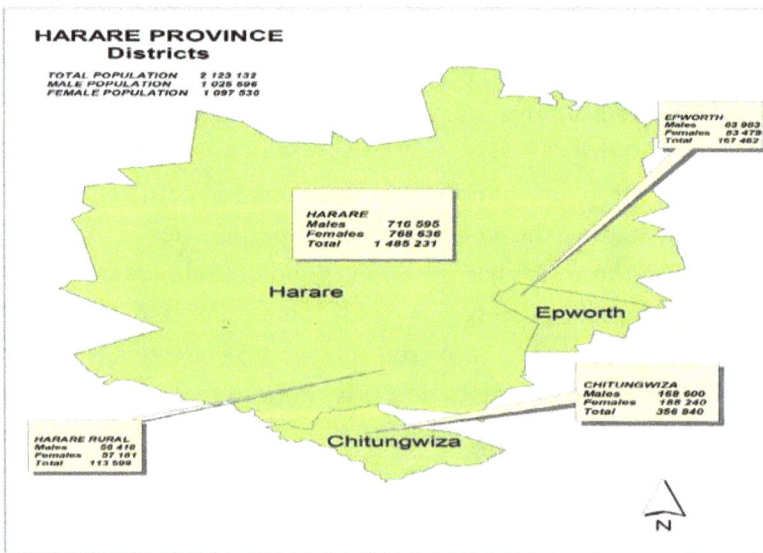

From: Harare Province Population Census 2012

Historical Context of Poverty in Chitungwiza

The history of poverty in Zimbabwe urban population has its roots in the British South African Company (BSAC) of 1890 to 1923. This administrative colonial government was immediately followed by the Rhodesia self-government of 1923 to 1967. The Unilateral Declaration of Independence (UDI) of 1965 to 1980 was the final white colonial regime that shaped the political and economic repression of Rhodesia. Throughout those dark years especially for the Africans, the "urban poor" population grew to unprecedented levels. Barrett, Carter and Little (2006) note of the magnitude of poverty in Africa citing the need for new approaches to reduce poverty especially in urban poor populations. The "very unfavourable historical hand" remains a hard blow for African communities who must confront residual effect of poverty and deprivation. This created an almost permanent damage in various aspects of Zimbabwean population especially in urban African townships.

Alongside legislative and statutory instruments, colonialism was an adjunct of exploitation "of man by man" which reinforced poverty and deprivation in the generality of the African poor. The Southern Rhodesia Order in Council (1898) and the Native Locations Ordinance of 1906 were aimed at retaining and expanding white urban land interests. The 1906 legislation sanctioned the establishment of native locations separate from white residential areas. The separation was justified by concerns for health and security needs of whites. In lucid terms whites remained paranoid that most blacks were criminals who posed health risks to their minority and privileged population.

The Land Apportionment Act (1930) (Amended in 1941) provided African population with limited urban housing. The Natives (Urban Areas) Accommodation Registration Act of 1946 ensured that the whites had full control of urban land and continued with discriminatory practices that disadvantaged the African population, for example implement a raft of 'Pass Law' provisions. The law also ensured that the provision of council housing was tied to one's duration of urban employment. Urban accommodation was provided to the husband working in labour employment. Wife and children were expected to live in Tribal Trust Lands. It was therefore illegal for any wage labourer to live with families in employment-linked houses, (like Rugare Township) or council accommodation (infamous 1907 Matapi Hostels in Mbare).

Native Husbandry Act Number 52 of 1951; Land tenure Act Number 55 of 1969 were complimentary with each other in apportioning land in terms of racial categories. The Land Apportionment Act (1930 a1941) was repealed and replaced by the Land Tenure Act (1969) The Land Tenure Act denied the right for Africans to own or lease land. Africans in townships such as in Southerton, Houghton Park, Kambuzuma and Mufakose (Marimba Park) could own houses and not the land on which the houses were built.

The concept of "progressive development" is a theme debated in poverty and deprivation discourse. Colonial Rhodesia is accused of facilitating the plundering of resources at the expense of the majority African population. As highlighted by Van Onselene (1976), Moyo (1995, 2009) the provision of urban housing in Harare was directly linked to provision and expansion of the manufacturing base. It was part of managing sanctions imposed on Rhodesia after it declared independence in 1965 in its designs to avoid facilitating majority and inclusive rule in that country. Primitive accumulation of capital, for which sourcing cheap labour was part of managing UDI, became the focus of mitigating the effects of international sanctions on Rhodesia.

It became necessary to bring more factors of production into use and this meant increased cheap labour. Under the said project, *"Chibaro"* or forced labour created chronic poverty levels characterised by poor housing, unemployment, poor service provision, sub-standard education for Africans and poor infrastructure. It is the period in which apartheid style of government was implemented by colonial Rhodesia in which the black working class remained marginalised in African Townships like Rugare, Mbare, Mufakose and Harare National.

Evolution of *Chirambahuyo*[66]: Another Elevation

...There were several squatter camps which emerged in the colonial days including *Chirambahuyo* at the edge of Harare. The colonial regime was ruthless on the perpetrators and illegal settlements were often destroyed and razed to the ground..."[67]

Chirambahuyo squatter camp was a peri-urban illegal resettlement project for rural refugees fleeing from the brutal war of liberation of the 70s and 80s. Chief Seke Mutema *(Shava Mhofuyemukono)* had long running battles with the colonial establishment as he fought for his people's rights to land entitlement. Chaeruka and Munzwa (2009) noted that "...a combination of 'rural push' and 'urban pull' factors help explain Zimbabwe urbanization trends". What is not highlighted in that study is the Chimurenga war of liberation as a 'push' factor for communities who had abandoned rural homes at the height of Zimbabwe's liberation struggle.

The situation obtaining at the time was that urban centres were safe places of refugee, hence massive rural-urban migration trends to Harare peri-urban. For population fleeing from war frontiers of Manicaland and Mashonaland East provinces, *Chirambahuyo* became

---

[66] In Zimbabwean culture, 'Huyo' is a what is a 'pound' of a 'pestle' carved meticulously out of stone. 'Huyo' crushes grain against 'guyo' the latter is the bigger hammer stone. Thus, 'huyo' crushes grain to mealie meal usually against a stone surface called 'guyo'. The two objects ambiguously represent both destruction and reservation and life but are often viewed as a symbol of both power and resilience. Both symbolizes the concept of regeneration through creation of a staple diet called 'hupfu' or [mealie] meal. ('Chiramba' as a verb which can be used interchangeable as a noun. It means refusal, or resistance as an adjective) Use and meaning may depend on the context. Kuramba kukuyiwa is -in the lateral sense – refusal or dismissal of oppression. Chirambahuyo therefore, refers to survival, power and strength in resistance. Squatters would return in collective adversity even after their camp had been demolished to the ground by Rhodesian soldiers to reconstruct it. Chirambahuyo as a squatter camp was a symbol of unity, toughness and resistance against colonialism. Squatters refused to be vanquished. They never capitulated.

[67] Chirisa, I., Bandauko, E. and Mutsindikwa, N,T. (2015) 'Distributive politics at play in Harare, Zimbabwe: case for housing cooperative'. Bandung: Journal of the Global South Open Access Research, 2015, http://link.springer.com/article/10.1186/s40728-015-0015-9/accessed/05 Mar 2017.

169

the safe port of arrival. Decades after war time rural-urban migration trajectories, settlement and housing pressures have not abated. As at the time of this study, there are war veterans still trying to settle in ZRHC.

In 1980, Zimbabwe inherited a highly marginalised and poor urban population. Chirambahuyo was later to be transformed to be part of Chitungwiza African township status at independence in 1980. The United Nations poured in aid under UN-HABITAT to replace slums with what came to be known as "match box houses". From December 1980 refugees moved from cardboard and plastic tents to somewhat habitable poor-quality structures. Core house units comprised of a toilet and a bedroom built from prefabricated material under asbestos roof. Adversely and ironically, foreign aid perpetuated the problem of dependency in that it did not address or break the fundamental causes of deprivation in the circle of poverty. As summed up by Schlyter (2003) "Chitungwiza has a legacy of poverty, much of it derived from wartime squatter camps such as Chirambahuyo which were demolished after independence to make way for new urban communities based upon home ownership"

In what appeared to be a crush programme in July 1980, dangerous materials like asbestos and other "ultra-low costs" building materials was sourced by international aid agencies to "avert a humanitarian crisis" in post-independence Zimbabwe. This presents complex problems bigger than humanitarian crisis itself because over the years, Chitungwiza has had high rates of people suffering from mesothelioma, respiratory diseases and chrysotile-related asbestosis. Camus, Slemiatycki and Meek (1998); Kupakuwana (2007) confirm that industrial asbestos cause lung cancer and mesothelioma for which there is no known cure yet. Cost implications for maintenance of asbestos confirm that houses with asbestos based material require extensive repairs and removal work. Many households in Chitungwiza cannot afford these repairs and renovations, ending up living in perilous conditions.

The "match box" style of housing is blamed for overpopulation of housing units into a vicious circle of poverty because housing units ended up accommodating more than their capacity. Studies by Bhamu, Mhlanga and Mushayabasa (2014) suggest high levels of

HIV/AIDS when percentage of prostitutes in especially poverty-stricken communities is high. This deduction links with the belief that the ill-planned transformation of slums is one of the principal causal factor of moral decadence and prostitution which has characterised Chitungwiza City since colonial times.

Furthermore, Chitungwiza came to be known as a "dormitory township" a derogative acronym for a pool of cheap labour living under squalid conditions. It provided wage labourers to nearby transport, textile industries and in heavy industry area of Workington, situated in the precincts of the then Salisbury capital city. Women worked mostly as 'nannies' as they were called in colonial Rhodesia. Chitungwiza supplied maids in the apartheid style "whites only" suburbs of Hatfield, Queensdale and Cranborne; and as cleaners and baby minders in the "coloureds only" suburb of Arcadia. A sizeable number of young men worked as general hands in light industrial areas of Graniteside. Some worked as gardeners in low-density whites only residential areas like Eastley and Waterfalls. Like many other African townships in Harare in 1980, Chitungwiza had endemic poverty levels, serious food shortages, undernourishment, poor transport and reticulation. It did not have clean water systems. It lacked hygiene standards and had no access to recreational facilities. It had limited medical facilities and experienced high mortality rates thus.

While Chitungwiza has grown to population levels of 356 840 residents (Government of Zimbabwe 2012 Census), aspects of poverty and housing shortages continue to be carried forward as baggage from colonial days. Housing shortages especially in the new millennium appear to be a by-product of inept, ineffective and highly corrupt local authority of Chitungwiza Town Council (CTC)

I use data from the population census results of 2012 describe the characteristics of my population. ZRHC is a sample of this population obtained through snowballing. In terms of demographics Chitungwiza has an average household size of 4.1, while number of yearly population births stands at 12 668. Total fertility rate stands at 3.3 while general fertility rate is 116.9. Under 5 mortalities is 71 while infant mortality rate stands at 46. The number of yearly under 5 deaths U5 MR times Births/1000 stands at 904. Chitungwiza has a population of 6-16 who have never been to school which stands at 1.8; while population of 6-16 of those school going age that remained out of school stands at 4.5.

What is important for this research is that these selected indicators confirm that the population of Chitungwiza is growing exponentially although growth may not necessarily be matched with adequate provision of resources. The composite index combines social indicators into composite deprivation index and helps to trace the poor and deprived. Section on data analysis represents a breakdown of profiles of the population by category.

Zano Remba Housing Cooperative

Zano Remba Housing Cooperative was mooted at government level by the then Minister of Local Government and Housing Dr Witness Mangwende, in the 1990s. This was a way of alleviating the housing shortages in Chitungwiza after years of neglect by the colonial regime of Rhodesia. As the cooperative transformed itself into a housing company, it was tasked by the government of Zimbabwe to deal with people who were affected by the effects of sanctions, civil servants who had been made redundant following Wold Bank policies like ESAP. It was necessary to work with local community leaders in the area. Christopher Chigumba, who had been a Councillor for Chitungwiza Town Council and a local Member of Parliament agreed to establish a community-based housing cooperative in 2002. Zano Remba, went into full operation in 2004, registering 3000 two-roomed cottages for individual families by 2008. The Cooperative was subsequently registered in terms of The Cooperative Societies Act Chapter 24:05 which governs the operations of housing cooperatives in Zimbabwe. Housing Units and stands were allocated to mainly homeless people in Chitungwiza South Constituency, Unit L, for nominal prices to cover the costs of setting up two-roomed core houses in the estate. The cooperative allocated basic housing units comprising of two rooms, a small kitchenette and a toilet on an average of 246 square metres. The first phase of allocations involved 3000 structures of brick under asbestos.

Buyers were expected to complete remaining civil works including plumbing and water installation services and electrification of the units. Following the economic crisis of 2008 caused by the imposition of sanctions, it became virtually impossible for contractors to finish construction projects of those housing units. Out of corruption and greed, local councillors conniving with local political structures invaded the estate, re-allocating incomplete housing units to rival desperate home owners. It is the 'double allocation' of stands and housing units that caused the regression of the estate into anarchy, housing demolitions and a permanent state of relative deprivation. Land Barons put up some fierce and tough struggles in exploiting new home seekers thereby running it down in poverty, conflict and deprivation.[68]

Methodology: Self-Administered Questionnaires

The research relies on self-administered questionnaires as a method of social enquiry and data collection. Questionnaires as a research instrument are designed to be simple and easy to follow. Mathew and Rose (2010) define questionnaires as "a list of questions each with a range of answers [arranged] in a format that enables standardised and structured data to be gathered". Thus, effectives of questionnaires are in their implied control, standardisation of questions and uniformity of responses. The research also collects different but related type of data including facts, descriptions, knowledge, opinions, attitude and values from research participants.

---

[68] The Herald (2015) "Land baron cashes in on desperate home-seekers" 5 November 2015, http://www.herald.co.zw/land-baron-cashes-in-on-desperate-home-seekers/accessed 17Mar 2017

The Herald (2015) "Six land barons up for $300 000 fraud" 30 November 2015, http://www.herald.co.zw/six-land-barons-up-for 300-000-fraud/accessed 17Mar 2017

Press Reader.com – Connecting People Through News (2016) http://www.pressreader.com/zimbabwe/the-herald-zimbabwe/20160422/281716714549075/accessed 17 Mar 2017

Test Questionnaires

Test questionnaires were administered test questionnaires to gauge the mood of respondents and to check on the structural appropriateness of my methodology. It was essential to check on levels of understanding and conceptualisation of poverty issues. It was appropriate to check on questionnaire criterion - for validity in terms of time frames and anticipated interview duration. Test surveys gave clues and impressions of how this fieldwork was likely to be received especially in this highly-politicised environment. The fact that there were multi-pronged investigations in the estate at the time - about corrupt councillors and land barons made it hard for communities to open and accommodate strangers. There were also tensions and intra-party violence on the ground. In short, the atmosphere was fragile and volatile.

Studies in fieldwork confirm that it is essential to understand the mood of the population under investigation. This is so because it gives a clear idea of the quality of data and findings that one is likely to adduce from interviewees. Outsiders were at that time treated with suspicion and caution. The researcher considered approaching political leaders at party branch level to seek clearance. This option was discounted on the basis that it was potentially political and therefore likely to distort findings through bias and distortion. If the researcher should deal with labels such as "spies", "outsiders", "detectives" and Central Intelligence Organisation", then it makes data collection hard, arduous and laborious.

Last, before we went into this field for research, there had been many personnel from Non-Governmental Organisations (NGO), Urban Development Corporation (UDCO), surveyors from the Surveyors General's Office, Officials from the Ministry of Health and Child Welfare – all of which appear, among other things, to have promised development and eradication of poverty, provision of schools and facilities.

Structure of Questionnaire

Part A is compilation of demographic data, notably date of birth, size of family, and ages of children. Certain information like names and address details are anonymised to protect respondents. We do not gather information of national registration identity information in line with ethical protocols. Sections on demographic anonymity are the point at which research participants start to construct their storylines without researcher interventions. Participants tend to gain trust and confidence in data elicitation when they feel that questions are less intrusive but personal.

Part B is a summary of employment status or income source. What the research gains is establishing the nature of employment status by ticking the box which best describes participants' occupational role. Rather than ask direct questions of monetary returns, figures or gains, "Source of Income" in this section is a credible measure of poverty. This section helps to construct tentative co-relationship indexes of deprivation. Five categories of employment, namely Formal, Informal, Self-Business, Pensioner and Unemployed are presented as tick boxes. This category is extensively debated in the findings.

Data collection from Zano Remba Housing Cooperative is factual because it is designed to solicit opinions and information direct from research participants. This is done is a structured and methodical manner. I have included closed ended questions like "Are you registered with a Medical Practitioner"? A "Yes" or "No" answer helps to quantify statistical information in figures or percentages of research participants who have access to a Medical doctor. Access is also an aggregate measure of both relative and absolute poverty.

Part C asks about access to or sources of water. Five aspects namely - Communal, Well, Borehole, Communal tape [or other sources] are arranged as tick boxes. All participants are asked the same set of questions in a "tick box" style of self-administered questionnaires. From the Housing Cooperative in question's point of view, uniformity of questions reinforces a degree of fairness and consistence. At the level of this research, a random selection of households is selected for completion of self-administered questionnaires.

Part D enquires on number of rooms used by each household; while E is centres on education and access to schools by children of research participants. Section F is on Security and Empowerment. The fulcrum of this research is anchored on cutting down of costs. I also considered the possibility of getting quicker response rates. At the same time, social desirability bias was eliminated by "the absence of interviews" thereby strongly pointing out to honest and natural answers.

Data Capturing and Processing

I used the CSPRO computer-based data processing package. Here is how it works: Data from questionnaires is configured into known categories for easy processing. In terms of this research, data was captured on categories determined by and outlined on the questionnaire. This is called sequencing. CSPRO is a statistical package that is easy to understand and clear in quantifying frequencies. It has high accountability levels for data entered and certainly a narrow margin of error. Data is transferred from questionnaires and keyed in to CSPRO to create data capturing template. Data from the template is transferred to SPSS for analysis.

Findings: Strategies for Poverty Alleviation

The Zimbabwe Agenda for Sustainable Socio-Economic Transformation (Zim Asset) was formulated in October 2013 for accelerated economic growth. It identifies four clusters, namely Food Security and Nutrition, Social Services and Poverty Reduction, Infrastructure and utilities and Value addition and Beneficiation.

i.   Zano Remba Housing Cooperative falls under Social Services Poverty Eradication cluster. This research confirms that generally there are high levels of poverty in Unit L Seke, Chitungwiza. The study confirms that of tools used to measure levels of poverty in the constituency. The eight aspects are outlined in the questionnaire attached as an appendix. These are Employment, Education, Health, Housing, and Access for children to schools, Access to facilities like nurseries, Access to safe drinking water and Security/Empowerment.

ii.   From this research, we gather evidence that there are high levels of unemployment in Zano Remba Housing Cooperative. Unemployment is a key indicator of poverty levels. The deployment of statistics in terms of percentage distribution by employment status confirms that only 18.6% of the working-class population is in formal employment; while the rest is deployed as 81.4% outside formal employment. This the population is recorded as informal traders in self-employed business, pensioners or unemployed. - (Refer to the distribution chart on employment)

iii.   Registration with a Medical Practitioner (Doctor) is another significant indicator. Healthcare distribution graph by GP Registration is a product of the question "Are you registered with a Doctor". Non-registration is confirmed by 66.3% as compared with 32.6% who are registered. However, registration with a Doctor does not necessarily imply that registrants afford paid access to healthcare or a Medical Practitioner. If the majority are unemployed, then they may not be covered by medical aid.

iv.   From a representative sample of those who filled in the questionnaire, 79.1% indicated that they own their houses (They are Landlords) as compared to 20.9% who are either lodgers or other. That strong distribution of home ownership confirms the fulfilment of one of the Zim Asset clusters cited above – viz Social Services and Poverty Reduction. Home ownership is evidence of stability and settlement and confirms considerable success in implementation of poverty reduction strategies.

v.   Although the respondents score adversely (thus confirm the existence of high levels of poverty in Zano Remba Housing Cooperative) in other poverty-related indicators, there is evidence that the Cooperative fulfils Social Services and poverty eradication cluster. The distribution of those who own houses is positively skewed towards government policy of Zim Asset. This interpretation is consistent with growth targets for Zim Asset especially in terms of exponential growth year on year end in construction (From 2013 to 2018, recoded as the 10.0 at lower limit to 15.0 upper limit. (Refer to Growth targets for Zim Asset – Ministry of Finance and Economic Development)

Percent Distribution by education Level

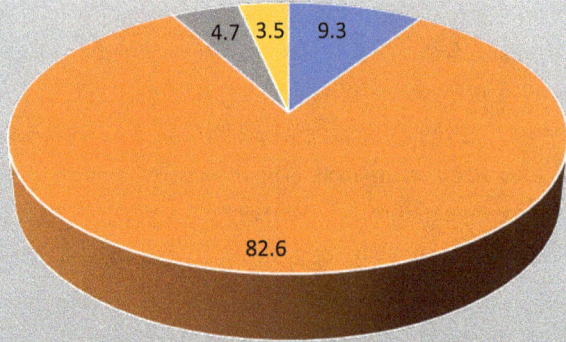

4.7 3.5 9.3

82.6

Primary   Secondary   Tertiary   Vocational

Percent Distribution by Employment status

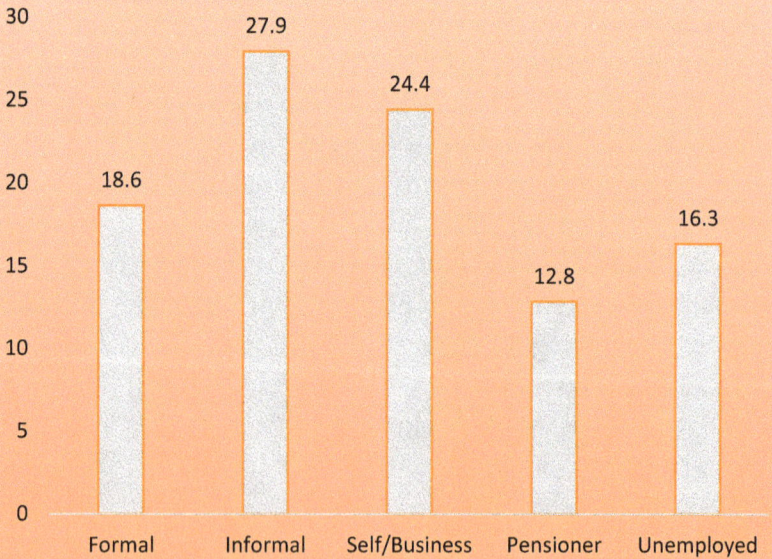

27.9	
24.4	
18.6	
12.8	
16.3	

Formal   Informal   Self/Business   Pensioner   Unemployed

30
25
20
15
10
5
0

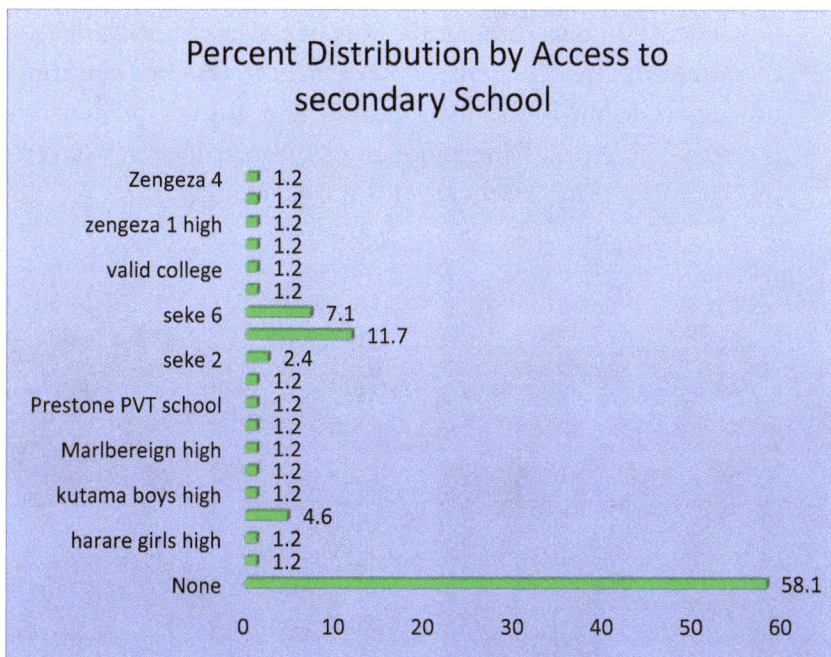

Percent Distribution by Access to secondary School

Zengeza 4	1.2
	1.2
zengeza 1 high	1.2
	1.2
valid college	1.2
	1.2
seke 6	7.1
	11.7
seke 2	2.4
	1.2
Prestone PVT school	1.2
	1.2
Marlbereign high	1.2
	1.2
kutama boys high	1.2
	4.6
harare girls high	1.2
	1.2
None	58.1

Local Strategies for Poverty Alleviation: Zim-Asset

At Zimbabwe government policy level there is evidence of full commitment to World Bank initiated Interim Poverty Reduction Strategies Programme (PRSP) of 2002[69]. This does not withstand the fact that a year earlier the USA government crafted and imposed sanctions under ZDERA (2001)[70]. By formulating the Zim Asset Policy, the Government of Zimbabwe has been able to:

i.   Implement a country driven and owned policy of poverty reduction predicated on broad-based participatory processes involving vulnerable groups and the poor.

ii.   Focus on outcomes that benefit the poor, for example, housing cooperatives including Zano Remba have been able to deliver tangible results to the poor. In the diagrams which highlight frequencies in terms of responses, 71.1% of the sample are

---

[69] World Bank (2002) A Sourcebook for Poverty Reduction Strategies: Volume1: Core Techniques and Cross-Cutting Issues. Edited by Jeni Klugman, Washington DC, USA.

[70] Zimbabwe Democracy and Economic Recovery Act (ZDERA) (S.494) passed by the United States government in 2001, Amended 2018,

Landlords. Although other indicators of poverty show variables that confirm widespread poverty in the estate, this research confirms that home ownership is the most critical step towards elimination of poverty. The World Bank annotation "measure to attack poverty" is precisely what Zim Asset cluster is focusing on.

Frequencies

Size of family				
Size of family	Frequency	Percent	Valid Percent	Cumulative Percent
1	2	2.3	2.3	2.3
2	3	3.5	3.5	5.8
3	22	25.6	25.6	31.4
4	23	26.7	26.7	58.1
5	19	22.1	22.1	80.2
6	6	7.0	7.0	87.2
7	5	5.8	5.8	93.0
8	3	3.5	3.5	96.5
12	1	1.2	1.2	97.7
15	1	1.2	1.2	98.8
45	1	1.2	1.2	100.0
Total	86	100.0	100.0	

1. Employment

Employment	Frequency	Percent	Valid Percent	Cumulative Percent
Formal	16	18.6	18.6	18.6
Informal	24	27.9	27.9	46.5
Self/Business	21	24.4	24.4	70.9
Pensioner	11	12.8	12.8	83.7
Unemployed	14	16.3	16.3	100.0
Total	86	100.0	100.0	

2. Education

Education	Frequency	Percent	Valid Percent	Cumulative Percent
Primary	8	9.3	9.3	9.3
Secondary	71	82.6	82.6	91.9
Tertiary	4	4.7	4.7	96.5
Vocational	3	3.5	3.5	100.0
Total	86	100.0	100.0	

3. Are you registered with a Doctor?

Are you registered with a Doctor?	Frequency	Percent	Valid Percent	Cumulative Percent
Yes	28	32.6	32.6	32.6
No	57	66.3	66.3	98.8
DK/Missing	1	1.2	1.2	100.0
Total	86	100.0	100.0	

4. What access to water do you rely on?

What access to water do you rely on?	Frequency	Percent	Valid Percent	Cumulative Percent
Well (Tsime)	53	61.6	61.6	61.6
Borehole	33	38.4	38.4	100.0
Total	86	100.0	100.0	

5. How many rooms do you have?				
How many rooms do you have?	Frequency	Percent	Valid Percent	Cumulative Percent
1	11	12.8	12.8	12.8
2	33	38.4	38.4	51.2
3	10	11.6	11.6	62.8
4	3	3.5	3.5	66.3
5	5	5.8	5.8	72.1
6	1	1.2	1.2	73.3
7	17	19.8	19.8	93.0
9	1	1.2	1.2	94.2
22	1	1.2	1.2	95.3
23	1	1.2	1.2	96.5
33	1	1.2	1.2	97.7
63	1	1.2	1.2	98.8
72	1	1.2	1.2	100.0
Total	86	100.0	100.0	

6A. Access to Local Nursery?				
Access to Local Nursery?	Frequency	Percent	Valid Percent	Cumulative Percent
None	78	90.7	90.7	90.7
best pre-school	1	1.2	1.2	91.9
best pre-school	1	1.2	1.2	93.0
precious kids	2	2.3	2.3	95.3
Precious kids	2	2.3	2.3	97.7
Precious Kids	1	1.2	1.2	98.8
PRECIOUS KIDS	1	1.2	1.2	100.0
Total	86	100.0	100.0	

6D. Access to Vocational or Polytechnic

Access to Vocational or Polytechnic	Frequency	Percent	Valid Percent	Cumulative Percent
None	80	93.0	93.0	93.0
Trust academy	1	1.2	1.2	94.2
UZ	1	1.2	1.2	95.3
University of Zimbabwe	2	2.3	2.3	97.7
Young African skills Centre	1	1.2	1.2	98.8
Young African skills Centre	1	1.2	1.2	100.0
Total	86	100.0	100.0	

6E. Other (e.g. correspondence, distance learning)

Other (e.g. correspondence, distance learning)	Frequency	Percent	Valid Percent	Cumulative Percent
none	85	98.8	98.8	98.8
1	1	1.2	1.2	100.0
Total	86	100.0	100.0	

7A. Do you own your own house?

Do you own your own house?	Frequency	Percent	Valid Percent	Cumulative Percent
Yes	68	79.1	79.1	79.1
No	18	20.9	20.9	100.0
Total	86	100.0	100.0	

7B. Do you have access to Police or Legal System?				
Do you have access to Police or Legal System?	Frequency	Percent	Valid Percent	Cumulative Percent
Yes	79	91.9	91.9	91.9
No	5	5.8	5.8	97.7
DK/Missing	2	2.3	2.3	100.0
Total	86	100.0	100.0	

7C. Do you have access to mobile telephone or internet?				
Do you have access to mobile telephone or internet?	Frequency	Percent	Valid Percent	Cumulative Percent
Yes	83	96.5	96.5	96.5
No	3	3.5	3.5	100.0
Total	86	100.0	100.0	

Source: Statistics from Zano Remba Housing Cooperative Questionnaire
April 2017

An image of total destruction of property belonging to a legitimate owner in Zano Remba Housing Estate - rival terrorist gangs had obtained such properties through a corrupt Councillor. – *Picture by Munoda Mararike*

Conclusion

This Chapter has examined several fundamental issues especially in context poverty measurement and strategies for poverty reduction. It has also established that indicators of poverty are both monetary and non-monetary. I use a case study of Zano Remba Housing Cooperative to highlight that poverty is not only associated only with insufficient income, but consumption, lack of access to health, education and gloom prospects for families and relatives. I argue that the situation obtaining in ZRHC was brought about through biting socio economic conditions which was caused by ZIDERA economic sanctions. I also use ownership of houses (Landlord status) as an important indicator for social status and poverty.

I conclude by observing that chronic poverty in Zano Remba Housing Cooperative is also a product of historical colonial forces that were discriminatory and brutal towards squatters fleeing from the Chimurenga war of liberation in the late 1970s. The situation is drawn from colonialism and imperialism – with the Rhodesian regime discriminating against Africans.

The sub-culture of poverty started to set in as Chirambahuyo squatter camp in the 1970s war of liberation has continued to grow on an exponential and linear levels. Current housing problems at Local authority level are also a result of pre- and post-independence stagnation, years of under investment, poor planning and decades of neglect. The main reason why it was complex to eliminate poverty and housing shortages was dates to the counter effects of Rhodesian regime discriminatory practices. This research opens a new front for further inquiry in terms scholarship rapporteur in sociological approaches to inequality, political economy, poverty and relative deprivation.

References

Barrett, C.B., Cartel, M.R. and Little, P.D. (2006) 'understanding and reducing persistent poverty in Africa: introduction special issue' *Journal of Development Studies,* Vol (42) 167-177

Bhamu, C.P., Mhlanga, A.N. and Mushayabasa, S. (2016) 'exploring the impact of prostitution on HIV/AIDS transmission' *International Scholarly Research Notices,* 1, 1-10.

Bryman, A. (2016) *Social Research Methods,* Oxford University Press, UK

Camus, M., Siemiatycki, J. and Mech, B 'nonoccupational exposure to chrysotile asbestos and risk of lung cancer' *N.E. J. Med* (338), 1565-1571

Chaeruka, J and Munzwa, K. (2009) 'assessing regulatory framework bottlenecks for low cost housing in Zimbabwe' *UN-HABITAT and Government of Zimbabwe* 1-49

Chigwedere, A.E (1980) *From Mutapa to Rhodes: 1000 to 1890 AD,* ISBN 10: 0333281586 / ISBN 13: 9780333281581, Published by MacMillan, 1980

Fiegehen, G.C., Lansley, P.S and Smith, A.D. *Poverty and Progress in Britain 1953-73,* Cambridge University Press, Cambridge, UK

Government of Zimbabwe (2005) *The Cooperative Societies Act* (24:05) Harare: Government of Zimbabwe

Government of Zimbabwe (2013), '*Zimbabwe Agenda for Sustainable Socio-Economic Transformation (Zim-Asset),* Harare: Government of Zimbabwe

Government of Zimbabwe (2012), *Population Census Results Harare Province.* Harare: Government of Zimbabwe

Gray, D.E. *Doing Research in the Real World,* Sage, London, UK.

Kupakuwana, P. (2007) 'a critical analysis of asbestos removal project cost implications'. *Cost Engineering,* Vol 49 (11), 30-35, Found at http://www.academia.edu/861062/A_Critical_Analysis_of_Asbestos_Removal_Project_Cost_Implications/Accessed April 23, 18

Mathews, B and Rose, L (2010) *Research Methods: A Practical Guide for the Social Research Sciences,* Pearson Education Limited, Edinburg Gate, United Kingdom.

Moyo, S. (1995) *The Land Question in Zimbabwe,* SAPES Books, Harare, Zimbabwe

Moyo, S. (2010) *Emerging Land Tenure Issues in Zimbabwe.* ISS Book Chapter. Found at http://www.aiastrust.org/index.php/publications/land-tenure.html/Accessed April 23, 18 Volume 32, Issue 2 July 1991, pp. 345-347

Mudenge, S.I.G (1988) *Mutapa Politics – A Political History of Munhumutapa,* c. 1400–1902. Harare: Zimbabwe Publishing House; London: James Currey, 1988

Mufuka, K., Muzvidzwa, K. & Nemerai, J. (1983) *Dzimbahwe: life and politics in the golden age 1100-1500 A.D.* 1st Ed, Harare Publishing House; Zimbabwe.

Runciman, W.G 'Relative Deprivation and Social Justice. A Study of Attitudes and Inequality in Twentieth Century England', *The British Journal of Sociology,* 17:4 430-434, 1966

Schlyter, A.M. (2003). 'Multi-Habitation: Urban Housing Life in Chitungwiza. Zimbabwe', *Uppsala: Nordic African Institute,* 1-77.

Townsend, P (1979) *Poverty in the United Kingdom: A Survey of Household Resources and Standards of Living.* Penguin Books, Hazel Watson, Aylesbury, United Kingdom, Found at http://www.poverty.ac.uk/system/files/townsend-book-pdfs/PIUK/piuk-whole.pdf/Accessed April 23, 18

UN-HABITAT (2006) "UNHABITAT Zimbabwe review of activities in Zimbabwe since 2006: Towards a comprehensive and inclusive human settlement development strategy and policy", Harare *UNHABITAT,* Zimbabwe. Found at https://s3.amazonaws.com/academia.edu.documents/3744299 1/Muchadenyika_2015_Habitatl_Intl_Vol_48_Slum_Upgrading ___Inclusive_Municipal_Governance_in_Harare..pdf?AWSAcc essKeyId=AKIAIWOWYYGZ2Y53UL3A&Expires=1524445 102&Signature=EL696DfNFbQTy30Lb2ZWUITw6CY%3D& response-content-disposition=inline%3B%20filename%3DSlum_Upgrading_and _Inclusive_Municipal_G.pdf/Accessed April 23, 18

Van Onseleen, C. *Chibaro: African Mine Labour in Southern Rhodesia 1900-1933.* Pluto Press, London

Williams, Chancellor, (1987) *Destruction of Black Civilization: Great Issues of a Race from 4500BC to 2000AD,* Third World Chicago Press, USA

World Bank (2002) *A Sourcebook for Poverty Reduction Strategies: Volume1: Core Techniques and Cross-Cutting Issues.* Edited by Jeni Klugman, Washington DC, USA. Found at http://documents.worldbank.org/curated/en/15693146813888 3186/pdf/298000182131497813.pdf/Accessed April 23,18

World Bank (2002) *A Sourcebook for Poverty Reduction Strategies: Volume2: Core Techniques and Cross-Cutting Issues.* Edited by Jeni Klugman, Washington DC, USA. Found at http://documents.worldbank.org/curated/en/68165146814731 5119/pdf/298000v-2.pdf/Accessed April 23,18

Wright, E.O (2002) 'The Shadow of Exploitation in Weber's Class Analysis', *American Sociological Review*, Vol. 67, 832-853.

Appendix 1

QUESTIONNAIRE: INDICATORS OF ECONOMIC SANCTIONS-INDUCED POVERTY: A STUDY OF ZANO REMBA HOUSING COOPERATIVE.

- *Please choose answers that applies to you by ticking in the right boxes*
- *Please answer Y for "Yes" and N for "No" for some questions as indicated*
- *This information will be used for academic research: Confidentiality will be maintained.*

SECTION A: DEMOGRAPHIC DATA:

Name (Optional)   _____

DOB   _____

SIZE OF FAMILY   _____

AGES OF CHILDREN   _____   ____   ____

_____   _____   _____

SECTION B: EMPLOYMENT: [Tick correct answer]

☐ Formal

☐ Informal

☐ Self/Business

☐ Pensioner

☐ Unemployed

SECTION C: EDUCATION: [Tick answers applicable to you]

☐ Primary

☐ Secondary

☐ Tertiary

☐ Vocational

☐ University

SECTION D: HEALTH:

Are you registered with a Doctor? [Tick Yes or No]

☐ Yes

☐ No

What access to water to you rely on?

☐ Council [inside my home]

☐ Well [Tsime]

☐ Borehole

☐ Communal tape

☐ Other   Specify _____

SECTION E: HOUSING:

How many rooms do you have?

☐ Write the number in the box

SECTION F: EDUCATION FOR CHILDREN: [You may tick more than one answer below]

☐ Access to local Nursery – Name of Nursery:

_____

☐ Access to local Primary School – Name of School:

_____

☐ Access to Secondary School – Name of School:

_____

☐ Access to Vocational or Polytechnic – Name:

_____

☐ Other (e.g. correspondence, distance learning) – Name:

_____

SECTION G: SECURITY AND EMPOWERMENT: [Put a Y for Yes or N for No to what applies to you below]

☐ Do you own your own house?

☐ Do you have access to Police or Legal System?

☐ Do you have access to mobile telephone or internet?

Thank you very much for your precious time to complete this questionnaire.

Chapter 7

Remarks on Imperialism and Plundering of African Resources by the West: A Posthumous Collection of Articles written by Chinondidyachii Godfrey Tichafara Mararike, BL, (Z'bwe), LLB (Z'bwe) [1961-2009][71]

'... Like those who fight against sleaze, bigotry and oppression whose automatic AKs are proof of their humanity... – so is my pen – chino

Snapshots of Chinondidyachii's Intellectual Terrain

"… Mr. Mararike also criticized two prior attempts by activist Peter Tatchell to attempt citizen's arrests against President Mugabe during trips to Europe. 'Heads of state, either from Europe, Africa or Southeast Asia, enjoy immunity; they ought to be protected properly in terms of their security when they visit other countries,' he said. 'It is not [appropriate] for Peter Tatchell to try these tactics. If anyone attempted to make a citizen's arrest on Tony Blair or on George W. Bush, it would not be accepted. President Mugabe is not guilty of human-rights abuses to the extent to what has been put across in the media'…"

Mr. Mararike says the Zimbabwean government has and will continue to bring to justice supporters of the government or the opposition who resort to violence. "…The aim and policy of ruling party, ZANU PF, is that allegations are properly investigated because

[71] I thank all who helped in compilation of these articles for all the effort and hard work to preserve the indelible memories of Chinondidyachii, a very sharp and intellectually astute brother: a coruscating and – like a soldier – 'decorated' lawyer. I am indebted and intensely grateful to Munyaradzi Hatendi and Kudakwashe Mazuru of Zimbabwe Newspapers, Harare. I thank Gamuchirayi Mujere for extracting and converting PDF files.

191

we want to ensure that we run a peaceful country, where there is no breakdown of law and order," he said.

From http://www.zimbabwesituation.com/old/feb25_2003.html

Cablegate: Media Report U. S. Under Fire: Harare

Monday, 28 October 2002, 7:56 am
Cable: Wikileaks
Ref: 02HARARE2346
This record is a partial extract of the original cable. The full text of the original cable is not available.
UNCLAS HARARE 002346
SIPDIS:
DEPT FOR AF/PD, AF/S, AF/RA
NSC FOR JENDAYI FRAZER
LONDON FOR GURNEY
PARIS FOR NEARY
NAIROBI FOR PFLAUMER
E.O. 12958: N/A
TAGS: PREL KPAO KMDR ZI
SUBJECT: MEDIA REPORT U. S. UNDER FIRE; HARARE

1. Under headline "Bush wants to create space for decision strike on Iraq" the October 28 edition of the government-controlled daily "The Herald" carried the following written by Chinondidyachii Mararike on page 8:

2. "Will the U.S. go ahead and launch military strikes against Iraq or will Saddam Hussein comply with Bush's ultimatum that `Iraq complies with all the relevant UN resolutions?' Surely these are not the right questions to ask. What is right to ask is why now, and after months of dilly-dallying, has Bush seen it fit to seek UN approval for America's so-called war on terrorism? Is the issue simply that of weapons inspections or is there a greater and even more sinister agenda than the inarticulate Bush is either able or willing to articulate?

". . .The point then is that Bush's 12 September 2002 speech to the 190-member UN General Assembly was intended to provide international cover for American unilateralism, and thus give legitimacy to Bush's need for a regime change not only in Iraq but in other states that stand up against U.S. domination and control.

". . .Surely if Bush had concern for upholding human rights then his government would not support, arm and underwrite the Israeli army to mount military campaigns against innocent Palestinians. And if America has respect for the rule of law then it would understand the Zimbabwean government's commitment to correcting the injustices of colonialism and contemporary U.S.-supported neo-colonialism and not impose punitive sanctions against our entire leadership. I think it's time somebody reminded Bush, and his `blind' Caucasian American followers, that America is not the only superpower in the world but that people in countries continuously resisting U.S. imperialism are in fact the superpowers..."

Zimbabwe: Part 1
Imperialists Seek to Dominate Third World
OPINION
By Chinondidyachii Mararike,
13 January 2003 *www.herald.co.zw*

Harare — This is the first part of the article in which Chinondidyachii Mararike examines imperialism. The second part will be published next Saturday. [Article follows this contribution – see below]

We embrace 2003 buoyed by that stunning victory over the forces of imperialism, and in the knowledge that Zimbabweans will greet their next challenges with courage and determination - and not complacency and insouciance.

The suffering that Africans endured at the hands of colonial imperialists is no different from what they are enduring under today's neo- imperialist thugs, and clearly shows how contemporary imperialists absorbed the habits of their forefathers.

The refugees fleeing Western-inspired civil wars in Africa, victims of imperialism, are dwellers of plastic palaces, or of mud-walled affairs with roofs of palm fronds.

Africa's squatter camps in Ouagadougou, Abidjan, Freetown, Monrovia, Kisangani, or in Kenya's illegal human settlement of Kibera, are homes to groups of small, wide-mouthed and hungry children who together with their distraught neighbours stare while the Britons, French, Israelis, and Americans sun themselves in some of Africa's tourist equivalents of a British Empire, rubbing salt in the wounds of the poor who watch in horror at the drunken revelries and pampered ignorance.

Imperialism is when Morgan Tsvangirai's MDC calls for sanctions against the innocent people of Zimbabwe and when Kenyan dancers in colourful print outfits and white-fringed skirts die dancing barefoot for foreign tourists milling in the lobby of an unnamed hotel for a pittance.

Since when have the coasts of Africa been a paradise for the local African peoples, when most are forced to work for subsistence wages, serving unquestioningly every demand of pampered Westerners? Since when have the tourist resorts of Africa played host to honest and philanthropic Europeans?

No, comrades - no way *vehama!*

Now that is the "modern" face of imperialism, tourist-style, in which the imperialists do not care about what the "security" forces of their respective "elected" Western governments are doing on their behalf in Liberia, Sierra Leone, Uganda, Ivory Coast, Rwanda, Burundi, Palestine, Afghanistan, Iraq, the DRC, and Angola. And all because imperialism is deceptive: it blends political calculation with sheer diplomacy.

Imperialism is terrifying and wicked. And for Sigmund Freud who was writing at about the time when imperialist ideas were taking a modern shape, it is the obscene pleasure of the death drive, and the self-destructive instincts, which seduces the imperialists into killing other races out of sheer selfishness.

What makes the imperialist most impregnable is how he embraces his own destruction, not just dismembering others.

On this theory, which one can find in both Fascism and Nazism, imperialism is in thrall to the petty suburban logic of living as long as the victims fear death. Imperialists, therefore, believe they free themselves from death only when they accept their own death,

194

indeed more like the revolutionary who risks his own life when he or she takes up arms to fight the imperialist - but there the comparison ends!

That is why Zanu-PF and other African ruling parties understand that the "ism" at the end of imperialism suggests a philosophy crafted out of frightening monsters that kill other non-Europeans for exploitation, for fun and for purposes of domination.

Zimbabweans understand how imperialists operate, that is, through nourishing their socio-economic and political systems of domination by making those in the third world perpetual servants.

Through these systems of control, they spread their tentacles of hegemony, what Antonio Gramsci, refers to as "the way in which the consent of the subordinate classes to their domination is achieved".

Once achieved, hegemony ensures that the dominant ideology permeates every facet of human existence. Religion, language, food, clothing/dressing, taste, morality, customs, and political principles are some of the arenas of hegemony. Indeed, it perpetuates an order in which a Western way of life and thought is dominant, and one concept of reality prevails throughout the dominated society.

This way, the dominated are unable to respond to the spectre and genre of exported Western religious culture with anything else other than the pleasure of familiar horror - to use an oxymoron. In the meantime, Messrs Donald Rumsfeld, George W. Bush and Tony Blair are busy trying to convince the world that they are the most effective defenders of universal democratic values. In fact, all they are defending are the undignified liberal values of today's Western-dominated world order.

Now that is imperialism. The terror of imperialism is founded upon the kind of right-wingers for whom any fundamental criticism of the West by anybody in the so-called developing world is so inconceivable that it can only be a symptom of insanity.

Britain, defeated by Zanu-PF in the 1966 to 1980 anti-colonial and liberation war, and also in the 2000 to 2002 Third Chimurenga - has learned that Cde Mugabe is still as sharp as he was since the 1960s when he came out to fight against the forces of imperialism.

That is why the tabloid press seeks to portray President Mugabe as an insane person. That is why Britain portrayed the Zanla war as a "gorilla" rather than a guerrilla movement, even though the British government was aware that this was Zanu-PF's legitimate armed wing during the liberation struggle. That, too, is why the West cannot quite stomach Zanu-PF's defeat of the neo-colonial form of imperialism in Zimbabwe. And too, why the opposition has no means of repelling Zanu-PF's anti-imperialist juggernaut.

Yes, Zimbabwean revolutionaries embrace 2003 determined not to allow the imperialists to underestimate us after what we have achieved because Zanu-PF has raised the tempo as the opposition's delusionary days turn to a distant memory. Zanu-PF is determined to give fresh evidence of its own distinction.

But much more than all this is because Davira Mhere acknowledges that President Mugabe is a one-man nemesis for imperialism, and for any imperialist stooge.

He, Africa's most loved and famous son, has dominated international forums in thought and deed. He is a man who makes his imperialist opponents uncertain. Concentrated and conscious, committed but controlled, the revolutionary suffers no disastrous lapses in discipline.

Zimbabweans have put up a good fight and must until this imperialist beast is defeated and killed completely. To these, the veterans of Zimbabwe's Third Chimurenga, we dedicate this poem, the Lyrics of Africa's Revolutionary Tune, and declare that:

The same courage, determination and unity of purpose that won us Phase 1 will win us Phases II and III, because President Mugabe's revolution is a Zanu-PF revolution.

A Zanu-PF revolution is a Zimbabwe-led revolution for the total liberation of Southern Africa and the rest of sub-Saharan Africa.

Zimbabwe should export this revolution to its neighbours, where the remnants of the racist white farmers went to settle.

Once successfully exported, the revolution's momentum will deny the beleaguered imperialists any room to manoeuvre, and will force them to either retreat or engage us on our terms – ostensibly because the resources they are stealing from our neighbours will not be available to them.

And with our hero, President Mugabe (the one who brought down 'whites') continually assaulting imperialism and vowing to fight on, Africans will not turn the other cheek in compromise.

Africa has the highest number of imperialist victims divested from their land. They dwell in deplorable shanties and refugee camps, and remain insulated from their history and decent existence.

The imperialist, bereft of any ounce of conscience, inflicts untold suffering to their victims. It is these victims that Tony Blair and George W. Bush think they can root out with Nepad. It is these that in the so-called Third World the West thinks it can root out with IMF and World Bank structural schemes.

For the imperialist victims, the effects are disastrous. This is what Europe desires - to have Africans overlook the fact that it is they, the Europeans, that are plundering the continent's abundant natural and human resources. Consequently the new post-colonial state in Africa is contenting with rampant capitalism and relentless exploitation.

"In the Southern African context in particular," writes the Sunday Mirror's Scrutator, "the socio-political and economic dynamics attendant to the liberatory and transformative process" continue to be "threatened by the combined forces of globalisation" and an increasingly Western-induced hostile environment in which reactionary MDC-style opposition parties "are forging closer ties with former colonisers and agents of globalisation".

Zimbabwe's task is, therefore clear: to export the revolution to countries in Africa whose current institutional arrangements and societal perceptions are still based on or stem from imperial structures dominated by foreign private sector interests and therefore, perpetuating inequitable entitlements and access to African resources.

When Zimbabwe's liberationist volcano explodes, its lava will scorch and smoother the resisting settlers on the continent. Mugabe's Revolution must move forward and through phases - Phase II makes Africans the primary beneficiaries of Africa's abundant mineral and other natural resources. Phase III sees the complete Africanisation of our commercial and industrial sectors.

In tandem with both phases should be the development of Afro-centric epistemologies, representations, discourses, and narratives in which the central tenets of African culture and religion as in *Mwari-via-Vadzimu neMasvikiro,* languages, architecture, dressing, food, music, jokes and general way of life, occupy the middle ground of the values that inform our activities.

Sure we cannot afford to throw a protective blanket over this revolution, for to do so would be to throw away what we have achieved for Zimbabwe and Africa and in the process squander this most rare opportunity when we can successfully export this revolution to others whose land remains in the talons of imperialists.

The fact that Mugabe's Revolution is already spreading fast into Namibia and South Africa, and has found resonance throughout the world makes our task less cheerless indeed.

That, indeed, is why we hear all these people chanting: Pamberi neZanu-PF, Swapo neANC! - (Pamberi!)

© Chinondidyachii Mararike is a Zimbabwean lawyer, writer, political analyst, and secretary-general of Davira Mhere.
http://www.raceandhistory.com/selfnews/viewnews.cgi?newsid10
43807365,41594, shtml

Zimbabwe: Marechera Abhorred Tyranny of Any Kind
ANALYSIS
By Chris Kabwato,
Financial Gazette, Harare - 22 August 2002,
http://www.fingaz.co.zw

I wanted to have this article published last week on August 15 (three days before the 15th anniversary of Dambudzo Marechera's death) but then decided to wait for the President's Heroes Day speech.

Foolishly I had hoped that the speech would announce some major turnaround from the suicidal path that our leaders have chosen. But my hopes were dashed, and I should have just gone ahead and written what I felt about Dambudzo and about the Dear Leader.

Dambudzo Charles Marechera died on August 18 1987. He was only 35 years old. Marechera was born in Vengere, Rusape, on June 4, 1952.

In 1973 he was expelled from the then University of Rhodesia together with other students for protesting against racial discrimination on campus.

He enrolled at Oxford University in 1974 but did not complete his studies for a variety of reasons mainly to do with his own non-conformist attitude.

In 1979 Marechera stormed the literary world with his debut work, The House of Hunger. Later he published The Black Sunlight and Mindblast.

I never met this writer who appeared almost daily in newspapers and magazines and seemed to have close acquaintance with controversy.

I only got to read his work six months after his demise when I enrolled at the University of Zimbabwe to study for my BA (then derided as Bachelor of Anything).

In that atmosphere of leftwing student politics it would have been easy to dismiss Marechera as a "post-modernist decadent bourgeois" writer. In fact, two of my lecturers called his work "a private voice" meaning his was largely "art for art's sake".

But for five students who enrolled at UZ in the BA English programme - Morris Vambe, Albert Nyathi, Nhamo Mhiripiri, Robert Muponde and myself - Marechera was a hero. Indeed, we became quite obsessed with his life and works - we knew House of Hunger from back to front, had loved Mindblast and Nyathi could recite many of the poems from the top of his head.

He, in particular, called Marechera "buddy".

The only other student not in our class who was equally passionate about Marechera was Munoda Mararike. Mararike was instrumental in organising Marechera memorial events in the Africa Unity Square. Musaemura Bonas Zimunya and Rino Zhuwarara, contemporaries of Marechera, fuelled our interest in the writer through their perceptive and sympathetic lectures.

Both lecturers had been Marechera's colleagues and together were part of the generation of students hounded into exile to further their education.

Fifteen years after his demise, Marechera still lives in the imagination of a lot of people. As I remember the life of the young writer taken away in his prime I wonder what he would have thought about the current Zimbabwe.

Would he have gone into exile? After all, when he had just arrived from exile in the early eighties he had immediately wanted to go back were it not for some government officials who sabotaged the intention. So, he stayed on.

But I have no doubt he would have remained a thorn in the government's belly. He might have done a repeat of his famous solo demonstration against Ian Smith in 1973 or thereabouts but it would have been against the darker twin of that most obdurate and suicidal leader.

He might have had to re-issue House of Hunger and say here is what the new Zimbabwe has become - a place where "every morsel of sanity is snatched the way some kind of birds snatch food from the very mouth of babes".

But that is mere speculation. All that would have remained constant is that he would never have betrayed his honesty and integrity. When a writer moves into the beyond he lives behind his work and that is what really survives him.

Marechera left a small but very potent corpus of work. I do not know how widely read he was outside universities and colleges. After all he was a writer that all agreed could be "difficult". So, I can only speak for myself.

I do not think Marechera was a great writer. Charles Mungoshi is certainly a much better writer. The value of Marechera lies in his influence on the writing of literature in Zimbabwe. I know for a fact he influenced the work and ideas of Muponde, Zenenga, Mhiripiri and Nyathi. Muponde has written quite extensively on Marechera and Mhiripiri contributed an essay to a sourcebook on the late writer's life. Mhiripiri is now a writer and an academic, Nyathi is a poet, Muponde and Vambe are academics, Zenenga is an academic and dramatist.

As we grapple in the dark searching for a way out of the malaise created by Mugabe and his henchmen, Marechera's life and work provide a source of inspiration. I am inspired by his search "for knowledge with the hardness and brilliance of a diamond". I am inspired by his vision that it was even more important that writers became critical of their own governments after independence. He would have found rich material in the tragi-comedy of our own Joseph Goebbels. After all he had foreseen him in the character Rix the Giant Cat in his work, Mindblast. He would have read his poem Oracle of the Povo to the president if those paranoid bodyguards would have allowed him within a radius of 40 km near the dear leader. He would asked him repeatedly as he did when he was living "Why is that writers and the Party are separated when the revolution is over?"

May the ideals of Dambudzo Charles Marechera live on in those that will not accept tyranny of any kind.

Zimbabwe Won't Allow West to Destroy Economy
Opinion.
Chinondidyachii Mararike in UK,
22 January 2003, *www.herald.co.zw*

The Mugabe Revolution is far from being over. The fight is on, and imperialism must be slaughtered once and for all. The West is fighting us, fighting an economic and propaganda war against the innocent people of Zimbabwe, their Government, their President and their ruling party.

So, when we sing of *Mukaona VaMugabe vachitonga iwee . . . ndicho chitenderano chatakaita, isu veZanu-PF* (If you see Cde Mugabe ruling, it's the covenant we signed, us members of Zanu-PF), we are simply referring to the mandate that we gave Comrade Mugabe, the mandate to fight and defeat imperialism. That was the deal and still is.

We have always known that the fight against imperialism is a protracted struggle. We will win because we are united, and we stand united against the imperialists who are interfering in our political and economic affairs.

We are united because we are brothers and sisters, sons of the soil, daughters of the soil and the veterans of the 1966 Chinhoyi battle. We are the cream of *Zanla's Chifombo* Military Academy High Command in Zambia.

We are graduates of the Chitepo College of Ideology and survivors of *Nyadzonya and Chomoio* in Mozambique. We are the veterans of the Second Chimurenga and heroes of the Third. So, we stand united against a common enemy. We are President Mugabe's scholars and we preach revolution.

We are revolutionaries, leaders, war veterans, chiefs, *sadunhus,* patriots, intellectuals, *chibwidos, mujibhas,* and ordinary folk ready to move the revolution forward with Cde Mugabe at the helm, our Commander-in-Chief!

And if yesterday the enemy failed to divide us then today the enemy cannot divide us. We remain united and we will win. United in purpose, in leadership, in Zimbabwe, in Africa.

Of course, I am talking here about the totally ridiculous story published recently - what the imperialist newspapers gleefully referred to as President Mugabe's "exit plans from politics" and which, predictably, caused undignified hysterics in both the opposition MDC camp and the British and Western media circles.

The racists and their local stooges were at it again, this time attempting to seize the propaganda initiative and control the political debate, what we call *kubaya kana kuti kudhaura muforo* so we unwittingly plough around it. The usual media gambit, you see, of setting both the pace and agenda of political discourse.

Ah, we have no problems with that, not at all. All we need to do is *kubaya wedu muforo,* and as sure as the sun will rise every morning the imperialists will plough around it.

Soon after his arrival at Lusaka International Airport for the occasion to honour Dr Kenneth Kaunda with the Grand Commander of the Eagle of Zambia on January 14, 2003, President Mugabe declared: 'Never will I go into exile. I was born, grew up and fought for Zimbabwe. I will die in Zimbabwe and be buried in Zimbabwe's soil'.

Invoking the revolutionary spirit of another of Africa's luminaries, Kwame Nkrumah, and in the presence of Comrades Kaunda and Nujoma, President Mugabe vowed he would not surrender to the imperialist forces, adding: "The only good imperialist is a dead one."

The articulate and erudite intellectual wins the battles.

Kudhaura muforo mutsva is what I have just done and am doing right now.

Watch and listen carefully when we say that as leaders, decision-makers and opinion-makers, we must recognise that what is over, or almost over under Mugabe's Revolution, is Phase 1 - and this brought land to the then long-suffering people Zimbabwe in 2002.

This fight we won. But our President says we should fight and defeat imperialism. In Lusaka he told the invited guests that "the fight against neo-colonialism requires men and women of strong will and irreversible determination to defeat it".

This is a fight for Zimbabweans to engage in and win as the nation braces itself for the challenges that lie ahead in 2003 and beyond.

This is a war for Africans to fight and win as the continent embarks on subsequent phases of the revolution, so our land ownership assumes a total and enduring meaning to us and all Africans at home and abroad.

That is why this war is not an event but a process, indeed a phased operation that will always be with us for as long as imperialism continues to rear its ugly head on our continent.

Winning the economic and propaganda war is our starting point and immediate priority. Thereafter, we shall swiftly embark upon the next phases, so we can take the war into the areas in which the arrogant and wasteful West still holds a stranglehold on our political and economic activities.

Our next, and equally important, objective is to ensure that we own everything on and underneath our soil, for beneath it there is a new undertow of meaning, a meaning as obvious as it is legal: a landowner owns the land and everything on and underneath it. That, now, is our discourse - our new *muforo*.

What we are talking of right now is our total and complete takeover, ownership and control of our vast mineral resources.

We will not sit back and allow the West to mess us about, to mess our economy and starve our people when we can sell our diamonds, platinum, gold and uranium to Thailand, Singapore, Nigeria, Malaysia, Ghana, China, Libya, Saudi Arabia, Pakistan, Syria, Iran, Iraq, Libya, Korea, Venezuela, Cuba, Lebanon, Japan, China . . . and in the process take away business from thieves in London, Washington, Brussels, Paris, Berlin, or Copenhagen.

We are taking over the mines, so we can market our God-given resources to countries with which we enjoy excellent relations and use the money to buy food for our people from wherever we can source them.

Yes, indeed, Africa is free to trade with whoever it wants. We have what they want and need, and they have what we want and need. And we know what we want.

We now open a new diplomatic offensive, that's what it is. And that is where we are going as a people, as a nation. And that's how far-sighted Mugabeism is, a philosophy that in Zimbabwe has created a new, democratic order - and will soon do so in Southern Africa and beyond. And in turning ourselves into anti-imperialist weapons, we force a point because as anti-imperialist soldiers we accept that the risk of death is a symbolic statement that under imperialism the way we live is even direr than non-existence.

We are fighting to win, and to win against a deceitful, arrogant and racist enemy. We're fighting on behalf of King Lobengula who in 1888 wrote to the Queen of England objecting to the Rudd Concession, insisting he had been deliberately misled by British negotiators and therefore "would not recognise the paper, as it contains neither my words nor the words of those who got it".

In her mean and imperialist response of April 1889, the queer queen Victoria arrogantly told King Lobengula: "It is impossible to exclude the white men".

Britons and their European counterparts still believe that "it is impossible to exclude the white men" from African land and resources, from African politics, and from African attempts to liberate themselves. We are fighting to win against a stubborn and divisive enemy.

This then is not the time to flinch or retreat, for the imperialist by his very cowardly nature will always pursue a retreating person. Courage and determination won us Chimurenga Phase 1, and that is why 2002 was largely a victory *Jikinya* dance marking our successful land reclamation exercise and the final phase in the destruction of the MDC party. The journey has started, admittedly, but we still have a long way to go.

From: https://www.mailarchive.com/ugandanet@kym.net/msg02641.html

Bush wants to create space for decisive strike on Iraq

OPINION
By Chinondidyachii Mararike
Posted: Monday, October 28, 2002, *www.herald.co.zw*

Will the US go ahead and launch military strikes against Iraq or will Saddam Hussein comply with Bush's ultimatum that "Iraq complies with all the relevant UN resolutions on weapons inspections, human rights, the repatriation of prisoners of war, and the state sponsorship of terrorism?"

Surely these are not the right questions to ask. What is right to ask is why now, and after months of dilly-dallying, has Bush seen it fit to seek UN approval for America's so-called war on terrorism? Is the issue simply that of weapons inspections or there is a greater and even more sinister agenda than the inarticulate Bush is either able or willing to articulate? Will Bush go for North Korea whose officials openly revealed, on 19 October this year, that the country had "nuclear weapons" and "more powerful things (presumably chemical and biological weapons) as well?"

And surely how can the US claim it is able to re-order the whole world and yet is today paralysed by a murderer in its own backyard, the so-called sniper whose marksmanship has so far claimed ten lives and yet has avoided detection by vanishing into Washington DC's permanently chaotic rush-hour traffic?

These, indeed, are the questions to ask for the truth is you cannot expect to arrive at the right answers if you ask the wrong questions.

The point then is that Bush's 12 September 2002 speech to the 190-member UN General Assembly was intended to provide international cover for American unilateralism, and thus give legitimacy to Bush's need for a regime change not only in Iraq but in other states that stand up against US domination and control.

Whether Saddam is a realistic threat or isn't is not the real issue; uppermost in Bush's mind is to find ways to shift responsibility onto the UN so he can confer to America a moral high ground in its quest for a global strategy that supports US post-Cold War imperialism.

The US President's seeming concern for the UN as an international institution of repute also carries with it a hint of self-serving, and reeks of deception and double standards of the worst kind.

While Bush spoke of his desire to work with the UN Security Council to hammer out the necessary resolutions that would give Saddam one last chance to avoid invasion, he also challenged the UN to "salvage its credibility" and "serve the purpose of its founding or it will be irrelevant".

Yet it is ironic that the US itself and Britain, countries that were instrumental in establishing the UN after the Second (largely) European Tribal War of 1945, and with the stated aim of ensuring "lasting peace by ending the scourge of war", should themselves engage in precisely what the UN was designed to prevent.

Bush's strategy is designed to put the world body in a dilemma: if the UN refuses to tow the US line then it would not have lived up to the purpose for which it was formed.

In the event then Bush would ignore and by-pass it and, under the guise of a war on terrorism, launch military strikes against Iraq.

If, on the other hand, the UN complies with Bush's demands, then the US would exploit the opportunity and craft a resolution loaded with what Anatol Lieven (Guardian 13 September 2002) called "so many conditions that Baghdad would be certain to reject it, leading to an immediate Anglo-American attack".

Bush's courting of the UN reveals his belligerence, his attempts to hoodwink the international community so he can create space for a quick and decisive strike on Iraq.

Fortunately, most people, particularly African and Middle East leaders, know that the Bush (who seemed quite happy and enthusiastic to demand action from the UN against those who deny others human rights and generally flout international law) presides over a nation that imprisons people on the flimsiest of suspicion, denies them access to legal representation and visits from relatives; and that the US is a "nation" that has its own torture camp in Cuba, hidden away from the world.

Examples of the pretexts upon which the US has based its quest to destabilise other countries abound.

On August 5, 1964, for instance, the US reported that the North Vietnamese had fired on American warships in the Gulf of Tonkin.

Before that, support in the Congress for the involvement in the Vietnam War had been doubtful but on August 7 the "Gulf of Tonkin incident" led to the US Congress voting for troops to be sent to Vietnam, with only two votes against.

The Tonkin incident never happened - in fact, it was a lie - but American troops went to Vietnam nevertheless, resulting in the deaths of millions of innocent Vietnamese and only 65 000 young Americans, mostly of African descent.

In that war, the US - committed to upholding the basic human rights of others on mother earth - used chemical weapons, Agent Orange, destroying much of Vietnamese forests and poisoning a lot of the country's fertile agricultural land!

As it turns out, even the dog's breakfast tossed to the assembly by Bush - empty commitments to standards of human dignity shared by all, to a system of security defended by all, to Palestinian independence, and the US's immediate return to the Paris-based UNESCO after 18 years of absence - cannot hide the fact American policy has increasingly turned this safe planet into a combustible world.

It may be important to note that the US pulled out from the body in 1984 during Ronald Reagan's presidency and when the organisation was under the leadership of Senegal's Amadou Mbow who promoted an equitable new world information order then (as now) opposed by Western countries, particularly Britain and America.

This "tolerant" Atlantic democracy has, since 1945, continuously bombed the innocent, and has also used weapons of mass destruction on a large-scale - and in the form of atomic bombs and chemical weapons, often resorting to the most barbaric tactics ever known.

Using a series of fabrications to deceive the world, and also in the hope that this would result in a change of leadership, successive US Presidents have bombed defenceless and peace-loving nations: China (1945-46, 1959-53), Japan (1945), Korea (1950-53), Guatemala (1954, 1960, 1967-69), Indonesia (1958), Cuba (1959-61), Congo (1964), Peru (1965), Laos (1964-73), Vietnam (1961-73), Cambodia (1969-70), Lebanon (1983-84), Grenada (1983), Libya (1986), El Salvador (1980s), Nicaragua (1980s), Panama (1989), Bosnia (1985), Somalia (1994), Sudan (1998), Former Yugoslavia (1999), Afghanistan (1988, 2001-02) and Iraq (1991 to date).

Presumably what Bush would have the world believe is that his hard-line stance on Saddam is based on just demands for global peace and security but, in the case of Iraq, the world recalls the main factors which earlier terminated the endeavour to have the UN weapons inspectors re-admitted into the country. In 1996, a failed US coup against the Iraq leader used Unscom information, that is, the inspectorate had been used as espionage agents.

In 1997, the US declared that it intended to invade Iraq anyway, which meant that it was irrelevant whether or not Iraq submitted to the inspection process. In 1998 Operation Desert Fox used Unscom information to find its bombing targets and the US - together with its 54th State, Britain - bombed the Iraqis.

The inspectors were ordered out of Iraq because of these re-bombings and thus signalled the termination of the inspections processes, and Unscom.

Today its successor Unmovic - headed by an impressively "neutral" Swede, Hans Blix - is ready to move in: to locate bombing targets. Yet in spite of this record - in which the neutrality and actual purpose of weapons inspectors is questionable - Unmovic is today insisting on new inspection teams to go into Iraq. On Unmovic's team are personnel from the two countries to have repeatedly bombed Iraq, and whose policies are geared towards an Iraq regime change: the UK and its former colony, US. This approach, needless to say, is not in any way compatible with the weapons inspection process, and flouts international law - including every conceivable UN resolution.

Speaking of which, it must needs be pointed out that both the US and Britain are guilty of double standards in that the technical difference between the extant UN resolutions on Iraq and those on Israel is statistically misleading. The US has forced through all the resolutions on the former while vetoing many more resolutions critical of Israel's illegal occupation of, and terror tactics in, Palestine.

England which today has pledged to stand "shoulder to shoulder" with the US has done nothing to deal with Unionist terror in its backyard but, instead, has turned on the IRA, a liberation movement fighting against Britain's stranglehold on Irish territory, Northern Ireland, but which Westminster describes as a terrorist organisation.

The White House policy makers and so-called Pentagon hawks should stop deluding themselves into thinking that America's reliance on high-tech gadgetry gives it the right to unilaterally extend its hegemony over all countries and societies on planet earth without meeting with some form of resistance. It is this kind of thinking that, in America, continues to produce the kind of psychotic individuals who imagine themselves God and thus enter into bizarre dialogues with authorities whilst continuing to kill innocent people and, like the US' Zodiac the Killer of the 1970s, to kill across several state boundaries and, in the process, tying staggering amounts of state resources into embarrassingly fruitless searches!

Bush should know that the pain, disruption, fears, and anxieties the American feel and experience today, and also what those who lost relatives and friends in the Bali bombing have been going through these past few days, is exactly what a lot of people in Vietnam, Angola, DRC, Palestine, Nicaragua, Somalia and other countries the American military mighty has visited live and have lived with on a daily basis.

Surely if Bush had concern for upholding human rights then his government would not support, arm and underwrite the Israeli army to mount military campaigns against innocent Palestinians. And if America had respect for the rule of law then it would understand the Zimbabwean Government's commitment to correcting the injustices of colonialism and contemporary US-supported neo-colonialism and not impose punitive sanctions against our entire leadership.

I think it's time somebody reminded Bush, and his "blind" Caucasian American followers, that America is not the only superpower in the world but that people in countries continuously resisting US imperialism are in fact the superpowers. It is these same people - Africans, Asians, Persians, Arabs, Chinese - who today don't accept what Bush and Blair are saying, who refuse to be taken to those old dark days of Darwinian Caucasian superiority, who love their children, their peace and their countries.

Rather the US President ought to concentrate on finding this man with a telescopic high velocity gun that today is terrorising the residents of Baltimore, Washington DC.

Blair, on the other hand, must solve the dispute with Britain's grumbling fire fighters, revamp the crumbling British education, and put a stop to the unending series of notorious scandals involving Britain's paedophile priests.

© Chinondidyachii Mararike is a Zimbabwean lawyer, political analyst and Secretary General of Davira Mhere.
http://www.uscrusade.com/newsupdate/printnews.cgi?newsid1035 797041,.39229,.shtml

Zimbabwe: Donnelly Must Shut Up
OPINION
By Chinondidyachii Mararike
8 November 2002. www.herald.co.zw

Harare — A clause in the Criminal Procedure and Evidence Act clearly states that "a witness who gives evidence of good character cannot seek protection under the rules that exclude cross-examination on "character evidence".

Britain's High Commissioner to Zimbabwe, Brian Donnelly, has done exactly that. He has thrown away the shield and, in the process, has bared his chest to a barrage of arrows issuing from the prosecutor's tight bow.

On Friday 1 November 2002, Donnelly - who regularly expresses his outrageous MDC political opinions and is generally given to interfering in our country's internal affairs - gave an interview to the Zimbabwe Independent.

We in Davira Mhere are astounded that this supposedly experienced and senior British diplomat should think it the height of diplomatic finesse to toy with a newspaper known for its anti-government views, and which in reality is simply a mere mouth-piece that amplifies the preposterous anti-Mugabe utterances issuing from the dirty mouths and cursed pens of unforgivable reactionaries, myopic racists and the MDC party's pocket-sized politicians.

It should come as little surprise to anybody, not least those responsible for the kind of drivel that regularly appears in the pages of the so- called independent Press, why our normally affable and dignified President and his Cabinet ministers are choosing to dispense with the niceties of diplomatic etiquette when dealing with this loud-mouthed British diplomat.

For this reason, and several more, Davira Mhere condemns Donnelly for seeking to portray his country's human rights record as somehow superior to ours when we know the opposite to be true.

Commenting on what the so-called independent paper referred to as "Harare's political fall-out with London", Donnelly openly stated that it was "not a fight (with Zimbabwe) that Britain seeks and wants . . . it could quickly be ended if the Government were to change course and put into practice the democratic values it repeatedly says it believes in".

As if this insult to Zimbabweans was not enough, Donnelly proceeded to repeat his oft-quoted remarks that the famine that has hit the whole of Southern Africa is, in Zimbabwe, "man-made". He went further to claim that his country respects the rule of law and upholds human rights.

If his country respects the rule of law, and by that we mean the sovereignty of independent states, Donnelly must explain why Britain seems so much interested in poking its long nose into the domestic affairs of Zimbabwe, and too why much of Britain's foreign policy is a bundle of glaring contradictions and ridiculous grand-standing.

Today, as we speak, over half a million of Britain's immigrant population – victims of Britain's barbaric and racist foreign and domestic policies - endure hardships.

There are, in Britain today, and standing outside the doors of Westminster and Windsor Castle right now, thousands of people with neither food nor shelter, sleeping rough, and all driven by want and poverty.

Surely Donnelly, who so often is given to portraying himself as a paragon of virtue, must provide explanations as to why his country turns the other way whenever the deplorable plight of Britain's "blacks" crops up for discussion in the House of Commons.

But instead, we see Donnelly arrogantly beating his chest so hard when his country, a colonial dinosaur, insists it wants to travel, and at great expense, distances of more than 6 000 kilometres, across the Mediterranean Sea, the Sahara Desert and the mighty Kilimanjaro - supposedly to give aid to Africans in Southern Africa.

In his interview with reporters from the Zimbabwe Independent, Donnelly insists Britain has the interests of ordinary Zimbabweans at heart, adding that "Britain would not withhold food aid to influence local policies because the masses would suffer", and also that he did not "think it is right that the poorest and most vulnerable sectors of the society should pay the price."

This is rich coming from UK's envoy to Zimbabwe. For a man whose office in Harare has gained notoriety for the shabby manner his officers habitually treat ordinary African folk seeking assistance with visa processing and other information relating to requirements for students intending to study in UK colleges and universities, Donnelly must just shut it up for Chaminuka's sake.

He has been a thorn in the Government's flesh for quite some time now, this Donnelly, and his tendency to shoot his mouth carelessly in all directions, and also to voice his wild and outrageously way-off-the-mark political opinions, have not helped Britain's relationship with Zimbabwe.

And yet, despite losing so often in his various political battles with Minister of Information and Publicity, Prof Jonathan Moyo and Permanent Secretary Cde George Charamba, Donnelly seems unable to read the clear 'please back-off' message pinned on Zimbabwe's political wall. Now is the time, perhaps, that somebody tells this British envoy that Zimbabwe is not Serbia and President Mugabe is not Milosevic. I'll do it.

On reading Donnelly's interview in the Independent, I was suddenly reminded of a letter that I wrote to the same British "diplomat" in June 2001. Therein I raised serious concerns at the racist way and disgraceful manner exhibited by his office when dealing with a simple and straightforward UK Entry visa application submitted by one of my African clients.

Though the Caucasian officer that I spoke to on the phone denied the racist charges mentioned therein, the letter – a most iconoclastic piece of drama ever received by Her Majesty's servant, I guess, and thus likely to ring a bell in Donnelly's head – elicited a quick and positive response. My client's UK Entry visa application was granted within two days of his office's receipt of the letter.

Reproduced here - except for the names and specific dates that have been slightly altered, and the few paragraphs shifted – are extracts from the said letter, and Britain's envoy to Zimbabwe cannot deny ever receiving it. The hope is, it will put paid Mr Donnelly's claims to altruism and concern for the ordinary Zimbabwean. It went like this:

"Re: Application for United Kingdom Entry Clearance Visa - Miss Rusununguko Igidi (or Mrs Rusununguko Mashoko-Minzwa Muchakaura)

I represent the above-named and please note my interest. I must, from the outset, state that my client had initially taken legal counsel on this matter from one of your own kind. She has now approached me, chamangwiza musvetusi wemagandanga ekuchamhembe, to handle this matter on her behalf.

Now I don't want to ask this question but tell me what you are up to you white folk working in the offices of the British High Commission (BHC), right in the middle of Zimbabwe's beautiful capital city, Harare, and at the intersection of Samora Machel and Leopold Takawira *"Bhuru rekwaChurumhanzu"* . . .

A timely reminder, perhaps, that unlike Britons who have consigned cultural traditions to history's junk pile, Africans are not unlike other non-European races: we do have a culture and traditions that we follow, and that are legacies passed from generation to generation.

Samora Machel and Leopold Takawira are therefore no ordinary street names nor are they a result of political accidents.

Both commemorate a Mozambican and a Zimbabwean who willingly inherited the formidable legacies left by Jomo Kenyatta and Dedani Khimathi – leaders and commanders of the Mau-Mau warriors, they who liberated Kenya from British colonial oppression.

Hey, listen you hear, that's a formidable foursome. There is no kidding about it. But it becomes even more portentous now when you consider that up there, and just a few blocks from your offices, President Mugabe continues to hold fort – alert and ready to defend the Munhumutapa Kingdom his people have inhabited from time immemorial.

This Mugabe man, you're right to presume, is the only lingering tooth on sub-Saharan Africa's often-turned and slapped jaw; indeed, he is a Dingani rolled into a Nehanda into a Nkrumah into a Lumumba into a Biko into a Malcolm X into a Ben-Bellah into a Che Guevara and into a Magama Tongogara.

And by the way, this last hero - whose courage and fearlessness dealt a deadly blow to colonialist settler scum - decorates a street not far from where you are operating.

Oh, wait a minute. I think I am getting carried away! I'll ask the question properly: "If my client's husband was Caucasian - or 'white' to use an inappropriate but nevertheless popular term; okay 'white' - would you have treated his wife and him this way; this rough and shabby fashion?" I am here talking about how the officers in the Immigration Section of your office have deliberately mishandled my client's simple and straightforward UK Entry Clearance visa application.

A certificate to confirm my client's marriage to Mr Mashoko-Minzwa Muchakaura, properly solemnised in terms of the Marriage Act [Chapter 5:1], has been shown to your officers. Her husband - who was born in Britain but was brought back home to Zimbabwe as an infant - is a British citizen currently living here in the UK. He is working and makes his national and income tax contributions to the fiscus. So where is the rub, as they would say? That he happens to have a bank overdraft is surely no reason for your officers to turn my client back saying her husband is not in a position to take care of her.

Now this thing, which has annoyed my client, is starting to annoy me also. What with all the nightmares of her queuing up at your offices from dawn till noon, and after all those many visits at which you request her to bring to you this or that document, the usual false promises from your officers that they would phone her back: would you yourself not be annoyed? See her sit back and say 'the Office of God, and his angels, have spoken, and spoken the last word' – is this what you want her to do?

On all these occasions, your officers have deliberately refused to disclose their names to the Applicant one would be right to see visions of espionage and not of officers performing public functions. Yet they have the temerity to ask her to produce pre-marriage love-letters exchanged between her and her boyfriend-now-turned-husband, and which when brought are opened, read, scrutinised, copied and then used to provide the butt of snide jokes at exclusively Caucasian social gatherings, that kind of stuff you know - how fair is that?

I am concerned that the reason your officers have given for refusing to grant my client a visa - her husband's bank overdraft - militates against the law, offends against public morality, confounds common sense, and is a terrible and outrageous travesty of justice. It is totally ridiculous to allege that a husband's possession of a bank overdraft makes him unfit to look after his wife.

With the greatest of respect, your officers' decision is unreasonable in the extreme and, not unnaturally, and denies basic human rights to my client. Besides, it collides with the universal principles of natural justice and touches upon a raw nerve. If the law were to decree that husband and wife are not permitted to live together on account of either spouse having a bank overdraft, then few couples would be living together.

Now, let somebody tell me whether or not it is a crime to have a bank overdraft; to have facilities that, in England, are afforded to any Tom, Dick and Harry so long as they are working, and have no previous judgements against them. And if it is a crime that the Applicant's husband is creditworthy then surely this world is full of criminals just as it has hypocrites, and these include the British and French governments whose creditworthiness enabled these two sister states to secure bank overdrafts and loan facilities to build the Channel tunnel - and from the Japanese! Did you know that?

Your officers further argue that if the Applicant were to join her husband now, the bank overdraft would strain both, financially, to the extent he would be tempted to resort to public funds. My client's husband Mr Muchakaura is, after all, a British citizen - born in Britain, currently working in Britain, paying taxes in Britain, having National Insurance (NI) contributions deducted from his income, and legally and justifiably in possession of a British passport. The fact a bank granted him overdraft facilities shows he is creditworthy, and I am proud to say he is because he is in gainful employment – and by choice.

Further, given that Applicant's husband is a British citizen, then surely Mr Muchakaura is entitled to certain public benefits that his national insurance and income tax contributions warrant, and/or in the event he loses his job or simply decides not to work. So, would his wife, just like the wives of unemployed British citizens would! What better way to demonstrate his principles and pride than that he was at work within seven days of his 1999 entry into UK?

Surely members of the public are entitled to complain when officials make bizarre decisions predicated on erroneous perceptions, unfounded suspicions and absurd assumptions wherein any non-Caucasian who migrates to Britain is suspected he does so ostensibly with an eye on public funds. And yet, as all this happens, intellectual sterility shields from view the reality that no African with an iota of common sense would derive pleasure and satisfaction from living on Britain's paltry state handouts, nor choose to live in exile in a cold, snow and sleet-ridden island when Africa is there to offer a sunnier and more picturesque alternative!

I do not need to knock any of my diaspora-dispersed African brothers and sisters who, blinded by Western capitalism, continue to plunge headlong into a whirling pool of poverty, trapped in a cycle from which there is no escape. It's a life of the damned I mean, the kind of life led by (some of) those who, as it happens, are earmarked for hard labour and eventually, and in the minds of those dominating them, end symbolising an imaginary and allegedly inferior race.

The same ones, our African brethren and sisters, daily struggle against both economic and psychological enslavement because of the irreparable if not permanent brain-damage inflicted on them during the "log-carrying" ordeals of slogging in the 'white' man's sugar and cotton plantations – yes slavery, that "endlessly bleeding wound" – why would my client opt for such a life?

Officer Donnelly, I am no politician myself – and neither do I suspect you to be one - but why your officers think my client, or her husband, would seek to transform into an art form the embarrassing hat-in-hand spectacle of scrounging for public funds is for you to explain. Applicant's husband is no illegal immigrant in Britain, nor is he an asylum-seeker, and not Ronnie Biggs even, Britain's so-called Great Train Robber – is he?

It has to be pointed out that, on a previous occasion, your officers have also questioned the validity and authenticity of the British passport held by my client's husband. Yet, for all these troubles, he (Mr Muchakaura) had twice before used the same passport on his way into and out of Britain. They are sick, those British immigration officers who spent more than an hour questioning him for carrying an identity that ought not be part of him but for 19th Century European imperialism; a medal to the theft-addicted and hooligan victor in recognition of the part he is playing to fleece and filch riches from the African continent. So here he was, defined as 'British' but then not quite so, because as an African, he 'deserved' to be treated less favourably in comparison with his Caucasian British passport-holder counterparts.

Are there parallel laws for African British citizens and Caucasian British citizens? Your officers' shabby treatment of my client's husband: is it because he is an African British citizen or because him and his wife have an intimate connection to Zimbabwe, a country whose political and diplomatic relationship with Britain is currently frosty?

But then again how can my client be blamed for the sins of miscreants who in fact, sinned against her ancestors? You know, and everybody knows it wasn't the likes of my client who put together a force that invaded Zimbabwe in 1890, the so-called Pioneer Column - hence the land issue. That dishonourable honour went to somebody else, in fact to Cecil John Rhodes, for it was him who chose Starr Jameson – an irredeemable psychotic according to Rhodes – and at the time, a 22-year-old British subject - no, object - take command of the invading forces.

Why bring my client and her husband into all this? And if your officers cannot allow my client to join her UK-residing husband, then into which river shall we chuck your Western "till death do us part" mantra – into the sluggish Thames or the crocodile-infested Limpopo? Surely if anybody needed any convincing about the extent to which my client feels a sense of injustice about the way her application has been handled at your Harare offices, then these facts should – hopefully.

Look, I believe that every individual has the right to choose the kind of life they intend to live, and to live wherever they wish – subject, of course, to compliance with the law. How, tell me then, do your officers normally deal with cases involving non-African couples but with circumstances similar to those of the Applicant and her husband? Are you denying entry visas to wives of Caucasian British passport- holders on the same basis you have denied my client?

Can you confirm whether or not your officers are aware of the existence of, and familiar with, the provisions the Immigration and Nationality Act, its relevant regulations; and also, the various pieces of legislation and juridical pronouncements coming from the European Community (EC) and European Court of Justice (ECJ)? So why can't the same good goose and good gander be judged under similar laws?

My client and her husband are entitled to better treatment from public servants employed by countries that daily espouse phrases such as "the rule of law", "human rights" and "ethics". Of course, sooner rather than later both will be returning to Zimbabwe in Africa, a country and a continent that, better than anywhere else in the western world, offers people the chance to bring up children in relatively safer environments. Or, for that matter, with less industrial pollution, freedom from the expenses of going to a zoo to see animals, more natural as opposed to genetically modified food, and beef from grass-fed cows and not the herbivores-turned-carnivores' animals to which the mad-cow disease and CJD are inextricably linked?

It is not my intention to drag issues that are deemed emotive in this age of political correctness, but I do so because all of them are not peripheral to my client's visa application. Indeed, the charade surrounding this case leaves one with the impression your officers have devised a ploy to 'transform' the Applicant into some kind of a monkey that has to visit your offices regularly to beg incessantly for a paper that she is entitled to in the first place.

How else then do you explain the constant taunts and ceaseless embarrassments that she and her family have endured for this long, and on no less than eight occasions, and which your officers' predilection to the procrastination and prevarication has made worse? And her being separated from her husband for no apparent reason to follow - is this not a case, on the facts and on the face on the case, of your immigration officers deriving pleasure when they see the Applicant incessantly coming into your offices, waiting in a long queue, and emerging from there clasping thin air?

It sure is a disgraceful thing that your officers have caused a simple visa application to degenerate into a charade that in turn has generated more heat than light - and without its share of farcical fuss. While I understand that an Immigration Officer has discretionary powers in such matters, I am also aware that the exercise of those powers should be in accordance with the rules of natural justice, and of which fairness, reasonableness and compliance with any existing statutory provisions are the most sacrosanct.

Already in your possession is evidence of the existence of a properly solemnised marriage, of her husband being a British citizen, and that he has both a job and the capacity to look after his wife.

Your officers cannot, in exercising of that discretion, afford to ignore or overlook these facts.

I am all for justice, fairness, personal responsibility and dignity of self and for others in the community of Homo sapiens and, as a matter of principle, I intend to pursue this case relentlessly through the British courts and, if need be, vigorously through the British political establishment until a logical and fair conclusion is reached. Now given that nothing stops anybody from taking their grievances to the highest office in the land, there ought to be no reason why Britain's Home Affairs Secretary Mr David Blunket, and British PM Tony Blair cannot be my client's ultimate destinations!

In addition, now that I know as I have always suspected that the actions of Britain's Zimbabwe-based Immigration Officers smack of the kind of impropriety frowned upon by the law, I must sound a warning that this letter is a prelude to legal action. I do not take for granted that you'll reflect on all the issues raised herein but rather grant the optimism that you will re-consider the reasons for your refusal to grant the Applicant an Entry Clearance visa into the UK.

I am therefore writing to you directly with a view to appealing to your professional conscience (if you have any) so this matter can be expedited without much further ado, and within the ambit of existing legislation, and also in the spirit of justice and fairness. I ask that you kindly bring your better judgement to favourably bear on this case.

I thank you in anticipation of your most favourable response."

There you are comrades; the MDC party spokesman Brian Donnelly is exposed once again!

Zimbabwe: Howard's Latest Act of Madness
Opinion
By Chinondidyachii Mararike
15 October 2002. www.herald.co.zw

Harare — Glass-housed Caucasian Australia should think twice before throwing stones at Great Zimbabwe's stone-built palace of agrarian reforms.

It ought to know that the main battle in imperialism is over land. And when it comes to who in Zimbabwe owned the land, who had the right to settle and work on it, who kept it going, who won it back, and who should now plan its future, all African organisations in Europe, America and the Caribbean clearly recognise that President Mugabe is a grand narrative of emancipation and enlightenment that has mobilised people in the former colonial world to rise up and throw off neo-imperial subjugation and domination.

The Australian Prime Minister John Howard should know, if he doesn't by now, that Zimbabwe's land reform programme has the support of all African progressives the world over.

And that he himself - including all his Australian, New Zealand, American and Canadian kith and kin - are prototypes of the Robinson Crusoe category who created fiefdoms for themselves in distant non-European lands. Howard should check his politics at the door before he enters the Zimbabwean political arena.

We boldly wish to remind Howard that Australia was established as a penal colony in the late eighteenth century, mainly so that England could transport an irredeemable and unwanted excess population of criminals or felonies to a place originally charted by Cook.

It was expected to also function as a colony replacing those lost in America. The pursuit of profit, the building of empire, and what in Botany Bay Hughes calls social apartheid together produced modern Australia.

Howard himself is a product of this criminal system, and is in the same category with Charles Dickens' Magwitch who, in Great Expectations, was prohibited from returning to England for both penal and imperial reasons.

This clearly shows that England could take its criminal subjects to Australia but would not allow them to return to their mother country.

For Howard to criticise Zimbabwe while standing on Australian soil is indeed a bad joke. It is a monumental misnomer given that the Australian Prime Minister is not only a biological mistake but a colonial businessman and who, like Pip in Great Expectations, is hardly an exceptional figure, and that all Caucasian Australians are to the natives of that country frightening outsiders with an abnormal and secure connection with the empire.

The problem we see in most Western countries is that they have embraced much of the rhetoric of the "New World Order" promulgated by the American government since the end of the Cold War – with its redolent self-congratulation, its unconcealed triumphalism, its grave proclamations of responsibility: we, in the "white" West are number one, we are bound to lead, we stand for freedom and order, and we uphold the rule of law and seek to protect human rights.

Howard has not been immune from this unfortunate and contemptible structure of feeling - and skewed thinking.

He thinks it the rule of law and the protection of human rights when he portrays an arrogant interest and a paternalist attitude towards what the West considers a lesser Third World, populated with lesser people of a dark hue and open to the intervention of so many Robinson Crusoes like himself.

What we in *Davira Mhere* express are sentiments similar to those being expressed by most children of decolonisation and other beneficiaries of advances in human freedom at home: Howard's latest act of madness, frogmarching Australia into imposing further targeted sanctions on Zimbabwe, amounts to an act of war against a legitimately or democratically elected government.

We are ready to defend our independence. We are ready to export the third Chimurenga to Australia and thus assist our Aborigine brothers and sisters to reclaim their land from Caucasian Aussies.

We are already exporting the revolution to the rest of sub-Saharan Africa and beyond.

We are part and parcel of the newly-empowered roster of voices asking for our concerns to be addressed. We have seen Howard supporting and reproducing the imperial ideology of yesterday. We cannot afford to stand aloof.

The Zimbabwean intellectual and peasant remembers with sadness the country's colonial past which was punctuated with Rhodesia's senseless military attacks on defenceless villages and refugee camps in Zimbabwe, Zambia and Mozambique.

They recall the torture of prisoners during the 1966-1980 war of liberation, and of contemporary Western hypocrisy and double standards when discussing and reacting to Zimbabwe's Third Chimurenga.

Happily, for us, those British-cum-Rhodesians who, despite having taken part in the dastardly and murderous Rhodesian affairs or whose families lived in Zimbabwe as colonial dregs, raised the white flag by way of surrender in April 1980.

There is humiliation at having lost colonially-bequeathed land. They feel it is because of African "trouble-makers" and "tyrants" who continue to disturb the idyllic relationship between exploitative Caucasians and the dominated Africans in Zimbabwe.

Howard, himself the great-grandson of unreconstructed criminals, should not be allowed the chance to dismiss or forget the ravaged colonial peoples (in Australia and Africa) who, for centuries, endured (and continue to endure) injustices and unending economic oppression because of the alleged European superiority. The ruthless history of slavery and colonialism cannot continue anymore.

President Mugabe belongs to that revolutionary camp of Zanu-PF cadres who refuse to go on complaining about the past without taking any decisive action.

Indeed, Zimbabwe's President – conqueror of colonialism, fighter against neo-imperialists, *"Karigavangezi"* (the one who brought down whites), is a man of action.

He is a just, faithful and devout soldier. He is an intellectual of inimitable acuity who knows the truth about the terrible effects of both colonialism and neo-colonialism. Howard, on the other hand, is backed by a miscellaneous bunch of querulous European reactionaries and the so-called MDC intellectuals and wishy-washy media sceptics who work for the so-called independent Press, people who are mere appendages of imperialists.

The likes of Howard ought to realise that the imperialist's sense of power scarcely imagined that those "natives" who had appeared either subservient the white folks give up Angola, India, Kenya, Namibia, or South Africa and now Zimbabwe.

The warriors who fought in Mau-Mau, Frelimo, Swapo, PAC/ANC, Unip all know that President Mugabe is not a tyrant but a righter of wrongs in Zimbabwe, Africa and the rest of the world.

He is a true and determined defender of genuine freedom no matter the place or the cost.

Davira Mhere - together with other African organisations such as African-Caribbean Self-Help, Africa Strategy, Nation of Islam, and South Africa's Landless People's Movement calls upon the EU, America, Australia and other Caucasian Commonwealth countries to lift the sanctions imposed on Zimbabwe, and to lift them forthwith.

Davira Mhere, like Frantz Fanon who states that "colonialism and imperialism have not paid their score when they withdrew their flags and their police forces from our territories", flatly rejects the condemnation that Zimbabwe has been receiving from hooligan Western countries.

Yes, Fanon is right to add that "for centuries the (Western foreign) capitalists have behaved in the underdeveloped (sic) world like nothing more than criminals".

Africans everywhere will not sit idly and allow the white heirs to 18th and 19th century European imperialism in Australia, New Zealand and the EU to pass along their residual imperialist propensities to settler colonists in Africa, nor to punish Zimbabwe for correcting the injustices of colonialism and neo-imperialism.

* About the writer: Chinondidyachii Mararike is a Zimbabwean lawyer, writer, political analyst and secretary-general of Davira Mhere.

Zimbabwe: So-Called Independent Papers Publish Falsehoods Opinion
By Chinondidyachii Mararike,
19 December 2002, http://www.herald.co.zw

Harare — The two stories that appeared on December 16, 2002 in The Daily News and on South Africa's News24 bulletins provide further confirmation that the so-called independent media think they have a right to indulge in destructive criticism of both our Government and President Mugabe without allowing a similar level of scrutiny being given to such media's own underlying motives, agendas and methods or who has been paid for what.

While the Caucasian-sponsored Daily News was publishing a false story claiming that "five skeletons of murdered MDC supporters were recovered by police in a dip tank", South Africa's Western-controlled News24 was busy reporting falsehoods that "President Mugabe had arrived in that country to attend the African National Congress' national conference".

The latter even went further to claim that "the bridge over Eerste River was closed to public traffic as the President passed through" . . . and that "once through the venue gates, the President moved inside and access to the building was off limits to the media".

This indeed is the kind of yellow journalism that President Mugabe has often attacked and shows how imperialist stooges show their flagrant biases. The reason for this, I think, is to be found not so much in the independence of the so-called independent newspapers but in the staggeringly partisan nature of Zimbabwe's foreign-controlled papers.

These papers are carriers of foreign flags - and foreign causes – who not only fling their blessings at imperialists but also are paid to excoriate those who support revolutionary ideals. They regard support for the West, in particular the evil Blair/Bush alliance, as a qualifying condition for membership of the human race.

Zimbabwe has a very free and vibrant Press. This is unlike in the US or UK where the Press experiences permanent interference from either the government or the security forces. Our Government prides itself in scrupulously preserving an atmosphere of pluralism and freedom of speech, even under severe and emotionally charged conditions that surround us in Zimbabwe.

We certainly need freedom of the Press, protection of sources and public interest. Yet day in day out we read – in Zimbabwe's Daily News, Standard, Independent, and Financial Gazette – the kind of personal attacks on President Mugabe that even an angel would not endure quietly. Why single out Comrade Mugabe for personal attack and in the process besmirch his good name, that of his family, his Cabinet members, and country? These stories are not only untrue but wholly invented and grossly exaggerated as part of a campaign against the Government of Zimbabwe.

Politics cannot be used as an excuse for losing respect for others. It is therefore wrong when newspapers, particularly those which operate under the rubric of "independence", seem so obsessed with making scurrilous, rude and hostile remarks about President Mugabe, accusing him of things he has not done, and lampooning Mrs Grace Mugabe and whoever is remotely thought of as the President's relation.

We have read in the Financial Gazette about this farm belonging to Mrs Mugabe - and it turns out to be a charity project headed by a person who is not a relation of either the President or the First Lady. We read in The Daily News the shameless lies that Zanu-PF supporters allegedly beheaded a woman in Magunje in front of her two young daughters. As the Minister of Information, Prof Jonathan Moyo, clearly stated, "Stories like that, and they are many (that have appeared in the foreign-controlled newspapers), damage our country and cost us lots and lots of money to correct". Indeed, this species of journalism prompts a wearisome sense of déjà-vu because it occurs, almost invariably in the "independent" print media, and with clockwork frequency.

Zimbabwe's so-called independent papers and members of the opposition MDC party have, after the manner of foreign tabloids, described President Mugabe variously as a "terrorist", a "tyrant" and a "brutal" man". Many patriots in and outside Zimbabwe are concerned at how these papers' demonisation of President Mugabe is serving to divert attention from the Government's efforts to improve the lot of our people, and also at the actual and potential infringement of the liberty and freedom of our President.

President Mugabe is a human being, has a family to protect, and does have feelings and a personality like everybody else. And personality in politics – roughly defined as the agent of belief, the conduit to public interest - offers the ultimate yardstick against which to measure a leader's credentials, whether in politics or outside of it. Indeed, it is via his or her actions, and other instinctive vibes, that a leader registers what kind of a human being he or she is, and these are the prime concerns of the leader's immediate and peripheral subordinates - and electorate.

No one is in any doubt here that a new chapter –

which has so much significance in the lives of so many people – has been written in the Zanu-PF fairy tale: out of the 2000 defeat in the constitutional referendum, President Mugabe has returned to reaffirm his stature as one of the jewels of Africa with too many medals to prove it. We beat them (the imperialists) over the land issue and have withstood a whirlwind of propaganda ever since. Today

Zimbabweans are entering 2003 with land as a lucrative reward for the party's slaying of the imperialist giant in a three-year period of revolutionary activity laced with passion, drama and commitment.

Our Government's victory over neo-colonialism is an historic achievement for all Africans to savour, a culmination of a little over 100 years of relentless progress, and a reminder to those who on previous occasions have sought to dance on Zanu-PF's supposed grave that it would be safer first to check that the revolutionary party is properly buried before passing premature judgments on it.

It must be President Mugabe's disinclination to keel over that is baffling the opposition Press and causing it to resort to name-calling. It sure is a rare political leader who refuses to compromise his ideological beliefs, who refuses to be bought out to ditch his own people. But Comrade Mugabe is that rarity, as the world has seen from various examples of unselfishness during his long and successful political life. It is only now that Europe has learnt the dangers of underestimating his revolutionary commitment.

President Mugabe's great crime, it seems to our hypocritical independent Press, is for standing up for the interests of his people, of Africans. I can't see how it can ever be right to lampoon our President for giving land to his people. But, right apart, it is surely exactly the kind of distraction the foreign-controlled Press relishes and needs; and yet again, the ordinary people who are really suffering, and whose lives Zanu-PF is trying to ameliorate, get forgotten.

It has been proved now and again that tales of Zanu-PF violence that appear in the opposition papers have been used to whip up support against the Government and in the process act as recruitment machine for the MDC. The worst irony to emerge from all this is when editors of "independent" newspapers greet any criticism of their irresponsible activities with the argument that the

Government is trying to curtail Press freedom, and that it is Press freedom that the people want.

There sure is a whiff of hypocrisy about editors insisting they should police their own papers when recent events have clearly shown that the newspapers are not only irresponsible but will always raise the banner of Press freedom to avoid public investigations into their conduct. A good example is when the Standard's late Mark Chavhunduka saw no contradiction between his claim to the public's "right to know" and the Government's greater public interest in insisting that he discloses how his story of an alleged coup plot had come into his possession.

The reason, on the other hand, why The Daily News is struggling today has nothing to do with the Government but rather, is a consequence of the paper's gargantuan appetite for sensationalism; its misplaced belief that Mugabe-bashing is the best tactic to sell newspapers; its poor features, opinion, local and foreign news coverage; and the fact it has tied its fortunes to those of the MDC.

In November this year, barely a month after the US Assistant Secretary of State for African Affairs Walter Kansteiner said his "government was working with journalists from the private media, civic organisations and opposition to effect a regime change in Zimbabwe", the news editor of The Daily News, William Bango, joined the MDC information department as a consultant at about the same time when the Financial Gazette's entertainment editor Grace Mutandwa also left her job to work for the British High Commission's information department in Harare.

Granted people may like opinionated newspapers but then, surely, they want them to be truthful and fair. Buying a newspaper should not be the equivalent of buying the opinions of imperialists because that, itself, obfuscates the distinction between comment and fact.

Zimbabwe: UK Officers Guilty of Impropriety

Opinion.

Chinondidyachii Mararike in UK,
9 November 2002, *www.herald.co.zw*

Harare — This is the final of a two-part series in which Mr Chinondidyachii Mararike attacks the UK diplomat in Harare, Mr Brian Donnelly.

I do not need to knock any of my diaspora-dispersed African brothers and sisters who, blinded by Western capitalism, continue to plunge headlong into a whirling pool of poverty, trapped in a cycle from which there is no escape. It's a life of the damned . . . I mean, the kind of life led by (some of) those who, as it happens, are earmarked for hard labour and eventually, and in the minds of those dominating them, end symbolising an imaginary and allegedly inferior race.

The same ones, our African brethren and sister's, struggle daily against both economic and psychological enslavement because of the irreparable, if not permanent brain-damage, inflicted on them during the "log-carrying" ordeals of slogging in the 'white' man's sugar and cotton plantations - yes, slavery, that "endlessly bleeding wound" - why would my client opt for such a life?

Officer Donnelly, I am no politician myself - and neither do I suspect you to be one - but why your officers think my client, or her husband, would seek to transform into an art form the embarrassing hat-in-hand spectacle of scrounging for public funds is for you to explain. The applicant's husband is no illegal immigrant in Britain, nor is he an asylum-seeker, and not Ronnie Biggs even, Britain's so-called Great Train Robber - is he?

It has to be pointed out that, on a previous occasion, your officers have also questioned the validity and authenticity of the British passport held by my client's husband. Yet, for all these troubles, he (Mr Muchakaura) had twice before used the same passport on his way into and out of Britain. They are sick of those British immigration officers who spent more than an hour questioning him for carrying an identity that ought not be part of him but for 19th

Century European imperialism; a medal to the theft-addicted and hooligan victor in recognition of the part he is playing to fleece and filch riches from the African continent. So here he was, defined as 'British' but then not quite so, because as an African he 'deserved' to be treated less favourably in comparison with his Caucasian British passport-holder counterparts.

Are there parallel laws for African British citizens and Caucasian British citizens? Your officers' shabby treatment of my client's husband - is it because he is an African British citizen or because him and his wife have an intimate connection to Zimbabwe, a country whose political and diplomatic relationship with Britain is currently frosty?

But then again, how can my client be blamed for the sins of miscreants who, in fact, sinned against her ancestors? You know, and everybody knows it wasn't the likes of my client who put together a force that invaded Zimbabwe in 1890, the so-called Pioneer Column - hence the land issue. That dishonourable honour went to somebody else - in fact, to Cecil John Rhodes, for it was him who chose Starr Jameson - an irredeemable psychotic, according Rhodes - and at the time, a 22-year-old British subject - no, object -take command of the invading forces.

Why bring my client and her husband into all this? And if your officers cannot allow my client to join her UK-residing husband then into which river shall we chuck your Western "till death do us part" mantra - into the sluggish Thames or the crocodile-infested Limpopo?

Surely if anybody needed any convincing about the extent to which my client feels, a sense of injustice about the way her application has been handled at your Harare offices, then, these facts should - hopefully.

Look, I believe that every individual has the right to choose the kind of life they intend to live, and to live wherever they wish - subject, of course, to compliance with the law. How, tell me then, do your officers normally deal with cases involving non-African couples but with circumstances similar to those of the applicant and her husband? Are you denying entry visas to wives of Caucasian British passport- holders on the same basis you have denied my client?

Can you confirm whether or not your officers are aware of the existence of, and familiar with, the provisions of the Immigration and Nationality Act, its relevant regulations; and also the various pieces of legislation and juridical pronouncements coming from the European Community (EC) and European Court of Justice (ECJ)? So why can't the same good goose and good gander be judged under similar laws?

My client and her husband are entitled to better treatment from public servants employed by countries that daily espouse phrases such as "the rule of law", "human rights" and "ethics". Of course, sooner rather than late, both will be returning to Zimbabwe in Africa, a country and a continent that, better than anywhere else in the western world, offers people the chance to bring up children in relatively safer environments. Or, for that matter, with less industrial pollution, freedom from the expenses of going to a zoo to see animals, more natural as opposed to genetically-modified food, and beef from grass-fed cows and not the herbivores-turned-carnivores - animals to which the mad-cow disease and CJD are inextricably linked?

It is not my intention to drag issues that are deemed emotive in this age of political correctness, but I do so because all of them are not peripheral to my client's visa application. Indeed, the charade surrounding this case leaves one with the impression your officers have devised a ploy to 'transform' the applicant into some kind of a monkey that has to visit your offices regularly to beg incessantly for a paper that she is entitled to in the first place.

How else then do you explain the constant taunts and ceaseless embarrassments that she and her family have endured for this long, and on no less than eight occasions, and which your officers' predilection to the procrastination and prevarication has made worse?

And her being separated from her husband for no apparent reason to follow - is this not a case, on the facts and on the face on the case, of your immigration officers deriving pleasure when they see the applicant incessantly coming into your offices, waiting in a long queue, and emerging from there clasping thin air?

It sure is a disgraceful thing that your officers have caused a simple visa application to degenerate into a charade that, in turn, has generated more heat than light - and without its share of farcical fuss.

While I understand that an Immigration Officer has discretionary powers in such matters, I am also aware that the exercise of those powers should be in accordance with the rules of natural justice, and of which fairness, reasonableness and compliance with any existing statutory provisions are the most sacrosanct.

Already in your possession is evidence of the existence of a properly solemnised marriage, of her husband being a British citizen, and that he has both a job and the capacity to look after his wife. Your officers cannot, in exercising of that discretion, afford to ignore or overlook these facts.

I am all for justice, fairness, personal responsibility and dignity of self and for others in the community of Homo sapiens and, as a matter of principle, I intend to pursue this case relentlessly through the British courts and, if need be, vigorously through the British political establishment until a logical and fair conclusion is reached.

Now, given that nothing stops anybody from taking their grievances to the highest office in the land, there ought to be no reason why Britain's Home Affairs Secretary Mr David Blunket, and British Prime Minister Tony Blair cannot be my client's ultimate destinations!

In addition, now that I know, as I have always suspected, that the actions of Britain's Zimbabwe-based Immigration Officers smack of the kind of impropriety frowned upon by the law, I must sound a warning that this letter is a prelude to legal action. I do not take for granted that you'll reflect on all the issues raised herein but rather grant the optimism that you will re-consider the reasons for your refusal to grant the applicant an Entry Clearance visa into the UK.

I am, therefore, writing to you directly with a view to appealing to your professional conscience (if you have any) so this matter can be expedited without much further ado, and within the ambit of existing legislation, and also in the spirit of justice and fairness.

I ask that you kindly bring your better judgement to favourably bear on this case.

I thank you in anticipation for your most favourable response."
There you are, Comrades, the MDC party spokesman Brian Donnelly
is exposed once again!

West Making Fortunes from Plundered African Resources
Opinion
By Chinondidyachii Mararike
20 September 2002. www.herald.co.zw

And yet we have the same islanders insisting that the sanctions
Zimbabwe has imposed on Britain will hurt Zimbabwe more than
they will hurt Britons and continue to wallow in the dubious status
of greatness to the extent of prefixing this illusion to their country's
name, Great Britain.

This is madness I tell you! For nothing will ever change the fact
that Britain, two and half times smaller than Zimbabwe, is a poor
country.

The Island is so eager to resort to hooliganism and subterfuge
means to lay its pilfering hands on Africa's resources so that it can
keep its defence and manufacturing industries going.

Moreover, it needs to fend for and feed its skyrocketing
population of 62-odd million; fund and pay unemployment and other
benefits to all its indolent nationals that are on the dole, on
unemployment benefits.

As we speak, the University of London's School of Tropical
Medicine has for some time now been leasing land the size of another
English colony, Wales, from previous successive corrupt Nigerian
military rulers.

Without any resources and lamed by a terrible climate, Britain is
resorting to exploiting African countries and having its scientists
abuse African plants by carrying out genetic experiments intended to
prop up its pharmaceutical needs.

Indeed, Europe and America's bloated, diseased and greedy
populations are directly benefiting from Africa.

What chance then for Britain to turn to continental Europe for
salvation when Zimbabwe and Africa decide to seal their borders and

refuse entry to these imperialists; to turn to its European partners-in-sin and obtain the same resources it is stealing from Africa?

Then there is Holland, this Dutch country that continues to export flowers and beer to Africa as it did to South African Boers a century ago; this country with nothing except pot (as in mbanje) and prostitutes, and with a tarnished reputation and image already smudged by pornography, child fiddling and bombastic self-dramatizing apostasy?

To Sweden and Norway, the two Nordic countries for which there is not much to say except that one produced a boring rock band called Abba and the other gave its name to lobsters and some insignificant species of ugly rats? Then there is Luxembourg?

Ah, easy to stumble on that one!

The tiny country is afflicted by a conspicuous scantiness in resources synonymous only with its lack of a history.

Like Germany, Luxembourg came into existence only a couple of years ago, in fact in the 1870 after the 1814 Congress of Vienna had already given birth to most of today's European nations.

The two, and their neighbour Belgium, will surely do us a big favour by shutting their traps up. For Belgium left a horrendous legacy of cruelty in the Congo, cutting off breasts of African women as punishment for their having failed to reach the allocated quota demanded by the barbaric Belgian King Leopold in the Congo's Caucasian-run rubber plantations.

And that's not so long ago mind you, only recently in the late forties. Anybody who dares challenge this historical fact is welcome to visit the Congo and meet with women with single breasts — all victims of the Belgians' appalling and spine-chilling barbarism.

Or to Portugal, Italy, Spain, Poverty, Indigent and destitution, all being nouns capable of sitting comfortably together in one sentence, you suggest?

These are anything but rich countries, only infamous for the cruel and senseless torture of Christians and Muslims alike, the Spanish Inquisitions.

France, on the other hand, is known, not for the small deposits of iron and steel that were once mined in the Alsace-Lorraine district, but for its vineyards, Napoleonic legends and the July 14, 1789 storming of the Bastille.

And whilst still at it, the French must be reminded that the Storming of the Bastille was nothing more than the liberation of a bunch of seven criminals, including four forgers and an incestuous count, and by a group of naked drunks.

The truth about the capture of the grim old fortress (of Bastille) is just as shameful as most things French: Bonaparte's blood-cuddling campaigns in Europe; his notoriously frivolous, extravagant, lecherous and *pfambi* wife, Marie Antoinette; the scandalous Dreyfuss Affair; neo-Nazi Vichy regime and Jacques Chirac's government that today has turned into an art form of primitive agricultural methods - that have seen cows being fed on scientifically-treated human faeces.

But dies Moi, which in French is to say alas, Europeans would have us believe otherwise; have us believe that the disgraceful and despicable Storming of the Bastille was an act of supreme heroism.

But what we have seen, my Zimbabwean friends, is the French's reluctance to put this shameful episode behind them. Year in and year out the area around the Presidential palace, the Champs-Elysees, is a hive of activity.

They view white elephants and horses (stolen from Africa) and tanks and spectators pouring into an enclosure large enough to fill an area twenty times the size of Wembley, another of those architecturally overrated stadiums in England to celebrate. Do you see how backward and rearward these people are?

The only reason why Europeans continue to refer to our continent as 'poor', is because we have allowed them to do as they please. They control our resources and have us as the beasts of burden who daily will extract the same from our soil, pile them into trucks, and help ship Africa's heritage out of Africa, and for the benefit of Europeans.

These minerals have for centuries, enriched Europe, and at no cost to the plunderer. And now the same Europeans are telling us our continent is poor; want to brainwash us so we end up thinking Europe is rich, Europe is paradise, and Europe is heaven.

Listen Comrades, diamonds and gold are so precious to Westerners to the extent children poison their parents, so the former can quickly inherit or take jewellery to make a quick buck.

On the scary streets of London, people are daily murdered simply for the gold Rolex watches on their wrists. Gold the size of an ordinary human being's fist makes millions in Europe — earrings, necklaces, head and hand bands, tiepins, tooth-fillings, buttons — name it.

A gold-studded necklace or ring can cost as much as £30 000 in Britain, and you can calculate what this is in Zimbabwean dollars at today's exchange rate.

It can only be left to the imagination how much Britain makes from the many gold-studded necklaces crafted from a lump of gold enough to fill the palm of a toddler. Euro-American Caucasians, in other words, are making fortunes from diamonds or gold the size of an ordinary human being's fist — stealing from Africa.

Hey, did not Caucasians, out of this excessive love of gold and in 1851, head down under, to Australia, in what subsequently became known as "the gold rush". Did Hitler not send so many Jews to their early graves, sometimes not because of a sudden, explosive burst of Nazi xenophobic nationalism, but that the greedy Germans were melting gold fillings off their victims' teeth?

Today Africa stands as an inexhaustible reservoir of resources at Europe's disposal to loot with impunity. Euro-Americans continues to make use of African resources to build and service fighter planes that cannot be detected on the radar, develop nuclear arsenals, and power its factories and pharmaceutical industries. That Europe would not survive without Africa is therefore not an arguable point — but a fact.

A destitute, underfed and impoverished continent as was Europe before it met Africa, and still is, and which employs every means possible to get hold of our resources — theft and robbery, chiefly — so it can feed itself, and power its industries, cannot tell us that "Africa is a poor continent".

Rather we must insist that Europe trades with us on equal terms. We must stop the Anglo-Americans from resorting to uncouth tactics and arm-twisting gimmicks such as dominion over Africa's cultural, political and economic systems. We will not allow the long-nosed Caucasians to just march into Africa and grab everything from under our noses.

The British, their cousins the French, Caucasian citizens of Commonwealth Australasian, and EU countries that have imposed sanctions on Zimbabwe must now ask for our permission before they can come into our country to enjoy Zimbabwe's picturesque landscapes. And this, in part, explains why Zimbabwe instituted a visa regime on Britain and imposed sanctions on British politicians – starting with Blair.

Britain is anxious about what is happening in Zimbabwe. Britons are afraid that the rest of sub-Sahara Africa may embrace Mugabeism — this philosophical and practical weapon for use in Africa's anti-imperialist wars of today, tomorrow and for posterity. Once that happens Europeans would starve and, like dinosaurs, disappear from the face of planet earth. Now that would spark jubilations to last a lifetime!

Africa has everything that Africans needs. Africans can survive in Africa without any help from Europe. Europeans on the other hand, would starve, go mad and ultimately, die if Africans were to close their borders to entry by European misfits. Zimbabwe's travel bans on selected British officials — be extended to other EU countries, even — will therefore remain in place until these habitual kleptomaniacs are forced to give up on their sacrilegious attentions on Africa. That is what we, in *Davira Mhere,* are demanding.

© Chinondidyachii Mararike is a Zimbabwean lawyer, writer, political analyst and Secretary-General of *Davira Mhere.*

African leaders must not mistake Plunderers' for Allies
Opinion
By Chinondidyachii Mararike,
From *The Herald:* Wednesday, 10 August 2005, *www.herald.co.zw*

AFRICANS' problems stem from the fact that Africans see as friends and not enemies, those plundering African resources.

An extract from *'Heckling at Imperialist Hypocrisy'*, to be published in November 2005.

AFRICANS are making fools of themselves. They know they are making fools of themselves but are either afraid or unwilling to do something about it. The people who brought down the European empires in Africa in the four decades following Ghana's independence in 1957 through armed struggle, violent protests, rebellion and disobedience against colonial rule have acquired a unique capacity for being silly.

The tone and substance of the debates on solutions to the economic and social problems in Africa is superficial. We must appeal to Europeans for help. We must appeal to Western governments to cancel debts for the most-indebted African countries. We must appeal to Western-funded non-governmental organisations for humanitarian aid and charity. We must introduce Western-style democracy into our political systems. We should embrace liberalisation.

We should be the parties that care about Western concepts of human rights, rule of law and good governance. We should not be seen upsetting the West. In their despair they range widely, but without much focus, if any, on solutions beyond their own retention of power. Nobody is asking how the debts came about in the first place. And liberalisation and privatisation - nobody asks: 'To what end, and for whose benefit?' Is poverty, and its causes, a mystery? Is exploitation something that just happens? Does it not have perpetrators?

There is not a single wretched human being in the so-called Third World who does not stand in symbolic relation to the very open secret of Western imperialist domination, of European plunder and exploitation, of European terrorism and aggression, of European's misuse of power to deny Africans their right to genuine democracy, autonomy and self-determination. The misuse of power by Western governments, the materialism and greed of Europeans, and the inability of Africans to see through the hypocrisy, prejudice, bigotry of Europeans and failure to fight imperialists to achieve economic and social justice - all these are what, in the main, is hidden behind everything, behind the suffering of all non-European races in this world.

But, instead, many African leaders except President Robert Mugabe and, to a large extent, South African President Thabo Mbeki and President Benjamin Mkapa of Tanzania all seem unable to undertake a critique of power. They appear to believe that a consensus can be achieved between, on one hand, a resources-bereft West but now wealthy, rich and powerful through pillage and exploitation of African resources, and, on the other, a resources-rich Africa but now impoverished, diseased, scarred, and powerless because of the activities of European imperialists.

Most African leaders seem not to understand that while the Western governments maintain their grip on both African resources as well as the instruments of global governance and trade, there is hardly any possibility of remaining "outside revolution" of the powerful and powerless coming together in a great assembly of a great global chorus of the rich and the poor: These will sing from the same sheet. Indeed, a shared anthem of peace and love between the exploiters and exploited is about as meaningful, eh meaningless, as the old Coca-Cola advertisement.

The answer to the problem of power, especially power that is based on domination and exploitation of one race by another, and the answers to the problems of poverty, hunger, starvation, political instability, and internecine warfare in Africa, are all in front of their eyes. Building revolutionary political movements that deny the legitimacy of the powerful exploiters is one answer, and the other is to craft strategic objectives that seek to prise control of African resources from imperialist hands - to do, in other words, what people in Zimbabwe did through the Mugabe-led Revolution of Equitable Land Redistribution, and what the South Africans and Namibians are doing right NOW.

But African leaders are doing the opposite. By campaigning for more Western aid, debt forgiveness, philanthropy and charity, these leaders are portraying the enemies of Africa as the saviours, thus lending legitimacy to imperialist illegitimacy! This leads to the question of legitimacy – we are aware that through imperialist power Caucasians illegitimately acquired their riches, sustained through the violence, exploitation and the terror of subjugation, and deriving from ill-gotten wealth which remains evil and illegitimate.

These African leaders may be playing games, one is tempted to suspect, believing that praising the seemingly philanthropic intentions of the world's most powerful governments is more persuasive than criticising them. The problem is that in doing so, they give truth to the lie that Europeans in the West are genuinely altruistic towards Africa, and too that poverty in Africa is best solved through Western philanthropy. Thus, blinded by their spineless agonies, Africans do not see the obvious: they do not see that the problems afflicting Africa, such as poverty, relate to the fact that the global (read 'Western') economy is not accidentally, but deliberately constitutively unequal; that it produces poverty, and that any discussion on how best to address these problems that refuses or fails to pay attention to this very fact.

Europeans running Western governments do not make revolutions; people who refuse to consume mythologies do. Anyone with a grasp of basic development politics and has analysed the debt relief packages that Western governments have in the past offered to African countries, and are offering still, could and cannot fail to see that the conditions oppressive terms and conditions. The mind-set and practices are that aid packages contain enforced liberalisation and privatisation, usually in compliance with United States-led Western notions of democracy, good governance, rule of law and human rights.

Yet for some strange reason these pivotal facts make no impact on African ruling party leaders and politicians, a sign that their hunger for African economic empowerment, economic growth and prosperity, as well as political stability, peace and security, autonomy and national self-determination, is still perversely limited, if not non-existent. Thus, far from challenging the role Europeans have played in bringing about and in worsening Africa's socio-economic conditions, most African leaders are giving legitimacy to those Western imperialists responsible for plundering the continent's natural resources, and whose activities end up impoverishing the indigenous people of Africa.

Let me be more precise: The number of African leaders - current and former heads of state and opinion-makers seeking Western aid and debt relief to solve the continent's economic problems, is absurdly too high, far too high. Festus Mogae of Botswana, Abdoulaye Wade of Senegal, Yoweri Museveni of Uganda, Olusegun Obasanjo of Nigeria, former South African President Nelson Mandela and his sidekick Archbishop Desmond Tutu are all are often heard praising Western so-called humanitarian schemes as signalling a victory for the millions of people in Africa. It is true that Museveni has criticised US President George W. Bush for failing to deliver the money promised for Aids victims in Africa – and indeed he has been a lone voice! But he has never, as far as I can discover, said a word about how Western governments are sponsoring bandits who are killing more people in Africa than Aids does; or the role that Western governments have played in Africa's accumulation of debt through trade barriers; or accumulation of weapons destined for reactionaries and tribal warlords spearheading coups and internecine wars; or loss of resources through exploitation and plunder; or the collapse in public services.

All these to provide imperialists with justifications for neo-liberal policies that enable them to liberalize and privatize enterprises for concentration of wealth and power into the hands of settler colonists.

- *The writer is a lawyer, writer, political analyst, and secretary-general of Davira Mhere, an activist Pan-African organisation.*
https://www.mailarchive.com/ugandanet@kym.net/msg01362.html
Fri, 29 Nov 2002 04:55:34 -0800

Zimbabwe: Nothing Justifies Repeal of AIPPA
Opinion
By Chinondidyachii Mararike
The Herald, 21 May 2005, *www.herald.co.zw*

Harare — *THIS is the last part of an article by Chinondidyachii Mararike on the need to retain AIPPA and POSA as tools of defending Zimbabwe's sovereignty.*

HAS the so-called independent media renounced its pro-Western ideology, and has it become patriotic? Does it support land reform in Zimbabwe? Has it renounced its political partisanship or done anything to justify its call for the repeal of the Access to Information and Protection of Privacy Act (AIPPA)?

The reality is that nothing the "independent" media has done, or is doing, justifies the repeal of AIPPA.

Journalism as practised in the "independent" media in Zimbabwe has carried its pro-Western authority to the grossest, meanest and most brutal extreme, thus proving conclusively that this media is still aligned to the Western neo-liberal agenda of dominance and hegemony, and that the majority of "independent" media journalists remain informed by a false consciousness, saturated with thoughts, values, beliefs and ideologies of their Caucasian backers.

In addition, the "independent" media has developed a morbid and unhealthy faculty for lying, prattling outrageously about the absence of democracy and rule of law in Zimbabwe. On May 6, 2005, the Independent falsely reported that Reserve Bank of Zimbabwe Governor Dr Gideon Gono was "under pressure to quit his post". The other day, Tim Hughes, a South Africa-based journalist, had a piece in the Independent headlined "Plotting the Decline of a Tyrant"; the International Bar Association had another one packed with prejudice and ignorance on alleged "human rights abuses in Zimbabwe".

Additionally, the Standard and Independent regularly carry stories written by ghost writers to distort information on Zimbabwe. The real thing comes in all kinds of packages and doses at different strengths. For example, the two papers made a meal of the arrest of

242

two British journalists - Sunday Telegraph correspondents Julian Simmonds and Tobby Harden - which they held up as conclusive proof there is no democracy and Press freedom in Zimbabwe.

Feverishly clamouring for the triumphant verdict of acquittal of the journalists, it must have embarrassed the papers when, during the pair's trial in Norton, it turned out both had confessed to sneaking into the country under cover of being mere tourists but in reality to cover the March 31 parliamentary elections with neither proper accreditation papers nor valid visas, thus contravening both the Public Order and Security Act (POSA) and the Immigration Act.

The point to be made is that the "independent" media should not indulge in such intellectual beating of the air as to admit the violation of inviolable media laws, nor fail to recognise that the reign of law pervades the domain of journalism as much as it does that of history. And that history, the history of the Zimbabwe Revolution for Equitable Land Redistribution, and the West's stupid reaction to it, contains the greatest lessons for Africa and the world.

It is the solemn duty of journalists to manifest these lessons so as to save governments such as those of Britain and the US from formulating and following those unwise policies which always lead to dishonour and embarrassment, and to teach individuals to apprehend by the intellectual culture of history those truths which else they would have to learn in the bitter school of experience.

The tyranny that 'independent' media journalists propose to exercise over people's private lives seems to me to be quite extra-ordinary. People are disgusted by the lies, misrepresentations and falsehoods. Here, the definition of press freedom reflects a foreign value system that is an affront to African dignity, and to the sensibilities of patriotic and socially-conscious citizens of the world. As a natural consequence the 'independent' media has begun to create a spirit of revolt against itself. And these are the reasons why it is clamouring for the repeal of AIPPA, so it can repair its damaged image!

Frankly, I do not see how, with their lack of comprehension of what press freedom is, 'independent' media journalists could possibly use it in the proper sense. There is a simple explanation for this. The misuse, the origin of the misuse and the meaning that lies behind it all comes from a barbarous conception of the phrase; from a media community corrupted by Western ideology to understand or appreciate its role to country and nation. In a word, it comes from that monstrous and ignorant interpretation of the phrase "freedom of expression" to mean absolute freedom, which becomes infamous and evil when used as an excuse to subvert national interests.

There is no such thing as absolute freedom or absolute independence, any more than unfettered freedom of expression exists. Freedom is relative. The "independent" media in Zimbabwe interprets press freedom to mean absolute freedom to retail things that are ugly, or false, or disgusting, or revolting in fact, so that we end having the most indecent newspapers. AIPPA recognises this and recognises too that the 'independent' media in Zimbabwe is neither independent nor freedom-loving but intrusive and beholden to its Western benefactors, particularly England, the home of lost ideas.

It is absurd to imagine that this sector of the media craves for press freedom when it has shown itself to be completely irresponsible because it is answerable to the West to which it is totally dependent. In centuries before ours, the public nailed the ears of journalists to the pump. Luckily in 21st Century Zimbabwe we have AIPPA, and the Government will not be careless to rid itself of it!

"Independent" media journalists have clung with really pathetic tenacity to what in reality are the direct traditions of the 'Great Exhibition of International Depravity', traditions that are so appalling that they have seen journalists nailing their own ears to the keyhole. They take a real pleasure in publishing horrible things, often those that pertain to the private lives of individuals, and in looking to 'scandals' as forming a sort of permanent basis for an income.

The strategy, thanks to the West, is to encourage "independent" media journalists to drag before the eyes of the public some non-existent or fairly innocuous incident in the life of a senior Zanu-PF politician, or a great statesman like President Mugabe, a man who is a leader of political thought as he is a creator of a political force, and invite the public to discuss the incident, to exercise great authority over the matter, to give their views, to dictate to the man upon all other points, to dictate to his party, to dictate to his country; in fact to make him look ridiculous, offensive and harmful.

The "independent" media continues to exploit the country's economic problems as a mere opportunity for tragic writing, or for prescribing imperialist solutions to the country's problems, or for opposing everything that the government does. These past few weeks has seen the same media lampooning Zimbabwe's "Look 'East Policy" and deriding the Government's acquisition of two passenger planes from China.

It is the same media that puts down maize shortages to the myth of 'chaotic land reforms', telling the government to embrace demeaning NGO charity. Government should be wary when sections of the press reduce national interests to embracing IMF Structural Adjustment Programmes, to re-joining the Commonwealth and to returning African land to the defeated immigrant Caucasian racist immigrants of yesteryear.

This then is no time to assume that the West is about to tone down its propaganda against Zimbabwe, nor is the 'independent' media. Certainly the 'independent' media has not changed its colours, or agenda, or tactics. So, to what end is all this call for the repeal of AIPPA? Does press freedom, with as many meanings and interpretations as ideology dictates, boil down to allowing the private and international media to gang up to discredit Government over land reform in Zimbabwe?

But there is a story in that question. The call for the repeal of AIPPA hides another contentious Western agenda for "regime change" and ultimate re-colonisation of Zimbabwe – an item of far greater significance for country and continent. As it happens, the West's decision to loudly condemn land reform underscores its nervousness about possible spill-over effects in neighbouring countries, notably South Africa and Namibia.

In this broader sense, Western opposition to Zimbabwe, mostly through the hostile media attacks on our President, on members of the cabinet and those in the ruling party, is one piece in a much bigger contest between the West and Africa, and suggests that land reform has exerted pressures upon Caucasian tribes, and that these revolutionary pressures – pushing Zimbabwe, and Africa, on the cusp of a new cultural, political and economic world of growth, development, self-sufficiency, and stability based on autonomy, self-respect, self- determination, and sovereignty - which the West cannot stand to see replicated elsewhere on the continent.

A simple audit of 'independent' media houses we have in Zimbabwe reveals that the majority were formed for the sole or principal objective of 'governance' as defined and prescribed by the British, Americans and their Western allies but which, in reality, is the UK-US alliance's euphemism for its desire to topple the Zimbabwe government. Armed with this mandate, the 'independent' media engages in what is called psychological reactance tactics, the deliberate and systematic attempt to shape perceptions, manipulate cognitions and direct behaviour to turn the populace against its government and achieve the desired intentions of the propagandist.

Zimbabwe is therefore at war, a propaganda war with the West, and the 'independent' media provides the foot soldiers and muggers in this war in which both sets of combatants realise that the pen is mightier than the sword. When 'independent' media muggers continue shooting at Zimbabwe's sovereign body-politic, it certainly is unwise to ask of fellow countrymen, 'Are you willing to kick or punch the mugger in the nose?' Or, something advisedly more drastic!

Africa: West Must Give Africa Due Respect
Opinion
By Chinondidyachii Mararike
The Herald: 20 May 2007, *www.herald.co.zw*

Harare — HEY you Western folk, know now that from the shimmering swirl of waters where many, many thoughts ago the slave ship first landed on the islands of Goa, after which slave master and chained captives disappeared yonder in the grim forests of the West, three streams of thinking have flown down to our day: one swollen from the larger world here and overseas, saying, the multiplying human wants today closer and honest co-operation of races in satisfying them.

Hence arises a yearning for a new humanity based on equality and pulling all ends of the earth nearer – with African, Caucasian, Arab, Mongolian marching in unison.

To be sure, behind this thought lurks an afterthought of force -- the unavoidable insistence that the foundations of true emancipation from the talons of white domination and exploitation must be sunk deeper in the pan-African traditions of patriotism and permanent revolution, hence the need for Africans to quickly embrace armed revolutionary strategies to teach you a lesson or two about human dignity and decency!

The second thought streaming from the death ship is the thought of 1884 Berlin -- the sincere and passionate thought that somewhere between human beings and cattle, God created a tertium quid, and variously called it Negro, Native or simply Black; a clownish, simple creature, at times even lovable within its limitations, but ordained to walk along an imperialist path!

To be sure, behind this thought lurks an afterthought -- yes, with favouring chance some of these creatures might become human beings, but in sheer self-defence you westerners will not let them, thus you try to build walls around them so high and so thick that they shall not even attempt to jump over or break through.

And last of all trickles down a third and darker thought: the thought of the confused, half-conscious mutter of Africans who are black and whitened, crying, "Liberty, Freedom, Opportunity, vouchsafe for us, O white man, the chance of living like human beings".

These are the Morgan Tsvangirais, John Makumbes, Grace Kwinjehs, and a Sekai Holland: born fettered and historically constrained by the midwife of imperialism, and all ignorant of the world around them, the nature of imperialism, the function of government, and of individual worth and possibilities – indeed of nearly all those things which colonialism in its defence and neo-colonialism in its advance had to keep them from learning. Little wonder that much that a white boy imbibes from earliest social learning forms the puzzling problems of these lost African boys and girls in mature years!

Yet to be sure, behind this thought lurks an afterthought - suppose, after all, the whites are right, and we Africans are less than human beings? Suppose this mad impulse of emancipation burning inside the hearts of some us is all wrong, some mock mirage from the untrue?

You see, the problem with a lot of you western tribes are that you never seldom study or care to honestly and carefully understand the thinking of Africans – in fact, you forget or deliberately overlook that in each African is a throbbing human being.

Poverty-stricken some of them may be, yet "black" and curious in limb and ways and thought, capable of loving and hurting and hating: they also toil and tire, laugh and weep their bitter tears, and look in vague and awful longing at the grim horizon of their lives – all this even as you and I.

Admittedly, they have their loafers and rascals, these Africans, but the majority of them work continuously and faithfully for a decent return, which your erstwhile kith and kin farmers denied them, and your multinational companies deny them still. In the end it is un- rewarded labour or forced human toil or labourers with indeterminate wages, and the African writhing like a scotched snake while you continue to steal our gold, diamonds, nickel, and copper.

I remember once meeting a 70-year-old African man who had been employed as a farm hand. Forty-five years he had laboured on the farm – beginning with nothing and ending with nothing. This no doubt explains why his natural good nature was edged with complaint and his mood continuously changing into sullenness and gloom, now and then blazing forth in veiled but hot anger. What does such a mockery of freedom, of equality mean?

And sure, it is little consolation to him that the former farmer's wife is now a wretched and traumatised white widow, indeed a relic of other days sitting alone on a hectare among miles of hundreds of thousands of Africans who benefited from land reform.

Then we have the Australians, Anglo-Americans and their EU partners imposing sanctions on Zimbabwe as punishment for redistributing land to Africans, with Andrew Pocock and Christopher Dell and John Howard organising violent regime change.

This, of course, takes us back to that time when the United States cut aid to Zimbabwe as punishment for our co-sponsoring a resolution condemning US aggression in Grenada, as well as support for apartheid South Africa, and which – on July 16, 1986 – elicited an appropriate response from President Mugabe, then Prime Minister; a response which is relevant today as it was then:

I find it quite ironical, but what I find quite objectionable is the fact that the US of all countries, tends to use its aid as a weapon to coerce or impel countries that are the beneficiaries to toe a certain line, even contrary to their own political and ideological positions. Perhaps it is their tradition but of course... let it be known that when we fought for our independence and sovereignty, we never meant to sell it at all.

In words that seemed to anticipate Land Reform 2000, the President concluded chillingly: "...and so what I give you in the future is independent Zimbabwe with resources and determined population to exploit those resources and become their own masters and not beggars and beneficiaries."

Isn't it strange to relate, really, that the very shrill Caucasian voices lampooning and vilifying our land reform are themselves the greatest violators of human rights in the world?

Strange to relate indeed, for neither in Zimbabwe nor Africa can genuine economic and social progress be built on the African as an oppressed, exploited and turbulent proletariat.

Thus, it is much easier for you Westerners to arrogantly assume that you know all about Africans - their daily lives and longings, homely joys and sorrows, disappointments and ambitions; or, perhaps having already reached a priori conclusions in your own narrow and prejudiced minds, you are loath to have them disturbed by facts.

The Herald (Harare)
Zimbabwe: Africa Not Land of Poverty
By Chinondidyachii Mararike
The Herald: 28 November 2002, *www.herald.co.zw*

Harare — Reporting on the collapse of the ACP-EU summit in Brussels, Britain's far-right paper The Daily Telegraph (26 November 2002) states that: "Delegates from the world's poorest countries stormed out of a Brussels conference yesterday to show their solidarity for . . . Zimbabwe".

The Guardian went further to claim that the collapse of the talks could damage wider relations between the European Union and the ACP countries and hinder efforts to establish closer economic ties."

Is there no end to the wilful, deceitful, evil and decadent tactlessness of the West, comrades?

"Economic ties" for whose benefit, Africa or Europe?

What "wider relations" or "economic ties" does Europe have with Africa except those based on outrageous imperialist exploitation?

And the gluey motto of the 'modern' Western empire - is this not a bullies' charter iced with a religious resonance of charity? Our receiving of European aid need not blind us.

It is a fact that such seemingly charitable gestures are what in Europe gave rise to the primitive Spanish Inquisitions and much worse suffering?

Who is cheating whom?

Who says countries in Africa are the world's poorest?

Surely Europe cannot hope to deceive the world and simper on without being told a few home truths.

Precisely that I will do and am doing right now. Stark naked in its glorious beauty and choking almost to its summit with abundant resources stands Africa' tallest mountain Mt Kilimanjaro.

It is a proudly imposing and majestic landmark of uranium-joined toes, gold-girded hips, diamond-built breasts, copper-crusted neck, varied flora and fauna, climatic diversity (sub-tropical, tropical and tundra) and as Tanzania's Natural Resources Minister Mrs Meghy

250

eloquently put it on December 31, 1999, "by the miracle of the Almighty, snow at the summit of the Equator".

This continent's heartbeat is not only a microcosm of Africa but in several senses mirrors, symbolises, epitomises and provides a fascinating geographical anatomy of Africa, and will never cease to attract and at the same time surprise any intrepid traveller who happens to traverse this beautiful continent.

Matthew Parris, a discarded Tory MP and now an intermittent columnist of The Times but who as a boy growing up in Salisbury's suburbia was an enthusiastic beneficiary of Ian Smith's apartheid policies in Rhodesia, admitted just as much on 31 December 1999 when he led a motley crew of overawed Caucasian millennium mountain-climbers up the mighty mountain.

The West must really think God is African and of Africa as having the world's greatest wonders! For a fact, 75 percent of the world's gold output comes from the combined countries of Zimbabwe, South Africa and Ghana.

The Democratic Republic of Congo is not only richer in resources such as gold, uranium, diamonds, copper than the countries that make up the whole of Western Europe put together, but bigger in size as well.

Caucasians openly concede the fact that Angola and the DRC are not only cursed by riches but possess every imaginable mineral resource upon which Europe is dependent on for both its survival and progress.

Nigeria, the 4th largest oil producer in Africa and the 5th largest supplier of oil to America, is capable of producing food sufficient to feed both Africa and Europe.

Botswana boasts of inexhaustible diamond reserves: in fact, the country sits literally on not just ordinary diamonds, but diamonds of the highest quality. The Copperbelt is not in New York, but Zambia. It wasn't Africans, but Caucasians, who 'christened' Ghana the Gold Coast. And when it rains like the rain in that dull British film, Four Weddings and a Funeral, the people of Sierra Leone rush to the riverbanks to pick diamonds.

Zimbabwe, Namibia, Guinea and Mozambique all boast of iron and steel, copper and diamonds, cobalt and gold, tin, and aluminium, uranium and rutile.

A similar pattern and picture are replicated in almost all African countries.

Britain, whose immigrant settler ancestral kith and kin are responsible for the current problems we face in Zimbabwe today, is an island that boasts of nothing except snow, sleet, a diseased population, football hooligans and the depleted coal deposits that used to be along the banks of Newcastle-upon-Tyne - resources that today are of no use to anybody!

Zimbabwe: Imperialists Seek to Dominate Third World
OPINION
Chinondidyachii Mararike
The Herald: 13 January 2003, *www.herald.co.zw*

Harare — This is the second and final part of the article in which Chinondidyachii Mararike examines imperialism. The first part was published on Saturday.

We embrace 2003 buoyed by that stunning victory over the forces of imperialism, and in the knowledge that Zimbabweans will greet their next challenges with courage and determination - and not complacency and insouciance.

The suffering that Africans endured at the hands of colonial imperialists is no different from what they are enduring under today's neo- imperialist thugs, and clearly shows how contemporary imperialists absorbed the habits of their forefathers.

The refugees fleeing Western-inspired civil wars in Africa, victims of imperialism, are dwellers of plastic palaces, or of mud-walled affairs with roofs of palm fronds.

Africa's squatter camps in Ouagadougou, Abidjan, Freetown, Monrovia, Kisangani, or in Kenya's illegal human settlement of Kibera, are homes to groups of small, wide-mouthed and hungry children who together with their distraught neighbours stare while the Britons, French, Israelis, and Americans sun themselves in some of Africa's tourist equivalents of a British Empire, rubbing salt in the wounds of the poor who watch in horror at the drunken revelries and pampered ignorance.

Imperialism is when Morgan Tsvangirai's MDC calls for sanctions against the innocent people of Zimbabwe and when Kenyan dancers in colourful print outfits and white-fringed skirts die dancing barefoot for foreign tourists milling in the lobby of an unnamed hotel for a pittance.

Since when have the coasts of Africa been a paradise for the local African peoples, when most are forced to work for subsistence wages, serving unquestioningly every demand of pampered Westerners? Since when have the tourist resorts of Africa played host to honest and philanthropic Europeans?

No, comrades - no way *vehama!*

Now that is the "modern" face of imperialism, tourist-style, in which the imperialists do not care about what the "security" forces of their respective "elected" Western governments are doing on their behalf in Liberia, Sierra Leone, Uganda, Ivory Coast, Rwanda, Burundi, Palestine, Afghanistan, Iraq, the DRC, and Angola. And all because imperialism is deceptive: it blends political calculation with sheer diplomacy.

Imperialism is terrifying and wicked. And for Sigmund Freud who was writing at about the time when imperialist ideas were taking a modern shape, it is the obscene pleasure of the death drive, and the self-destructive instincts, which seduces the imperialists into killing other races out of sheer selfishness.

What makes the imperialist most impregnable is how he embraces his own destruction, not just dismembering others.

On this theory, which one can find in both Fascism and Nazism, imperialism is in thrall to the petty suburban logic of living as long as the victims fear death. Imperialists, therefore, believe they free themselves from death only when they accept their own death, indeed more like the revolutionary who risks his own life when he or she takes up arms to fight the imperialist - but there the comparison ends!

That is why Zanu-PF and other African ruling parties understand that the "ism" at the end of imperialism suggests a philosophy crafted

253

out of frightening monsters that kill other non-Europeans for exploitation, for fun and for purposes of domination.

Zimbabweans understand how imperialists operate, that is, through nourishing their socio-economic and political systems of domination by making those in the third world perpetual servants.

Through these systems of control, they spread their tentacles of hegemony, what Antonio Gramsci, refers to as "the way in which the consent of the subordinate classes to their domination is achieved".

Once achieved, hegemony ensures that the dominant ideology permeates every facet of human existence. Religion, language, food, clothing/dressing, taste, morality, customs, and political principles are some of the arenas of hegemony. Indeed, it perpetuates an order in which a Western way of life and thought is dominant, and one concept of reality prevails throughout the dominated society.

This way, the dominated are unable to respond to the spectre and genre of exported Western religious culture with anything else other than the pleasure of familiar horror - to use an oxymoron. In the meantime, Messrs Donald Rumsfeld, George W. Bush and Tony Blair are busy trying to convince the world that they are the most effective defenders of universal democratic values. In fact, all they are defending are the undignified liberal values of today's Western-dominated world order.

Now that is imperialism. The terror of imperialism is founded upon the kind of right-wingers for whom any fundamental criticism of the West by anybody in the so-called developing world is so inconceivable that it can only be a symptom of insanity.

Britain, defeated by Zanu-PF in the 1966 to 1980 anti-colonial and liberation war, and also in the 2000 to 2002 Third Chimurenga - has learned that Cde Mugabe is still as sharp as he was since the 1960s when he came out to fight against the forces of imperialism.

That is why the tabloid press seeks to portray President Mugabe as an insane person. That is why Britain portrayed the Zanla war as a "gorilla" rather than a guerrilla movement, even though the British government was aware that this was Zanu-PF's legitimate armed wing during the liberation struggle. That, too, is why the West cannot quite stomach Zanu-PF's defeat of the neo-colonial form of imperialism in Zimbabwe. And too, why the opposition has no means of repelling Zanu-PF's anti-imperialist juggernaut.

Yes, Zimbabwean revolutionaries embrace 2003 determined not to allow the imperialists to underestimate us after what we have achieved because Zanu-PF has raised the tempo as the opposition's delusionary days turn to a distant memory. Zanu-PF is determined to give fresh evidence of its own distinction.

But much more than all this is because *Davira Mhere* acknowledges that President Mugabe is a one-man nemesis for imperialism, and for any imperialist stooge.

He, Africa's most loved and famous son, has dominated international forums in thought and deed. He is a man who makes his imperialist opponents uncertain. Concentrated and conscious, committed but controlled, the revolutionary suffers no disastrous lapses in discipline.

Zimbabweans have put up a good fight and must until this imperialist beast is defeated and killed completely. To these, the veterans of Zimbabwe's Third Chimurenga, we dedicate this poem, the Lyrics of Africa's Revolutionary Tune, and declare that:

Nobody should say the Africans are dead because the Africans are alive, our banner shall never be lowered,
Our homeland is our land and culture and continent,
We are the heroes of the revolution and the colour red –
Just look and see how high we raise our revolutionary flag!
The African people are gallantly standing at attention,
The continent's youth is ever-present,
Ready to sacrifice their lives -
To inflict deadly blows on Western imperialism,
And to decorate our living crown with the enemy's blood!

Chapter 8

The New Scramble for Africa:
Re colonising the Continent

Neo colonialism is at work on two fronts – in Europe as well as in the underdeveloped countries. Its current framework in the underdeveloped countries is the policy of aid, and one of the essential aims of this policy is to create a false bourgeoisie to put brakes on the revolution and to enlarge the possibilities of the petty bourgeoisie as a neutraliser of the revolution.

Amilcar Cabral

Phases for Scramble for Africa

The scramble for Africa has been in three distinct phases. The first scramble for Africa was on 1884 when European nations visualised a continent with vast rich lands and mineral resources. What made access to this continent easy is that it was fragmented, poorly defended and had intra tribal wars resulting in divisions and disunity. Europe rushed in to steal the land and its resources in what is a classic case of unjust enrichment. Six years after this conference, the British colonialists arrived in Zimbabwe and started a series of wars with local African population aimed at dispossessing them of their land and rich mineral resources.

The second phase was played out outside the continent when the eastern bloc countries whose socialist ideology sought to incorporate the poor countries of Africa in what was a case of ideological indoctrination. The Soviet Union and other Eastern countries like China were accused by the West of backing African despots and dictatorship in order to easily access vast mineral resources. The West sought to maintain their grip and control of the continent through the provision of aid and maintenance of other neo-colonial ties. Although this battle for power and domination was played out as ideological warfare between the East and the West, the reality was that there were considerable direct interfaces with individual countries on both power blocs. For example, Britain maintained its stronghold by using a series of agreements and bilateral relations including the formulation of the Commonwealth group of countries. France extended its influence in Francophone West Africa while Portugal's presence was felt in Angola and Mozambique. America maintained its presence by backing African leaders who found themselves in neutral positions – for example in the Democratic Republic of Congo.

The third way in which the scramble for Africa is being reinforced is through globalisation of capitalist economies – by placing greater emphasis on free trade or voluntary exchange and the spread of technology like what is taking place in Rwanda at the moment. Rwanda is paraded as a gateway to Africa as European companies like VW and Heineken Brewery. British financial services sector companies like Deloitte, PWC and Ernst & Young, are leading the growth of the financial services sector in Rwanda. The UK Foreign and Commonwealth Office notes that "Bilateral trade in goods between the UK and Rwanda exceeded £21 million in 2014 up from £10 million 2012. UK exports to Rwanda, principally of machinery and pharmaceuticals, totalled £15 million. There are around 150 British companies registered in Rwanda. The UK is the biggest investor in the tea sector in Rwanda.

A British architect has done the design for Bugesera airport. Rwandair purchase of 2 new A300 from Airbus with Rolls Royce engines." https://www.gov.uk/government/publications/rwanda-business-guide/uk-rwanda-commercial-relationship

Rwanda is termed Fast Moving Consumer Goods (FMCG) economy but in reality, it is the gateway of capitalist penetration and western domination in Africa. Rwanda has been turned into a strategic satellite base for capitalism in Africa from where western companies will make inroads to the rest of the continent. The intention is to counter Chinese dominance in Africa. Foreigners hope to access resources and new markets because of its growing population. The scale of foreign interest in Africa is unprecedented. In Zimbabwe, the Unites States of America has built a 200-million-dollar embassy in Harare as they compete for presence with their

British counterparts. The Economist (07.052019) reports that between 2010 and 2016, 320 new embassies were built in Africa, the highest number in the post-war period. It is quite clear that one way in which Europe seeks to forge ahead with an imperialist agenda is through diplomatic engagements and extensions of its international relations. The same source highlights that China is now the biggest arms seller to sub-Saharan Africa and has defence-technology ties with 45 countries. Russia has signed 19 military deals with African states since 2014. Oil-rich Arab states are building bases on the Horn of Africa and hiring African mercenaries. https://www.economist.com/leaders/2019/03/07/the-new-scramble-for-africa

Why has it been easy for the west to sink their roots in Rwanda? It took place between two ethnic groups populating Rwanda: the Hutus and the Tutsis. On April 6, 1994, a plane carrying President Habyarimana, a Hutu, was shot down. Between April and June 1994, in a space of 100 days, an estimated 800,000 Rwandans were killed. A UN force (UNAMIR), watched as people were killed in the streets, as they claimed that they had "no mandate to intervene." It is from the ashes of this guilty conscience that Western Europe capitalised on to assert their capitalist agenda.

Africa as a bloc of 53 countries must unite to counter neo-colonialism and imperialism. For example, Africa needs to create a common market platform in which to negotiate with both the Western powers, China and Russia. China is using its financial muscle and aid to advance a new form of imperialism in the whole of Africa. The western powers on the other one hand, have used historical colonial ties to advance their economic interests. Africa needs to counter free market trade and military bargains in which its individual nation states are forced to compromise skewed deals and multilateral agreements. Africa needs that platform to strategically deal with Islamic fundamentalism and how to deal with oil rich Arab nations who have developed a keen interest in Africa's mineral resources especially in diamonds. The Africa that must deal with counteracting ideological must have values of democratic principles and diversity. It must be conscious enough to understand that Africa's best natural resources are being exploited for the sustenance of those who enslavement them rather than being exploited for its own enrichment and emancipation.

The Rush to Buy up Africa: Imperialism and Land Grab.

Data about transnational land deals are scarce and difficult to access, partly because of the high levels of secrecy around such deals (Cotula et al., 2009. If these are transparent deals, why the secrecy? Some of the land is acquired and disposed of to foreign governments and private land buyers corruptly using the ruling elite. Moreover, the acquisition and development of arable land is a highly dynamic process. It has grown exponentially since its emergence about a decade ago, and at the same time land deals undergo frequent change regarding their negotiation status (from intended to concluded or failed contract negotiations), areal extent (granted vs. allocated vs. cultivated area), and operational status (planned, started, cancelled, etc.) (Land Matrix Partnership, 2014). According to UK's Guardian Newspaper, almost 5% of Africa's agricultural land has been bought or leased by investors since 2000, according to an international coalition of researchers and NGOs that has released the world's largest public database of international land deals.[72]

The database, entitled *Dealing with Disclosure* lifts the lid on a decade of secretive deals struck by individual governments, investors and speculators seeking large tracts of fertile land in developing countries around the world. Since 2010, there have seen a flood of reports of investors snapping up land at rock-bottom prices in some of the world's poorest countries. But, despite growing concern about the local impacts of so-called "land grabs", the lack of reliable data has made it difficult to pin down the real extent and nature of the global rush for land.

The report, Dealing with Disclosure, published by Global Witness, the International Land Coalition and the Oakland Institute, looks at why it is vital to transform the secretive culture behind large scale land deals, and for the first time shows how it might be done. At present

---

[72] https://www.theguardian.com/globaldevelopment/2012/apr/27/international-land-deals-database-africa

decisions are being made in secret, with basic information unavailable even to those affected. The report argues that all contractual information must be made publicly available unless investors or governments can prove that this would harm commercial competitiveness or public interest – a principle it calls "if in doubt, disclose". The rush for land in developing countries has rapidly intensified since 2008, but the sector remains largely unregulated. Concerns are growing over the impact of big, secretive deals between governments and investors on communities and the environment. As more land is taken away from local communities, growing numbers of people are losing access to the resources they have relied on for generations, and ecosystems are being destroyed. Decisions and negotiations around land deals are frequently conducted in secret, without the knowledge, let alone consent, of affected communities. Without access to basic information such as contract terms or pre-project impact assessment studies, local communities and other parties cannot make informed decisions about the suitability of proposed investments.

This lack of information hampers efforts to hold governments or investors to account, making human rights and environmental abuses more likely. It also undermines governance and democratic processes and fosters high-level corruption, discouraging companies willing to operate responsibly.

Quoted from https://www.globalwitness.org/en-gb/archive/culture-secrecy-around-global-land-deals-must-be-lifted-protect-people-and-environment/

According to Anseeuw et al (2012) shortage of productive land in Europe is at the centre of the rush to buy up Africa. Evidence suggest that as prospects in global food and energy markets improved over the course of the 2000s, large numbers of agricultural investors sought access to Africa's cheap and fertile farmlands to establish industrial food and biofuel feedstock plantations. Many African governments met this renewed interest in their agricultural sector with great optimism since such investments promised to bring in much-needed capital in support of national agricultural modernization and rural poverty alleviation objectives. This has happened in Kenya were tracts of state land have been sold to British multinational corporations. Cotula, (2012) observes that many civil society organizations were quick to caution against the potentially devastating social and environmental impacts of commercial agriculture expansion. However, because land tenure regimes in many African countries are organized through customary arrangements that are often poorly protected by statutory law, it has been widely argued that the rising demand for farmland is increasingly exposing rural populations to involuntary land expropriation.

Large-scale land acquisitions for agricultural purposes have become a pervasive topic in current debates on sustainable rural development in the global South. Focussing on issues such as food security, land governance, agricultural transitions, and access to resources, these debates involve a broad range of actors, including development practitioners, policymakers, investors, activists, and researchers – all of whom are striving to understand the rapidly unfolding phenomenon. What is evident is that foreign governments are masking imperialism by hiding behind the tag of foreign direct investment in which acquisition of land is used as an excuse to rescue neglected land for agricultural development.

To date, much of the scholarly debate is on the legality of the Zimbabwe Land Reform programme, funding options and responsibility for the on the crisis. Western sponsored International organisations including the World Bank have hardly focused on governance of farmland investments and how the Zimbabwean populace can benefit from the evolution and functioning of its land tenure in the context of global (land) governance systems. Economic sanctions debates have bloated key and fundamental issues in the country's agrarian political economy or political ecology perspective. This literature produces critical insights into how global governance processes, notably the emergence of non-state mechanisms such as voluntary codes of conduct and certification systems, are produced and reproduced by contemporary world capitalist structures, corporate agro-commodity regimes, and an increasingly polycentric world order. Borras et al., (2013) share these views

The International Monetary Fund (IMF) Report of 2012 advances that 'farmland investments' are foreign direct investment (FDI) flows to many African countries. These began to surpass official development assistance (ODA) in the 1990s due to economic liberalization policies, agricultural FDI increasingly started to be viewed as a solution to rural poverty rather than the problem; for example, by promoting the uptake of modern farming practices, improving access to inputs, supporting smallholder integration into global value chains, and generating formal employment opportunities. Within this context, most African countries have started lifting capital controls, offering investors fiscal incentives, and reducing administrative bottlenecks by establishing 'one-stop investment centres for 'aid investors' who apply for the necessary permits and incentives that facilitate easy acquisition of land. Zimbabwe views such incentives as strategies to parcel out land acquired for peasants back to the colonial master and has challenged these development assumptions.

Economic Sanctions as a Recolonization Agenda

The United States of America announced extension of Zimbabwe's economic sanctions on 6 March 2019 for a period of one year. Donald Trump used Executive Order 13288, the President declared a national emergency and blocked the property of certain persons, pursuant to the International Emergency Economic Powers Act (50 U.S.C. 1701-1706), to deal with the unusual and extraordinary threat to the foreign policy of the United States constituted by the actions and policies of certain members of the Government of Zimbabwe and other persons to undermine Zimbabwe's democratic processes or institutions. Donald Trump alleges policy failures in Zimbabwe have contributed to the deliberate breakdown in the rule of law in Zimbabwe, to politically motivated violence and intimidation in that country, and to political and economic instability in the southern African region.

On November 22, 2005, the President issued Executive Order 13391 to take additional steps with respect to the national emergency declared in Executive Order 13288 by ordering the blocking of the property of additional persons undermining democratic processes or institutions in Zimbabwe.

On July 25, 2008, the President issued Executive Order 13469, which expanded the scope of the national emergency declared in Executive Order 13288 and authorized the blocking of the property of additional persons undermining democratic processes or institutions in Zimbabwe. According to the United States government, these actions and policies of persons cited 13288 'continue to pose an unusual and extraordinary threat to the foreign policy of the United States'. Building upon the 'national emergency' declared on March 6, 2003, and the measures adopted on that date, on November 22, 2005, and on July 25, 2008, to deal with that emergency, economic sanctions 'must continue in effect beyond March 6, 2019'.

It is therefore, in accordance with section 202(d) of the National Emergencies Act (50 U.S.C. 1622(d)), that President Trump extended Zimbabwe economic sanctions for 1 year the national emergency declared in Executive Order 13288.

The United Kingdom has gone on the offensive to pressure South Africa to 'deal with Zimbabwe' Baldwin encouraged Zimbabwe's southern African neighbours, particularly South Africa, to engage with the Harare government on the basis of its affiliation to the commonwealth membership and UN security Council seat. Through Morrison Baldwin, a Minister of State at the Foreign Office and Department for International development, Britain issued directives on pre-conditions for good governance. These lectures are reminiscent of President Mugabe's rule which was defined by anti-colonial rhetoric. War veterans of the Chimurenga liberation struggle have started to mobilise Zimbabweans against imposition of economic sanctions by the West on the basis of questioning their legitimacy effects and effectiveness.

https://www.businesslive.co.za/bd/world/africa/2019-02-05-britains-minister-for-africa-calls-for-more-sanctions-against-zimbabwe/

Conclusion: Legitimacy Overruled

Why are Zimbabwe economic sanctions illegal? The legality of sanctions imposed on Zimbabwe is debatable – from sender and receiver perspectives. From the USA point of view, they followed a due process of their legislative structures to put in place Zimbabwe Development and Economic Recovery Act 2001. At one other level, Zimbabwe questions the legitimacy of ZDERA on the basis that disputes between nations are dealt with by international law and not domestic law. According to the US law, "treaties shall be supreme law of the land". By virtue of the fact that the USA is a signatory to the UN Charter, Vienna Convention, Universal Declaration of Human Rights (UDHR), International Covenant on Cultural Rights (UCESCR), World Trade organisation (WTO); and General Agreement on Tariffs and Trade (GATT) - this places the legality of laws derived under USA domestic law into question. According to the UN Charter, Articles 32-38, all disputes between member states of the UN must be dealt with the UN Assembly and Security Council. No nation has the right to take aggressive and unilateral actions to solve disputes arising from the law. Solutions by the United Nations are collective and peaceful in the maintenance of peace.

Receiving countries like Zimbabwe interrogate sanctions legitimacy on the basis of their damaging and lasting impact. Sanctions destroys domestic currencies, causes mass unemployment, hyperinflation, escalation of domestic prices, business closures, political tensions, polarised societies, high crime rates, corruption, depopulation, rural urban migration and pressures on limited economic resources. Sanctions also cause rapid decline of buying power in poor communities, relative deprivation, high poverty levels and stratification of communities into class systems. There are no studies to confirm the extent of the impact of Zimbabwean sanctions on migrants overworking especially in Europe's poor working conditions - in order to sustain families through their external remittances. The International Court of Justice can make rulings against executive orders especially in consideration of their impact on health delivery systems. International law supersedes domestic law and. Zimbabwean sanctions are based on US domestic law which has been imposed on a sovereignty state. This is part of the wide imperialist agenda.

References

Anseeuw et al., (2012) W. Anseeuw, M. Boche, T. Breu, M. Giger, J. Lay, P. Messerli, K. Nolte, 'Transnational Land Deals for Agriculture in the Global South: Analytical Report' Based on the *Land Matrix Database, International Land Coalition*, Rome, Italy (2012)

Borras et al., (2013) S.M. Borras, J.C. Franco, C. Wang 'The challenge of global governance of land grabbing: changing international agricultural context and competing political views and strategies' *Globalizations*, 10 **(1)** 161-179

Cotula, et al., (2009) L. Cotula, S. Vermeulen, R. Leonard, J. Keeley 'Land grab or development opportunity: Agricultural investment and international land deals in Africa' Google Scholar

Land Matric Partnership, 2014 Land Matrix Partnership Land matrix newsletter – January 2014. Page 4 Retrieved March 14, 2019, from http://landmatrix.org/ Google Scholar

Chapter 9

Postscript: Zimbabwe Democracy and the Economic Recovery Amendment Act 2018 Flogging a Dead Horse before the Cart?

"...When there is no content in your character you get carried away and forget who you are..."

Upenyu Giles (UG) Chihota, 02/05/2018

On 22 March 2018 the US Congress amended the Zimbabwe Democracy and Economic Recovery Act 2001 through a Bill cited as "S. 2595 — 115th Congress: A bill to amend the Zimbabwe Democracy and Economic Recovery Act of 2001." www.GovTrack.us. 2018[73].

At the time of writing this report (April 2018), S. 2595 is a bill in the United States Congress waiting for President Trump's approval - A bill must be passed by both the House and Senate in identical form and then be signed by the President to become law.

The original Act of 2001 which is four pages in length has burgeoned to nine pages, incorporating changes demanded by opposition politics in Zimbabwe. The current bill is an incorporation of the Movement for Democratic Change (MDC) electoral reforms demands. These demands are designed to squeeze out ZANU PF and its liberation struggle ideology from political space in Zimbabwe.

Section 2 headed 'Reconstruction and Rebuilding of Zimbabwe' is a presumption that previous and enduring land reforms of ZANU PF are detrimental to social and democratic turf in Zimbabwe. The bill works on the premises that Zimbabwe needs to be 'reconstructed' and must be 'configured' to represent and protect Western interests including land, mines and mineral ores. ZANU PF perceives this move as attempts to propel western created opposition MDC to power for reasons of gatekeeping imperial Western interests.

---

[73] March 25, 2018 https://www.govtrack.us/congress/bills/115/s2595

In 5 (4) (2) the bill seeks to withhold funding for the African Development Bank for arrears clearance – revealing another punitive measure and sabotage directed at and designed to bring the Munangagwa-led government to its knees. Pre-election conditions in 6 (2) (a-f) are destined to foster western democracy that fosters neo-colonial imperatives – in terms of controls and governance. The enormity of demands is also implied to intimidate the ZANU PF revolutionary party into capitulation exceptionally at this pre-election time when it is in a dog fight for its legitimacy. According to ZANU PF, such overt threats not only go against the thread and reason of Chimurenga liberation philosophy but distort the history and mind-set of the younger electorate.

We also witness through the provisions of the same bill perverted efforts to dictate what to and not include into the Zimbabwean constitution. For example, under 6 (4) the US and its allies calls for statutory 'amendments' and updates of statutes again rendering their roles to those of dictators:

> "Laws enacted prior to passage of Zimbabwean constitution in March 2013 that are inconsistent with the new constitution are amended or repealed so that they are consistent with the constitution"

Who are they to call for insertions or invalidations of certain provisions of the law into the Zimbabwean constitution? Is it not striking coincidence that one such constitutional provision relates to the disbanded and moribund SADC Tribunal on Zimbabwean Land ruling? As far as President Mnangagwa's ruling ZANU PF party is concerned, implications are far reaching because recognising judgements from the said tribunal is tantamount to reversal of the land reform programme itself. (See Section 10, of the Bill, headed "SADC Tribunal Rulings" involving 18 disputes with original looters, so-called [dignified and exalted as] 'Zimbabwean Commercial Farmers'! Achume (2017) gives an apt summary of academic objective in legal interpretation of the SADC Tribunal at law:

> The final objective of my chapter is to offer a novel analysis of the international law doctrine on race-conscious post-colonial land reform

in southern Africa, which is at the heart of Campbell. Scholars to date have taken for granted the legal soundness of the SADC Tribunal's application of international human rights law in *Campbell,* which can be read to preclude race-conscious land reform even where this reform seeks to undo racialized land ownership structures rooted in colonial policy in the region. I challenge *Campbell's* racial discrimination analysis, arguing that a more nuanced approach is required by international human rights law and for southern Africa. Doing so initiates what must be a larger project more fully to understand international law's relationship to post-colonial land reform and racial equality in southern Africa[74].

The suggested changes by the US are an illustration of gross interference in terms of economic motives.

Different timeframes and same strategy

It is important for African scholars and their counterparts to understand that when imperialists seek vantage points, they make concessions even on terms and conditions that are inconsistent with their own precedent. They make exceptions to the general rules and convey what they term 'special cases' or even short gap measures. For the current crop of Zimbabwean politicians and policy makers to understand how imperialism work, it is important to examine key provisions of a similar and counter situation in which Zimbabwe experienced economic sanctions in its historical epochs. If we go back to the implementation and impact analysis of the sanctions under the UDI era in 1966, we note a similar formation in terms of how imperialists employed legislation to bull doze and manipulate their way into economic gains from sanctions. Here is how:

The Byrd Amendment Act of 1971 was enacted by the United States Congress in November 1971 to amend the Federal Strategic

---

[74] The SADC Tribunal: Socio-Political Dissonance and the Authority of International Courts, UCLA School of Law, Public Law and Theory Research Paper Series, Research Paper No. 17-04. Found at: https://papers.ssrn.com/sol3/papers.cfm?abstract_id=2907148 file:///C:/Users/Laptop/Downloads/SSRN-id2907148%20(1).pdf/Accessed 19 May 18

and Materials Stock Pilling Act which prohibited importation of chrome from Rhodesia and other socialist countries. The said act was created to allow an exception that allowed the United States to trade with Rhodesia in "strategic material" of chrome ore. Passing a legislation within the UDI at that stage was not only indicative of extremes of how capitalism work, but a contradictory measure of imperialistic designs. Thus, selective terms were designed to benefit international capital in situations were competing forces of trade were at work, where the capitalism faced socialism, where Russia faced the USA and Europe. The enactment of every legislation is underpinned by vested or competing interests, but more often than not, scholars don't read into caveats attached.

Rhodesia was a bastardized and irredentist outpost of imperialism, unrecognised by the United Nations-imposed sanctions following its declaration of independence in 1965. Empirical evidence from *Multinational corporations and United States foreign Relations, Volume 4, Parts 1-2, United States Congress: Committee on Foreign Relations. Subcommittee on Multinational Corporations,* page 77 point out to the fact that 40% of US chrome ore was from Rhodesia; while Rhodesia had 67% of world reserve of chrome ore. US importations were a multi-million-dollar industry in which the USA enjoyed the monopoly of looting the vital product at "depressed" prices. Other questions that African scholars may want to ask are – who benefitted the most from the Byrd Amendment Act? Did African Zimbabweans crushing under the racist and discriminatory Land Apportionment Act of 1941 gain tangible benefits resources from their land? We highlight that at that stage, spin offs from the Byrd Amendment Act were used by the settler government to reinforce their control of Rhodesia by consolidating their power in that colony. Rhodesia became the surrogate of white hegemonic power – and that power was based on white supremacy.

Because of the implications of the cold war of the 60s and windfall financial gains from a colony the US opted for the Byrd Amendment Act as a "facilitative exception" and not a control mechanism. They resorted to this – not only to undermine sanctions boycott but to strategically exploit crude profits out of colonised Zimbabweans. That aim is clear in terms of US Foreign Policy at that time[75]. Despite obvious US breach of terms and conditions of sanctions, 'Rhodesian' companies like Union Carbide capitalised on exclusive access to bring champagne on Caucasian dinner tables in Europe while Commanders Josiah Magara Tongogara, 'Rex Nhongo' Mutusva-Mujuru, Josiah Tungamirai, Dumiso Dabengwa, Alfred Nikita Mangena, Lookout Masuku and Tshinga Dube, were in trenches and on the frontline in Chimoio, Marogoro, Tembwe, Nyadzonya, Dzapasi ku Buhera, and Hwange.

With the amendment came the legitimisation of trading nickle and asbestos from Rhodesia (where Kamativi, Shabani and Mashava mines respectively worked on full throttle to achieve targeted production levels demanded by the United States). As of 1972, trading with Rhodesia was worth $13.3 million, rising to 17% of the US imports of chrome. Jones (1996) chronicles the American trade indiscretions in Rhodesia during the UDI sanctions era.

In the critique of Zimbabwe Democracy and Economic Recovery Act of 2001 as amended in 2018, what implications do Zimbabweans politicians draw from the foregoing dimensions?

i.   We see the USA crafting another similar repressive legislation 53 years later – in form of ZDERA which is exclusively designed to benefit and safeguard US trade and economic benefits in Zimbabwe. It is well known that, through modern and advanced methods of geological surveys and explorations, Zimbabwe is one of the richest countries on earth[76]. What has been extracted so far during the colonial and post-independence era represents a tiny proportion of its global ore resources;

ii.   Mugabe was considered first at independence in 1980 as a "dangerous communist" and after 2001 land reforms as a "brutal dictator". While he ruled Zimbabwe "with an iron fist" he was a

---

[75] Collier, EC (2011) Bipartisanship & the Making of Foreign Policy: A Historical Survey, Xlibris Corporation Printers, United States of America. Found at: https://books.google.co.uk/books?id=1BC6FroJAnsC&pg=PA163&redir_esc=y#v=onepage&q&f=false/Accessed May 5, 18: See Also Chapter One entitled "Meaning of Bipartisanship"; Chapter Two "Post War Record of Bipartisanship and Chapter Three "Perspectives on Bipartisanship Foreign Policy"
[76] Zimbabwe the richest country in the world. Found at: https://www.thepatriot.co.zw/old_posts/zimbabwe-the-richest-country-in-the-world/Accessed/May 06.18

stumbling block for international capital because of his anti-imperialist stance. The fact that the country is rich in terms of human capital development is a bonus for neo-colonial designs of the West. That completes the circuit for the creation of conducive "investment" environment!

iii.   By inserting in ZDERA, what political sociologists consider as "clauses of interests and gain" we witness a new level of economic and intellectual imperialism. Those clauses with hidden agendas are brought to the fore in subtle legal semantics, coded diction with double barrelled means that no ordinary man will understand. Zimbabwean politicians must be able to read between the lines to unpack the game plan being advanced through ZDERA

iv.   Proposed US amendments that deal specifically with the land question are part of their economic renewal agenda in Europe as they face ferocious competition for resources with former eastern bloc countries. Thus, demands for land and property rights are not only tributes to capitalism, but prerequisites necessary for underhand assault on a nation's de facto sovereignty. In Africa we call it stealing sovereignty from former colonies at the dead end of the night. Further "land audits" or "reforms" as advocated through ZDERA conditions for lifting of sanctions are part of the plan to lower white capital risk and threats! No investor wants to invest in high risk areas. Africans must be deeply disturbed by knowledge of the existence of such a strategy which spills over Zimbabwean boarders. One 'forgotten' Zimbabwean poet in the mould of Chino Mararike said Zimbabwe is the epicentre of liberation politics.

v.   We must highlight that the Zimbabwe African People's Union (ZAPU) was integrated to form the Zimbabwe African National Union, Patriotic Front (ZANU PF). Both organisations advanced the cause of nationalist and pan African principles to liberate Zimbabwe from the colonial yoke. Their core values of building a vanguard and revolutionary party were based on militancy and Marxist-Leninist of Mao thought. Freedom fighters used effectively tactics of infiltration, politicising the masses, hit and run ambush operations, extreme violence, the 'barrel of the gun' slogans, to purge counter revolutionaries, sell outs and to exterminate enemies of its struggle. The foregoing context was used to liquidate colonialism and capitalism in colonial Rhodesia. The period in which Zimbabwe's liberation struggle parties were formed in the 1960s was the height of cold war years. This means that continued regeneration of liberation party politics in addressing the land question and post neo-colonial struggles will never sit comfortably with international capital as is the case right now. The idea to neutralise-and-destroy liberation struggle parties is the reason for the existence of Tsvangirayi's the Movement for Democratic Change in Zimbabwe (1999); introduction by the West of multi-party system in Kenya (1992), Zambia's Movement for Multi-Party Democracy Chiluba 1990), Chafukwa Chihana's Alliance for Democracy in Malawi (1992); Tanzania's Party for Democracy and Progress *(Chama cha Demokrasia na Maendeleo)* The fore-mentioned parties are part of the proxy wars designed to preserve capitalism by reinforcing a new imperialist chapter in former colonies.

vi.   ZANU PF political party remains a robust system, a pan African ideology that herald freedom and emancipation of the African people. It is guided by the affirmative goal of empowerment, restitution and restoration of the African legacy. The fear is in the contagion effect of ZANU PF ideology of empowerment – whose impact is already felt in South Africa where the battle for land reform has now been set in motion. This is why the economic sanctions project is designed to obliterate the liberation discourse by fronting 'born frees' (those born after 1980) of Zimbabwe who are not linked to or conscious of liberation struggle politics. The American idea is to depoliticise and de-role Zimbabwean youths out of core nationalist values that guided founding their fathers to emancipation and independence. Creation of a new crop of political leaders in Zimbabwe is well under way – through perceptions and practices of instilling new cultures – of human rights, democracy and liberalism. You instil changes through influence and sponsorship of new socio-political projects that are different from the norm or the standard. That is how change is used as an agent to catch them young while they are still in their naïve stages of their growth. This is what the American agenda in Zimbabwe is all about. It is a new ideology. Political Sociologists are aware that ideology engenders a set of aims and ideas that directs goals and expectations. An ideology can also be conceptualised as a comprehensive vision with alternative ways of looking at things in terms of making comparisons of world views. Political scientists see ideology as sets of ideas proposed and imposed by dominant classes of a society to often weaker members of society. Could it be that the United States is targeting those who lack consciousness? What is the USA trying to change by targeting those whom they want to depoliticise and de link from liberation politics? But, academics are equally aware that the main purpose behind every ideology is to influence change in society, seek to influence adherence and conformity to the norms and values of those who are powerful. Influencing the thought process is in part what the USA seeks to do in Zimbabwe – especially in regard to youth consciousness. The USA wants to influence abstract thinking process of our youths so that they think like them, think like foreigners – and transform them to be their ideological messengers. That agenda is a trap because it is deceptive and reckless. It is as cruel as mind-mapping economic sanctions that hurt the poor the most. That is how change is brought. Zimbabwean politics has also identified that its people – particularly the youths, have been infiltrated by western imperialism. The question of the rule of law for example is often mostly advanced by those with assets both movable and immovable assets. When ZANU PF used seizing land as a weapon to advance post-independence black or rather African empowerment, whites who owned the means of production and most assets, riches and wealth started to be jittery and sought "protection" from the law. But ironically as perpetrators, whites had used the law during the colonial days to disempower and alienate Africans, discriminating them into barren and infertile tribal trust lands. By accusing imperialists of having 'stolen' the land from Africans in the first place, ZANU PF used the language which Caucasians do not want to hear of. Alarmed by the reality of an African renaissance and new awakening, the West started to selectively use inflationary and emotive language by accusing former freedom fighters of the armed struggle (War Vets) as 'violent ruthless thugs' who 'grabbed' land from white 'Zimbabwean' farmers. Now tell me: Who had stolen land from 'native' and 'kefirs' in the first place under the guise of the Pioneer Column on 22 September 1890? This is why, in the eyes of Europeans ZANU PF 'must go and must go now' because they are a threat to national and international security'! What is 'security'? Security is property rights. Security is land tenure, land rights and deed of transfer documents. Title deeds are a form of security that define property rights. What happens when government intervenes to restore land ownership through restitution and compensation especially from those who lay claims on immovable assets? Who owns most of that property in those former colonies? It is the Caucasians whose cousins are in Britain, Canada, Australia or New Zealand. That is where the crux of the matter is. Those cousins are shareholders in companies and multinational corporations including Rio Tinto, Anglo American Corporation, British-American Tobacco, Union Carbide, Barclays Bank, Boarder Timbers, Stanbic Bank, Bindura Nickle Corporation, Exide Batteries, Lever Brothers, Shell & BP, Coca Cola, Procter & Gamble, Colgate, Nestle Corporation – to mention but a few. You don't expect the Rhodesians to take such changes lying low. Zimbabwe is a war zone in which its reconnaissance is in different forms of trenches. Those with less tangible weaponry and mental software will win - but those whose soul and brains are part of stiff resistance to artificial intelligence; superficial and exploitative changes will also win.

Why is the US adamant in its support of opposition MDC? (i) It is their project created to frustrate land reform and empowerment; (ii). MDC supports market reforms that favour capitalism whereas ZANU PF advocates for market reforms designed to empower its people. Check on Zim-Asset versus MDC economic blueprint - The MDC's economic proposals are encapsulated in the "JUICE plan" – an acronym for "jobs, upliftment, investment capital and the environment; (iii). By redistributing land without compensation, a tit for tat that corrects preceding colonial and historical antecedents and banalities, ZANU PF deals a hard blow to imperialism, (iv). If MDC calls for restoration of property rights - it is a call to preserve capitalism. This is so because the heart of capitalism world over is property rights and profit accretion through creation of equity.

We all know that land is equity. ZDERA is therefore a formulation of a bible of capitalism in Zimbabwe which - of course, is being managed by and implemented for the benefit of MDC at the behest of their Western cohorts. We also all know that capitalist market reforms engender creation of stagnation and underdevelopment by perpetuating exploitation. Che Guevara was succinct:

> These characteristics are not fortuitous; they correspond strictly to the nature of the capitalist system in full expansion, which transfers to the dependent countries the most abusive and barefaced forms of exploitation. It must be clearly understood that the only way to solve the questions now besetting mankind is to eliminate completely the exploitation of dependent countries by developed capitalist countries, with all the consequences that this implies. [77]

In Chapter (vi) titled *The African Constitution Birth of Democracy,* Williams (1987) in his book *The Destruction of Black Civilization,* contends that what matters the most is the concept and application of African democracy as part of African judiciary system. Such a system is determined by evolution of their history derived from customary rules of their life. It is also shaped by humanly-constructed depravation and abomination in terms of dispossessions and disempowerment, colonial practices of theft by conversion and eighteen century imperialisms. It can never be 'primitive democracy' but part of systems and structures of their governance. Zimbabwe's constitution of 1979 is born out of coloniality and imperialism while the 2013 constitution is the ultimate process of addressing the evils of neo-colonialism – and that argument has always been crystal clear. *"Tonho"! sa President Mugabe na Madhuku*[78]*!*

Reasons why the West is wary about Zimbabwe

The information below is based on individual 2013/14 Financial Statements of selected companies that are listed on the Zimbabwean Stock Exchange (ZSE). These are Top 25 Zimbabwean Companies ranked by the value of their assets. Most of the companies have a

---

[77] Che Guevara, 1964. Found at http://abahlali.org/files/3295358-walter-rodney.pdf/Accessed 06 Apr 18

[78] See The Survival Strategy: Mugabe's 83 Birthday Interview on You Tube, at https://www.youtube.com/watch?v=5Mq0cVE7AmU/Accessed 22 Mar 18

foreign ownership status – particularly owned and controlled by foreign businessmen in different parts of the world. Some of the companies have subsidiary companies in Zimbabwe. In compiling this important data, we consider TOTAL ASSETS of these companies as their value: viz - the total values of EVERYTHING they own from Land & Buildings to inventory, Machinery etc.). In technical terms we focus and rank them on the basis of the value of their ASSETS and their Balance Sheets. In reality what is paramount is their net worth in form of their TOTAL VALUE in US dollars; and in terms of what the company owns - their DEBTS ranked for individual companies as based on the value of their ASSETS, notwithstanding their liabilities (DEBT). Value of companies are in United States Dollars[79].

1. OLD Mutual (ZW) $1.98 Billion (includes CABS)
2. CBZ Holdings $1,7 Billion
3. ZimPlats $1.4 Billion
4. Econet – $1,2 Billion
5. CABS – $852 million – 100% owned by OLD Mutual Zimbabwe
6. Delta Beverages $620 million
7. INNSCOR – $548 million (Includes National Foods)
8. Stanbic Bank (ZW)- $561 million
9. FBC Holdings – $477 Million
10. Standard Chartered Bank (ZW) - $407 million
11. ZB Financial Holdings – $383 million
12. Hippo Valley Estates – $363 million
13. Meikles – $354 million
14. Barclays Bank (ZW) – $293 million
15. AICO – $289 million
16. NMBZ – $260 million
17. Hwange Coal – $248 million
18. Masawara – $230 million
19. First Mutual Holdings – $213 million
20. Mwana Africa – $208 million
21. MBCA – $189 million

---

[79] This information is based on data obtained from Prale. Found at https://www.prale.net/top-25-companies-in-zimbabwe/Accessed12Agust18

22. SeedCo – $161 million
23. Zimre Property Holdings – $153.9 million
24. CFI Holdings – $133 million
25. National Foods (as part of INNSCOR) – $120 million

Any form of threat to their security triggers western governments to react like a rattle snake sensing danger. For the jittery Western governments, Robert Mugabe represented a danger and ZANU PF is a threat to their security! [80]

Zimbabwe's Cobweb of "Economic Growth": Post-ZDERA era

According to Jecheche (2007) efficiency measurement of the stock market is very important to investors, policy makers and other major players, who ensure long-term real capital in an economy. Maturity of the stock market efficiency level is perceived across the

---

[80] The zimbabwe government has compiled a list of 400 western companies and is mapping out strategies to ensure that the corporations adhere to the indigenisation regulations as their parent countries imposed illegal sanctions on Zimbabwe.

Youth Development, Indigenisation and Empowerment Minister, Saviour Kasukuwere said they have already compiled a full list of the companies with a clear roadmap being implemented to fulfil the indigenisation programme. He was responding to calls by President Mugabe, who stated [that these companies from the former coloniser and imperial America as well as other western nations should be the prime target for the indigenisation programme].

Kasukuwere cited an example of foreign banks such as Barclays, Standard Chartered that he claims are not willing to support farmers as they are opposed to the land reform programme. He also said that the corporates will not be allowed to loot the country's resources.

"We cannot have a situation whereby their countries imposed sanctions on us and they still operate freely, they should also be put under sanctions," Kasukuwere added.

In his address to ZANU PF supporters at the National Anti-Sanctions Petition Campaign Launch last Wednesday, Mugabe said time has come for Zimbabwe to take drastic action against companies whose governments are needlessly punishing the people of Zimbabwe with sanctions.

Please note: I acknowledge that this end note has been taken from an on-line article entitled "Zimbabwe compiles a list of 400 Foreign companies, targeted by Mugabe", Found at https://bulawayo24.com/index-id-news-sc-national-byo-1855-article-
zimbabwe+compiles+a+list+of+400+foreign+companies,+targeted+by+mugab
e.html/Accessed12August2018.

globe as a barometer of the economic health and prospect of a country as well as a register of the confidence of domestic and global investors. Singh (1997) highlights that, in principle, the stock market is expected to accelerate economic growth by providing a boost to domestic savings and increase the quantity and quality of investment. Stock markets also provide an avenue for growing companies to raise capital at lower cost. In addition, companies in countries with developed stock markets are less dependent on bank financing, which can reduce the risk of a credit crunch. Stock markets therefore are able to positively influence economic growth through encouraging savings amongst individuals and providing avenues for firm financing.

In reviewing developments in Zimbabwe Stock Exchange, Jecheche (ibid) traces the history of stocks and shares in Zimbabwe back to 1891 when the first stock-broking firm was opened in colonial Rhodesia by settlers. The first Stock Exchanges were set up a few years later in 1894 in Salisbury (now Harare) and Bulawayo. Later, two other exchanges emerged in Gwelo (now Gweru) and Umtali (now Mutare) around 1898. These exchanges were intended to meet the capital needs of the gold mining industry:

> The Zimbabwe Stock Exchange Act reached the statute book in January 1974. The members of the Exchange continued to trade as before, but it became necessary for legal reasons to bring into being a new Exchange coincidental with the passing of the legislation... During the late 1970s, the hope of independence and the end of sanctions led to a brief rise in share prices. By 1980, the RSE was a highly specialized market, which was likely to prove useful in the economy if a capitalist-oriented development strategy was adopted. On achieving independence from Britain in 1980, the exchange changed its name from the Rhodesia to the Zimbabwe Stock Exchange.

In the 1990s the Zimbabwe Stock Exchange (ZSE) was the second largest in sub-Saharan Africa after the Johannesburg Stock Exchange. The fastest growth of the ZSE occurred between 1994 and 1996, with capitalization rising at an average annual rate of 36% in US dollar terms. During 1998, Zimbabwe's stock market, once regarded as one of the most promising emerging markets in the region, saw a decline in turnover to 60% of the previous year's volumes and 88% of its value of shares sold. 1998's fall was attributed to high interest rates which attracted investors to the higher yielding money market and to a loss of confidence caused by a number of factors such as social unrest (including food protests and mass stay-a ways) and the government's stated intention to acquire commercial farms for resettlement (p. 6)

With the decline of the Zimbabwean economy, due to mainly the imposition of economic sanctions, hyperinflation rendered the Zimbabwean dollar useless and the US-Dollar was adopted as the legal tender for trading on the exchange in February 2009. Foreign companies that transacted business with local Zimbabwean companies severed links as penalties were incorporated into the Zimbabwe Democracy Economic Recovery Act in 2001. Because of threats for penalties became trade has been very thin, with very few foreign investors willing to risk trading on the market. The fact that at the inception of economic sanctions, some of the stocks were no longer trading at all underlines economic damages incurred under ZDERA.

Finally, economic recovery and growth in the post ZDERA era will - of necessity - consider both public and private investment as complimentary strategies. The incoming Mnangagwa government is emphasizing on opening the country for business by underscoring the role of government to improve the efficiency of financial sector of the economy. The government is pre-occupied with its direct role in enhancing human and physical capital in boosting economic growth.

Zimbabwe Stock Exchange (ZSE) - Listed Companies[81]

Company	Symbol	Sector	Price	Change	YTD	Date
African Distillers	AFDS	Consumer Goods	1.45	0.00%	-2.03%	10-Aug 18
African Sun	ASUN	Consumer Services	0.073	1.39%	52.08%	10-Aug 18
Ariston Holdings	ARIS	Consumer Goods	0.016	0.00%	-5.88%	10-Aug 18
ART Corporation	ARTD	Industrials	0.06	0.00%	-14.04%	10-Aug 18
Astra Industries		Basic Materials	0.043	0.00%	0.00%	03-May 18
Axia Corporation	AXIA	Industrials	0.25	0.00%	38.89%	10-Aug 18
Barclays Bank of Zimbabwe	BARC	Financials	0.0691	14.78%	15.17%	10-Aug 18
Bindura Nickel Corporation	BIND	Basic Materials	0.056	0.00%	1.45%	10-Aug 18
Border Timbers	BRDR	Basic Materials	0.2	0.00%	0.00%	10-Aug 18
BAT Zimbabwe	BATZW	Consumer Goods	25.65	0.00%	-28.15%	10-Aug 18
Cafca	CAFCA	Industrials	0.75	0.00%	150.00%	10-Aug 18
CBZ Holdings	CBZ	Financials	0.11	0.00%	-26.67%	10-Aug 18
CFI Holdings	CFI	Industrials	0.7075	0.00%	0.00%	17-Jul 18
COTTCO Holdings	COTT	Consumer Goods	0.002	0.00%	0.00%	04-Aug 18

---

[81] Zimbabwe Stock Exchange Listed Companies. Found at https://www.african-markets.com/en/stock-markets/zse/listed-companies/Accessed12August18. List produced as of 10 August 2018, courtesy of Zimbabwe Stock Exchange (ZSC)

Company	Symbol	Sector	Price	Change	YTD	Date
Dairibord Holdings	DZL	Consumer Goods	0.13	0.00%	-2.99%	10-Aug 18
Dawn Properties	DAWN	Consumer Services	0.016	0.00%	-20.00%	10-Aug 18
Delta Corporation	DLTA	Consumer Goods	1.9995	-0.02%	24.97%	10-Aug 18
Econet Wireless Zimbabwe	ECO	Telecommunications	1.2001	0.01%	30.22%	10-Aug 18
Edgars Stores	EDGR	Consumer Services	0.0662	0.00%	64.68%	10-Aug 18
Falcon Gold Zimbabwe	FALG	Basic Materials	0.025	0.00%	-86.49%	10-Aug 18
FBC Holdings	FBC	Financials	0.22	0.00%	10.00%	10-Aug 18
Fidelity Life Assurance	FIDL	Financials	0.102	0.00%	-7.27%	10-Aug 18
First Mutual Holdings	FMHL	Financials	0.17	0.00%	-12.82%	10-Aug 18
First Mutual Properties	FMP	Financials	0.06	0.00%	-1.64%	10-Aug 18
General Beltings Holdings	GBH	Industrials	0.008	0.00%	0.00%	10-Aug 18
GetBucks Microfinance Bank	GBZW	Financials	0.03	-9.91%	-18.92%	10-Aug 18
Hippo Valley Estates	HIPO	Consumer Goods	1.6875	-0.15%	-4.12%	10-Aug 18
Hwange Colliery Company	HCCL	Oil & Gas	0.038	0.00%	0.00%	10-Aug 18
Innscor Africa	INN	Industrials	1.4144	0.09%	41.44%	10-Aug 18
Lafarge Cement Zimbabwe	LACZ	Industrials	1.3	0.00%	-5.78%	10-Aug 18

Company	Symbol	Sector	Price	Change	YTD	Date
Mashonaland Holdings	MASHZW	Financials	0.0225	0.00%	-43.32%	10-Aug 18
Masimba Holdings	MSHL	Industrials	0.0398	0.00%	-44.72%	10-Aug 18
Medtech Holdings	MMDZ	Health Care	0.0001	0.00%	-80.00%	10-Aug 18
Meikles	MEIK	Consumer Services	0.35	0.00%	19.86%	10-Aug 18
Nampak Zimbabwe	NPKZ	Industrials	0.175	0.00%	-2.78%	10-Aug 18
National Foods Holdings	NTFD	Consumer Goods	5.6064	-0.05%	-13.75%	10-Aug 18
National Tyre Services	NTS	Consumer Goods	0.011	0.00%	-4.35%	10-Aug 18
Nicoz Diamond Insurance	NICOZ	Financials	0.0341	13.67%	-14.11%	10-Aug 18
NMBZ Holdings	NMBZ	Financials	0.12	0.00%	33.33%	10-Aug 18
OK Zimbabwe	OKZ	Consumer Services	0.2349	0.00%	17.45%	10-Aug 18
Old Mutual	OMU	Financials	5.1027	0.27%	-7.57%	10-Aug 18
Padenga Holdings	PHL	Consumer Goods	0.6025	0.42%	10.13%	10-Aug 18
PG Industries (Zimbabwe)	PGIN	Industrials	0.001	0.00%	0.00%	17-Jul 18
Powerspeed Electrical	PWS	Industrials	0.08	0.00%	6.67%	10-Aug 18
Pretoria Portland Cement	PPC.zw	Industrials	1.15	-3.97%	10.58%	10-Aug 18
Proplastics	PROL	Industrials	0.098	0.00%	28.95%	10-Aug 18

283

Company	Symbol	Sector	Price	Change	YTD	Date
Rainbow Tourism Group	RTG	Consumer Services	0.011	0.00%	10.00%	10-Aug 18
RioZim	RIOZ	Basic Materials	1.4	-4.57%	16.67%	10-Aug 18
Seed Co	SEED	Consumer Goods	2.5775	-0.10%	28.88%	10-Aug 18
Simbisa Brands	SIM	Consumer Services	0.4795	-0.10%	2.02%	10-Aug 18
Starafricacorporation	SACL	Consumer Goods	0.0128	0.00%	-36.00%	10-Aug 18
Truworths	TRUW	Consumer Services	0.014	0.00%	8.53%	10-Aug 18
TSL	TSL	Industrials	0.43	0.00%	16.69%	10-Aug 18
Turnall Holdings	TURN	Industrials	0.0135	0.00%	42.11%	10-Aug 18
Unifreight Africa	UNIF	Consumer Services	0.0252	0.00%	77.46%	10-Aug 18
Willdale	WILD	Industrials	0.006	0.00%	-17.81%	10-Aug 18
ZB Financial Holdings	ZBFH	Financials	0.3325	0.00%	-7.64%	10-Aug 18
Zeco Holdings	ZECO	Industrials	0.0002	0.00%	0.00%	10-Aug 18
Zimbabwe Newspapers (1980)	ZIMP	Consumer Services	0.013	0.00%	18.18%	10-Aug 18
Zimplow Holdings	ZIMW	Industrials	0.12	0.00%	53.45%	10-Aug 18
Zimre Holdings	ZIMR	Financials	0.02	0.00%	-22.78%	10-Aug 18
Zimre Property Investments	ZPI	Financials	0.017	0.00%	-29.17%	10-Aug 18

After ZDERA, the second stage of Zimbabwe penetration implicates several strategies designed to breach long term development. This entails Zimbabwe's controlled "Web of Economic Growth" in which Zimbabwean loans and borrowing powers from the World Bank and the IMF will be restored. There will be foreign aid in form of financial aid that Zimbabwe will be offered at punitive interest rates. After emerging from a total of 32 years of both colonial and post-independence sanctions, Zimbabwe is likely to be offered a costly financial aid and investment package that attracts punitive interest rates intended to shackle the country to huge debt. What Zimbabwe will earn from its rich mineral ores in form of profit will be cultivated back to the international capitalist organisations for repayments of financial aid.

Zimbabwe will record a health Balance of Payment based on the flow of money, loans and services that I prefer to call "toxic packages" designed to wipe out any form of surplus benefits destined for the poor. We already know that, as a strategy for sanctions bursting, some of the dirty deals during the post land reform sanctions era were funded through offshore capital into Zimbabwe. Zimbabwe is likely to be a destination of doggy financial aid -dangled to a state that has been isolated in the economic wilderness – a state that is prepared to declare that "We are open to business" at any cost. Zimbabwean politicians must remain guarded of sweeteners and inducements likely to perpetuate poverty and suffering of its citizens. We do not rule out IMF sponsored structural adjustment programmes re visiting the Southern African state as a harbinger of its complete demise.

John Perkins in his book titled *Confessions of an Economic Hit Man,* notes that:

> ...Some would blame our current problems on an organized conspiracy. I wish it were so simple. Members of a conspiracy can be rooted out and brought to justice. This system, however, is fuelled by something far more dangerous than a conspiracy. It is driven not by a small band of men but by a concept that has become accepted as gospel: the idea that all economic growth benefits humankind and that the greater the growth, the more widespread the benefits. This belief

285

also has a corollary: that those people who excel at stoking the fires of economic growth should be exalted and rewarded, while those born at the fringes are available for exploitation...

What matters here for Zimbabwe and developing countries is the fact that exploitation of the poor here to stay as a concept. A concept is defined as a fundamental category of existence. (Latin *conceptum* – "something conceived": a classical theory developed by Aristotle). The Cambridge English Dictionary notes that in contemporary philosophy, there are at least three prevailing ways to understand what a concept is: Concepts as mental representations, where concepts are entities that exist in the mind (mental objects); propositional attitudes and understanding of thoughts. Concepts do have characteristics – for example, the concept of imperialism and neo-colonialism can be perpetuated from generation to generation. In the case of Zimbabwe, Senator Byrd's proposal of sanctions imposition and management in the 60's is the same concept that was passed to George W Bush. What this means is that any fallacious concept is a conceptual weapon that is used to distort certain perceptions on new generations. The Western media and the pen remain supreme at conceptual distortions.

The question of aid that comes as a windfall to Harare in the post Mugabe / ZDERA era is propagated differently by aid activists. Moyo's (2010) narrative is that "aid has been, and continues to be, an unmitigated political, economic, and humanitarian disaster." The author rebuffs "orchestrated worldwide pity," because it leads to poverty, underdevelopment and dependency syndrome – all which do not empower communities in the end. Thus, in aid and dependency narratives, to increase aid to fight poverty may not necessarily imply so because it is a perpetuation of unequal ties though neo-colonialism, patronage and economic domination.

It is easy to control a dominated and weak populace, but it is another thing to create conditions that empower them eternally. Mugabe argued for empowerment through land distribution to landless peasants while the West insisted on giving dangerous genetically modified food imports to the poor. For example, one of the basis upon which the west continued to demonise ZANU PF

286

party in the post land reform era on 2000 was that it expelled aid agencies that were linked to opposition politics and food distribution. On the other one hand, the party welcomed aid agencies that were involved in empowering small scale and peasant farmers through the distribution of agricultural inputs.

The Circumlocution offices website notes that in Charles Dickens's *Bleak House,* in which Dickens highlighted the term Telescopic Philanthropy, he uses it as the chapter title[82]. Mrs Jellby is one of the protagonists who is obsessed with bettering an obscure African tribe but having little regard and hypocrisy to her duties as wife and mother; or the notion of charity beginning at home. She spiritually abandons her family to work on a philanthropic project to help people far away who she has never seen, namely The Borrioboola-Gha venture in deepest and 'darkest' Africa. Mrs Jellyby and Mrs Pardiggle in Bleak House are, respectively, guilty of 'telescopic philanthropy' and 'rapacious benevolence', neither of them helping to save the life of the child Jo, who dies of pneumonia. These poignant and colourful examples fly in the face of reality as to this day, especially in a first world country where beggars die on the streets in London's Kilburn High Street and Mayfair.

In a book entitled *A Game as Old as the Empire: The Secret World of Economic Hitman and the Web of Global Corruption,* Hiat (2007), the introduction to this book is punctuated by new confessions and revelations from the world of economic hitmen:

Economic Hit Men (EHMs) are highly paid professionals who cheat countries around the globe of trillions of dollars. They funnel money from World Bank and US Agency for International Development (USAID) and other "aid" agencies into the coffers of huge corporations and the pockets of few wealthy families who control the planet's natural resources. Their tools include fraudulent financial reports, rigged elections, pay-offs, extortion, sex and murder. They play the game as old as the Empire but one that has taken on new and

---

[82] The Circumlocution Office. Found at
http://thecircumlocutionoffice.com/bleakhouse/charles-dickens-telescopic-philanthropy/Accessed May 05 18

terrifying dimensions during this time of globalization. For millions of people globalisation has not worked (p. ix)

While they operate in the shadows of the illuminati and freemasons, they have even sponsored coups and other transgressions. They are involved in money laundering like the Iran Mossadegh atrocities, in South American states including Panama and Venezuela. Like the dirty trails of UK-based Cambridge Analytica in Nigeria and Kenya they have influenced elections through sponsored rigging. In the same book, the introduction by John Perkins highlights that:

> Several pundits criticize what some refer to as ... *radical accusation that economic forecasts* [that] are manipulated and distorted in order to achieve political objectives (as opposed to economic objectivity) [This is based on a notation that] foreign Aid is a tool for big businesses rather than an altruistic means to alleviate poverty (xi)

The narrative continues as Joseph Stieglitz in his book *Globalisations and its Discontents* sums up the strategy of EHMs. Zimbabweans may want to take note that Stieglitz is a former Clinton Economic Advisor and World Bank chief economist who was ironically, highly regarded by Bernard Chidzero – Zimbabwe's first Minister of Finance, Economic Planning and Development. A lot of Zimbabwean economic writers quote him extraneously:

> ...to make its [IMF's] programmes seem to work, to make numbers "add up", economic forecasts have to be adjusted. Many users of these numbers do not realise that they are not like ordinary forecasts; in these incidences GDP forecasts are not based on sophisticated statistical models or even best estimates of those who know the economy well, but are merely the numbers that have been negotiated as part of an IMF programme... globalization, as it has been advocated, often seems to replace old dictatorship of national elites and new dictatorships of international finance... (p.18)

The reason why the above instalment is important for Zimbabwe at this stage is that the country, run down by years of economic decline due to several factors including economic sanctions, is desperate to attract financial investment and aid under the banner "Zimbabwe is open for Business". Zimbabwe must sift through what comes through those doors to get rid of international economic miscreants. Bureaucrats and politicians must be sensitively aware of the existence of toxic aid packages designed to mortgage the country to international capital. It is also worthwhile noting that there are organisations that are prepared to act as EHMs without an iota of conscience or consideration - of the plight of the ordinary and majority of the Zimbabwean populace. We are aware that international private and dirty capital have attempted to sponsor rogue candidates for regime change agenda in African countries[83].

---

[83] See Shaxson, N (2008) Poisoned Wells: The Dirty Politics of African Oil, Palgrave Macmillan, USA – This is a book in which top British Conservative politicians like Jeffrey Archer and former British Prime Minister's son, Mark Thatcher are alleged to have been involved in a sophisticated conspiracy to topple Equatorial Guinea's leader Teodoro Nguema Obiang. The conspiracy was intercepted by President Robert Mugabe's regime – which tried and jailed the British hit man Simon Mann in Zimbabwe for trying to overthrow Equatorial Guinea's Prime Minister. Moco Placido (Severo Moto Nsa) the sponsored opposition presidential candidate was being backed by the Spanish government, UK, US and South African rogue military elements (led by Nick du Toit) of the apartheid era in what appeared to be a well-orchestrated regime change design dubbed the "Wonga Coup". Simon Mann was convicted in Harare on August 27, 2004 for trying to purchase from Zimbabwe military equipment worth $80 000.00 to use in the botched coup detat. For further reading, see Well Oiled: Oil and Human Rights in Equatorial Guinea
By Alex Vines, Human Rights Watch 2009
See Also Ex Rhodesian confesses terrorist raids into Zimbabwe from South Africa: Found at: https://bulawayo24.com/index-id-news-sc-national-byo-55655.html/Accesse4June18 In 1988 three South African Intelligence spies Kevin Woods, Michael Smith and Philip Conjwayo were arrested in Zimbabwe in connection with a bombing that killed the driver of the car transporting the bomb and injured several ANC members in Bulawayo. The three-code identified in South African intelligence as The Harare Three were kept in Chikurubi Maximum Prison from the time they were sentenced in November 1988 which suggests that MayHill's task may have been to try and free the three from the prison. Woods, Smith and Conjwayo were sentenced to death and their sentence was later commuted to life imprisonment by the Supreme Court. All three prisoners were former members of the Rhodesian intelligence and security forces. The three were recruited by the South African intelligence service after 1980 to carry out destabilisation activities in Zimbabwe. The trio was released from

We also bear in mind that there are organisations ready to sell financial aid packages for purposes of ensuring dependency and underdevelopment of Zimbabwe in what the book refers to as a 'debt trap' of nations. *Dirty Money: Inside the Secret World of Offshore Banking* is one such Chapter that chronicles history and documents the flow of capital from poor countries in Africa. That capital sadly enriches capitalists and their cabal in Europe. Tax invasion, bribes and kickbacks, capital flight and money laundering are attributes and symptoms of the death of many third world countries. The Human Cost of Cheap phones and other gadgets like laptops – DRC has suffered because of coltan and rutile, very precious minerals (found in large quantities and looted from DRC) – used to make semi-conductors in cell phones. In short, Zimbabwe must be warned in the new dispensation – of political debauchery perpetuated in the name of market reforms, aid packages and rescue packages.

The other chapters from this book place white mercenaries on the frontlines in the new scramble for Africa. Zimbabwe has good reasons – not just to be worried, but to safeguard its resources. By formulating hard bargains and trade negotiations in the post Mugabe era Zimbabwe is guaranteed to enter a phase of economic and political maturity designed to conquer imperialism. We want to establish why the western powers are keen on starting on a clean slate with "a new generation" in Zimbabwe – whose levels of consciousness on colonial matters has been deluged and compromised by fake globalisation mantra which means very little to villagers in Chiredzi and Chikomba Districts.

Zimbabwe needs to monitor robustly the insurgency of economic western sponsored Economic Hit Men [EHM] by educating the nation's younger economists on how to circumnavigate destruction and mirage of debt relief. A global system of exploitation can only be fought by communities and leaders who are aware of what global justice is all about, in an agenda that provides direction and empowerment to break the empire's web of imperialism and control.

---

prison on President Mugabe's mercy pardon in July 2006 after spending close to two decades at Chikurubi Prison.

Conclusion – Post-Election Positions taken by the USA, UK and the EU

The first post-Mugabe era elections were held in Zimbabwe on 30 July 2018 and were generally hailed to be peaceful despite the loss of lives in their aftermath. We will not discuss the causes of violence, counter-arguments and allegations in this conclusion. What is worth noting is that just before the said elections, the EU-appointed election delegation monitoring the elections noted that MDC opposition leader Nelson Chamisa made excessive and strenuous demands for a level playing political field. MDC maintained that if they lost the elections, then Zimbabwean Election Council (ZEC) would have rigged the elections in favour of ZANU PF[84]. What is important is not the merits of political parties' arguments or court appeal processes, but the reaction of key allies who have issues with Zimbabwe.

The EU issued a statement[85]:

The Heads of Mission condemn the *violence, attacks, and acts of intimidation targeted at opposition leaders and supporters.* These human rights violations have no place in a democratic society and contravene the fundamental tenets of international human rights standards … The Heads of Mission urge the government to respect the rights of the Zimbabwean people as enshrined in the Constitution. All allegations of incitement to violence or violent acts, as well as vandalism and destruction of property, should be investigated in accordance with the rule of law, and perpetrators held legally responsible…

---

[84] Zimbabwe elections: Opposition candidate Chamisa will not accept a 'fraudulent' victory by Mnangagwa as he warns of mass protests
'If they find that their vote has been ignored ... we do not control the people, they will do what they think is right,' Nelson Chamisa says, Found at The Independent, https://www.independent.co.uk/news/world/africa/zimbabwe-election-latest-mnangagwa-chamisa-zanu-pf-mdc-protests-violence-win-a8475276.html/Accessed18Aug18/

[85] European Union Delegation to the Republic of Zimbabwe, Joint Local Statement on Post-Elections Human Rights situation in Zimbabwe, Harare, 07/08/2018 - 11:07, UNIQUE ID: 180807_6, Found at https://eeas.europa.eu/delegations/zimbabwe/49178/joint-local-statement-post-elections-human-rights-situation-zimbabwe_en/Accessed18Aug18,/

The nature and tone of the statement is accusatory and biased in its effort to portray opposition leaders and supporters as victims of state perpetrated violence. There is no mention of opposition supporters and leaders inciting violence, encouraging anarchy through wanton destruction, looting and burning down of property, vehicles and orchestrating violence directed against the establishment especially the Zimbabwe Election Council. What would have been wrong -especially at a time when tensions were high – for the EU to call for restraint on both sides of the divide? The mission statement implores and apportions blame before any investigation has even been conducted to establish what transpired on the ground. We read a lot of signals into US's Donald Trump's renewal of ZDERA[86] after the said Zimbabwean elections of 30 July 2018 [87].

Post-election Zimbabwe remains divided with patriots and apologists expressing different interests regarding illegal imposition of sanctions. Regime changer pushers and sympathisers think that ZDERA is justified, while right wing revolutionaries believe in market reforms based on investment drive. The USA and its allies stand accused of deeply dividing Zimbabwean society for purposes of advancing new forms of imperialism, entrenched interests designed to meet former colonialists' selfish and exploitative business objectives. This is defined as a new struggle in the collapse of capitalism and financial markets triggered by the corrupt Enron scandals of the 1990's.

Elsewhere, we have talked of ZDERA seeking to plant clauses and caveats into the Zimbabwean Constitution. We have talked about ZDERA as a new form of imperialism designed to interfere with governance and democratic practices of Zimbabwe. We study imperialism that is designed to thrive under the patina of market reforms, skewed investment drive and multilateral relations with capitalism. We call for fairness and not David and Goliath relations of co-existence. We have talked about ZDERA as part of the grand

---

[86] Office of Foreign Assets Control (OFAC), Zimbabwe Sanctions Programme, Found at https://www.treasury.gov/resource-center/sanctions/Programs/Documents/zimb.pdf/Accessed18Aug18
[87] The Herald, Zimbabwe: Govt Slams 'Illegal' U.S. Sanction Renewal, Found at https://allafrica.com/stories/201808150525.html/Accessed18Aug18/

machinations of neo-colonialism and the subject of coloniality, displacement and exploitation. We talked about the subject of western-induced radicalization of political systems through various ways in Southern Africa as a strategy for decimating the liberation struggle parties. We talked of fear of the struggle for land restitution and reclamation as South Africa drafts its land reform programme. In a panic mode and reactions by African South Africans for total independence, Britain has threated South Africa of severe sanctions if they address land imbalances. What Britain is calling for is that Africans in that country should not be given land, (land must remain in Caucasian hands as Africans do not need this); The African National Congress (ANC) and Economic Freedom Party (EFP) agree that empowerment is what the Africans need not aid and donations. The agenda cannot be clearer as Zimbabwe continues to operate as a cradle of Pan-Africanism in the region. The last word is *"Aluta Continua"*!

References

Collier, EC (2011) *Bipartisanship & the Making of Foreign Policy: A Historical Survey*, Xlibris Corporation Printers, United States of America. Found at: https://books.google.co.uk/books?id=1BC6FroJAnsC&pg=PA163&redir_esc=y#v=onepage&q&f=false/Accessed May 5, 18

Hiat, S (2007) *A Game as Old as the Empire: The Secret World of Economic Hitman and the Web of Global Corruption,* Berret Cochler Publishers, California, USA

Jecheche, P. (2012) 'The effect of the stock exchange on economic growth: a case of the Zimbabwe stock exchange'. Research in Business and Economics Journal, Florida, USA

Jones, BC (1996) *Flawed Triumphs: Andy Young at the United Nations,* University Press of America, London England. Found at: https://books.google.co.uk/books?id=N7X1BXC-HSQC&pg=PA60&redir_esc=y#v=onepage&q&f=false/Accessed May 5,18

Moyo, D (2009) *Dead Aid: Why aid is not working and how there is another way for Africa* Paperback, Found at https://books.google.co.uk/books/about/Dead_Aid.html?id= Q0cCOAAACAAJ&redir_esc=y&hl=enAccessed May 09 18

Perkins, J (2006) *The New Confessions of an Economic Hit Man,* EDS Publications, Paperback, USA - Found at http://library.uniteddiversity.coop/Money_and_Economics/co nfessions_of_an_economic_hitman.pdfAccessed09May18

Singh, A. (2012) Financial liberalisation, Stock markets and Economic Developments, The Economic Journal Volume 107 Issue 442, Willey Online Library, https://doi.org/10.1111/j.1468-0297.1997.tb00042.x

Stieglitz, J (2002) *Globalisations and its Discontents,* Penguin Books, USA. Found at: https://www.amazon.co.uk/Globalization-Its-Discontents-Joseph-Stiglitz/dp/014101038X#reader_014101038X/Accessed 09 May 18